A CHARISMATIC THEOLOGY

A CHARISMATIC THEOLOGY:
INITIATION IN THE SPIRIT

Heribert Mühlen

Burns & Oates · London

Paulist Press · New York
Ramsey, NJ · Toronto

First published in Great Britain and associated territories in 1978 by
Burns & Oates, 2-10 Jerdan Place, London SW6 5PT and in the USA by
Paulist Press
Editorial Office: 1865 Broadway, New York, NY 10023
Business Office: 545 Island Road, Ramsey, NJ 07446

Original German version first published by Matthias-Grünewald Verlag
of Mainz, Federal Republic of Germany, copyright © Matthias-Grünewald
Verlag 1975-76

Translated from the German by Edward Quinn & Thomas Linton

ISBN UK: 0 86012 064 3

ISBN USA: 0-8091-2101-8

Set IBM by Tek-Art, Croydon, Surrey
Printed and bound in Great Britain by
Billing & Sons Limited, Guildford, London and Worcester

Contents

Preface   7

PART I: DOCTRINE AND EXHORTATION

Introduction   11

First week: Meaning   21

Second week: God   41

Third week: Separation   61

Fourth week: Jesus Christ   87

Fifth week: Church   111

Sixth week: Gifts of the Spirit   145

Seventh week: Discernment   167

Appendix I: Charismatic renewal and the unity of the
Church   196
Appendix II: Theological guidelines of the charismatic
congregational renewal in the Churches
of the Reformation   196

Notes   199

PART II: EXPECTANT PRAYER

Introduction 211

First week: Meaning 222

Second week: God 236

Third week: Separation 249

Fourth week: Jesus Christ 271

Fifth week: The Church 284

Sixth week: Gifts of the Spirit 309

Seventh week: Discernment 326

Appendix I: The renewal of the Church 347

Appendix II: A testimony of faith 354

Biblical quotations are from the Revised Standard Version. DS: *Enchiridion symbolorum, definitionum et declarationum de rebus fidei et morum*, ed. Denzinger and Schönmetzer, (Barcelona, Freiburg-im-Breisgau, Rome, New York,[33] 1965).

Preface

It is a good thing that an introduction to basic Christian experience in the Spirit can appear and be recommended as the fruit of Catholic-Protestant solidarity. This kind of solidarity belongs to the essence of the charismatic renewal. It is a sign of the presence and activity of the Holy Spirit. Charismatic renewal from the very beginning has been an ecumenical movement in a special sense, not as a rival but as a critical complement to other ecumenical efforts.

But even in charismatic renewal as a form of 'spiritual' ecumenism the problems of the past, the theological questions arising from Christian divisions, have not simply dissolved. If anyone were to think so, he would be thinking un-historically and showing a lack of charity to those who owe their spiritual life to the special character of their own denomination. As with individuals, so with the denominational Churches, the chances of a healing of the past can lie only in setting out afresh towards the common future.

Hence in this book also it is made clear that Protestants and Catholics do not come from the same ecclesiastical traditions. We often make use of different terms, we have particular customs without always being aware of this, we often link similar experiences and ideas with other meta-phors, symbols or propositions. Faced by the question of renewing his faith, the situation of someone who belongs to the Catholic Church is in fact in some respects different from that of other Christians, and then there are further differ-ences between Lutherans and Calvinists, between members of national Churches and other Churches, between Anglicans or Episcopalians and Methodists, Presbyterians, Baptists and so on.

In order to deal with this present-day situation — and not to act as if all theological questions were solved — Protestant colleagues have supplemented at some points, from a Protes-tant standpoint and for Protestant readers, the lectures and suggestions for prayer produced by Heribert Mühlen. This seems to us a more appropriate procedure than any attempt at a wholly uniform text. In this way it can be seen how much we have in common and where — to put it concretely — something which is properly Protestant has to be said. The preface to the second part of this 'initiation' contains further, complementary reflections on this point.

Hence there is no new charismatic theology; we are seeking and pleading for an awakening and a renewal of the whole Church and the individual Christian, on the basis of the teachings and practices of our Churches, all of which emerge from the encounter with the word of God. We are seeking this on our way to a future which is filled with increasing harmony, ever more intense love, ever greater courage to witness to the work of the triune God.

Part I
DOCTRINE AND EXHORTATION

Translated by Edward Quinn

Introduction

The present 'initiation' emerged, with the collaboration of Catholic and Protestant clergy, from seminars on faith organized for the *parish mission*. Behind it is a world-wide spiritual awakening which has led to the formation of prayer groups in all the major Christian Churches, and it describes the second phase of this awakening; integration into the actual life of local parishes.

This awakening in all the major Christian Churches heralds a new, realistic form of the Christian faith: social experience of God, removal of the taboo on a personal relationship with Christ, liberation to bear witness to the faith, missionary liturgy, church ministry as charism for the other charisms. At the same time the different spiritual traditions are by no means extinguished; they provide mutual aid so that each can purify its own heritage of historically-conditioned features and make it fruitful for the common future.

The way to a living community

Missionary testimony to the faith before one another and before the world is of the nature of the Christian Church, for this testimony is grounded in the event of Pentecost and is its *enduring origin*. Luke's introduction to his Acts of the Apostles is valid for all times: 'He charged them not to depart from Jerusalem, but to wait for the promise of the Father, which, he said, "you heard from me, for John baptized with water, but before many days you shall be baptized with the Holy Spirit . . . You shall receive power when the Holy Spirit has come upon you; and you shall be my witness in Jerusalem and in all Judea and Samaria and to the end of the earth" ' (Acts 1. 4f., 8). The gifts of the Spirit for the salvation of others have always been alive in the Church, but Christ distributes the gifts of his Spirit more abundantly at times of fossilization, of decline or even of historical change in the appearance of the Church. The itinerant prophets of the second and third Christian generations must be mentioned here as well as the great preachers of penance in the early Christian period and the Middle Ages. The mendicant orders' preaching apostolate was just as necessary to the Catholic Church as the Reformation of the sixteenth century. The fact that the latter involved a schism was the fault of human beings on *both* sides, as Catholics and Protestants more clearly recognize today.

One of the basic impulses of this Reformation was and is permanently relevant: the awakening and cultivation of the gifts of the Spirit promised to every Christian, guidance towards their acceptance in faith. It is however impossible simply to 'introduce' the exercise of the gifts of the Spirit as liturgical or structural reforms can be introduced. The acceptance of the gifts of the Spirit takes place in a very personal step of surrendering to Christ, of conversion and acceptance of one's own death (we do not proclaim ourselves, but the crucified Christ). Such a process as a whole cannot be started overnight in the parish, but — as all experience suggests — can only grow in small groups. The ideal would be for the leader of the parish with his assistants, with active members of the parish or also with those responsible for preparing young people for confirmation, to form such a prayer group. But neither does this grow up overnight, it needs an 'initiation' in the form of a seminar stretching over several weeks.

The present aid appears in two parts. The first part contains doctrine and exhortation and is for use by a parish or seminar leader or an individual. At the same time it provides information for those who want in the first place merely to know something about this spiritual awakening. But as he gets further into the book the reader will observe that the step of personal decision and surrender is not possible without the help of others (although God also rouses individuals to a living faith and to witness). The governing body of a seminary or college for the ministry normally assumes that the director must have accepted the gifts personally promised to him, before he becomes a witness and missionary mediator of ecclesiastical renewal. The first part of the book then serves as a basis for the weekly lectures or course of renewal.

It is obvious that the leader of the parish mission must adopt his exposition to the particular audience with which he has to deal. We have tried to avoid technical theological terms in this preliminary material. Specialist theologians will find some references in the notes.

The second part (*Expectant prayer*) is intended basically for those at a seminar and for anyone seeking renewal. It contains suggestions for prayer for every day for a period of seven weeks and is meant to be an aid to personal baptismal renewal and to the acceptance of the gifts of the Spirit. Both parts complement each other in regard to theological and pastoral initiatives and form a unity.

The thrust of the course takes a new turn after the first three weeks. Up to that point it is a question of each one's personal relationship to God, whereas in the subsequent weeks readiness to work for the salvation of others predominates. It proved advisable to extend the seminar to a period of fourteen weeks. At the first meeting there was a lecture followed by a discussion and during the rest of the week meetings in small groups with a personal exchange of views on experiences in prayer and on the individual's approach.

Personal turning to Christ

The title 'initiation' refers to the fact that it is a question of conveying experience and not merely providing information. A basic knowledge of matters of faith is assumed as provided by any basic modern manual, for example: *The Common Catechism: A Book of Christian Faith*, London & New York, 1975). With spiritual awakenings there is always a danger of wanting to replace doctrine by experience. Here however we shall try to convey the necessary doctrinal material in such a way as to reveal the experience from which it emerged. In some sections — particularly in the fourth to the seventh week — doctrine must predominate. On the other hand there are some elements of doctrine which cannot be conveyed merely by a neutral exposition. Personal exhortation is also part of an 'initiation'.

'One' or 'we' is no substitute for a more direct form of address. For example, in the very first week it is a question of the meaning of *my* life and not of the meaning of life as a whole. It is not 'we' who learn the meaning of life, but every time it is I myself in my personal relationships. Moreover, surrender to God, turning to Christ, is such a personal and at the same time social event that it can also be conveyed only in a personal and social way. The occasional use of the 'you' form of address refers to the fact that in relation to God every man is addressed in the depths of his personality. Doctrinal points — which of course have to be mentioned in this 'initiation' — are presented in the form appropriate to them.

In this connection the author may be permitted to recall the fact that readiness for renewal in the Spirit was conveyed to him in a personal way *by others*. A brief example may help. A priest called on me one day and began to talk in the usual way about theological questions. After about an hour he said, quite out of the blue: 'Shall we pray together?' This was a quite unusual question and invitation. A theology professor is simply not accustomed to pray with someone with whom he has been involved in a theological discussion and his first reaction is to regard such an invitation as demanding too much of him. I felt put out and very insecure. I could scarcely say 'No' to the polite and friendly question, so my colleague prayed with me, adoring, praising, glorifying God, in a very personal way such as I had never heard before. There was power and faith in this prayer and, above all, an awareness of the real presence of God around and between us.

A scholar is inclined to shrink from such immediacy to God, since he is accustomed to set up a screen of theological ideas and terms between himself and God. Academic theology does not lead without more ado to decision for Christ, to surrender to God. After this first encounter with a world-wide spiritual awakening there began a period of critical reflection in which the historical roots of the taboos on emotional faith became clear. Even within the Church faith has become very much a private affair and this is one reason for the inability of the Christian Churches to convey a truly personal faith and their ineffectiveness in modern society. The author therefore knows from his own experience the inner resistance, the initial feeling of embarrassment, when confronted with another's personal testimony of faith. The experiences recorded in this 'initiation' however do not come from a small, quasi-sectarian group, but are the sign of a world-wide, diffuse awakening. In face of this we must recall the words: 'Do not despise prophesying, but test everything; hold fast what is good' (1 Thess 5.20f).

Not a new movement, not a special spirituality

It must be emphasized that the charismatic renewal, for a variety of reasons, is not a 'movement' in the sociological sense. Movements arise from the fact that individuals or groups set themselves certain goals of reform and attempt with their ideas to influence or change society or the Church. As a diffuse awakening, this renewal has not been planned, organized, aimed at; in fact, it was not even expected. And it is scarcely possible to indicate any particular 'goal': we can only test this renewal to see whether it comes from God or not, for its inner dynamism is directed to a renewal of the whole Church in all its expressions of life. Assuming that the first impetus for this renewal comes from the Holy Spirit, it is of course always accompanied by human activities. It did not however begin with these. The charismatic renewal in the Church has no 'founder', no spiritual centre, no special theology (other than its perception of the partialities of traditional theology). It has no membership and no contributions, no programmes of action and only a very weak auxiliary organizational structure. Above all, it gathers no 'followers' who later cut themselves off from the major Churches and form sectarian divisions.

Nor is there any question of a new spirituality alongside other spiritual traditions. As it appears in its second phase, the renewal is so open in its approach that it also renews and intensifies the traditional forms of Christian spirituality. It can occur anywhere, where 'two or three' are assembled in the name of Jesus, irrespective of the group to which they otherwise belong. Personal and testifying prayer with one another and by one another is no less possible in the parish council and other bodies than in the family, in clergy gatherings, in youth groups and other associations. Charismatic renewal is an awakening to a spiritual *communication*, but not in itself a new spirituality. Baptismal renewal is a life-long occurrence which every Christian ought to allow to come upon him at some point in his life, even explicitly and in front of other people; and every Christian is granted certain gifts of the Spirit for service in and to the Church and the world. The parish priest or minister need not be anxious that a new 'association', a new group, is starting up alongside other associations. Charismatic renewal is a new historical form of the *basic Christian experience* and it is from the latter that all special formations emerge from the very beginning.

The ecumenical aspect

The 'initiation' presented here could not have come into existence had it not been for the spiritual impulses which first made themselves felt on the fringes of the major traditional Churches. Among the more notable stimuli were those coming from Pietism, from the Methodist-Baptist tradition and from that spiritual experience which has led from the beginning of the present century to the formation of what are known as the 'Pentecostal Churches.'

It is impossible *a priori* to question the true and authentic experience of the Spirit granted in these and other awakenings or to deny that the major Churches must face the question as to whether they have culpably closed themselves up against these experiences: whether they are to blame for the fact that new Churches have been formed, thus leading to further divisions in Christendom. Of course these religious experiences can and may be accepted in a *critical* spirit. Catholic and Protestant groups cannot take over from each other without more ado the other's understanding of the Church, theological interpretation of charismatic practice or style of biblical interpretation. On the contrary, it is in this encounter that each side has learned to love its own tradition all the more. At the same time it may be regarded as a special gift that Catholics and Protestants can produce *together* an initiation into the renewal of their *respective* Churches. The collaboration of *scholars* of different denominations is no longer unusual today. Over and above this, however, the charismatic renewal also justifies the hope that in the foreseeable future a tradition and spirituality common to the now separated Churches will be possible. At the same time what the Holy Spirit has effected and continues to effect in the respective Churches, despite the culpable division, can, may and must be preserved.

The initiation into the basic Christian experience does not claim to be the *sole* way to the living parish, to the renewal of the Church. God is not tied by human limitations. In any case it must be recognized that the Christian faith takes on a different appearance in different historical epochs. Only at the end of history, in retrospect, can the basic Christian experience be manifested in its wholeness: that is, when Christ lays everything at the feet of the Father and God is all in all. Every period in the history of faith inevitably shows a lack of balance which needs to be corrected. Does the worldwide charismatic awakening herald the beginning of a new epoch in that history? This renewal was not originally planned, organized, worked out in advance by men, and even in its continuation can be accepted only as a very personal gift from God. But then we ought really to apply the rules for the discernment of spirits (seventh week) to *test* whether it comes from God or not, whether human impulses or the promptings of the Holy Spirit are predominant. According to Paul the basic question at this testing must be: does this renewal serve to build up the Church or not? For our own part, we can only ask the Lord himself to show us *how* he calls us to that 'continual reformation' (Vatican II, *Decree on Ecumenism*, art. 6, 1) which is part of the historical nature of the Church.

Particular emphasis must be laid on the fact that *the inner dynamism of the charismatic renewal is directed, not to a new charismatic Church (Church of the Spirit), but to a charismatically renewed Church.* This has certain consequences for the practice of prayer groups. There can be no question of the formation of 'supra-denominational' prayer groups on the part of those who have given themselves personally to Christ, no question of emigrating mentally from their respective Churches. On the contrary each one should try to establish the renewal in his particular Church and to do so in a way corresponding to the tradition of his Church. The awakening of the gifts of the Spirit in *all* the major Christian Churches can lead to the restoration of our lost unity only under the further guidance of the Spirit of God.

One of the chief obstacles, which persists up to the present time, is the understanding of ministry in the Church. If this is to be a *living* ministry, a charism for the other charisms, then it must be assumed that the latter are themselves alive. Prayer groups therefore would have to emerge for the most part respectively in the Protestant and Catholic *local parishes:* that is, in the actual worshipping communities centred on word and worship. As experience shows, it is of great importance in all this for the traditional forms of worship to retain their sustaining power. The eucharistic celebration is often a climax of the prayer meeting. The eucharistic presence of the risen Lord makes people aware of the fact that his presence is not dependent on the personal involvement of the worshippers, but *is prior* to this. Prayer groups frequently disintegrate because they lack this pre-existent, objective, God-given meeting point.

If the charismatic renewal has its roots in the respective local parishes, this does not mean that inter-parochial prayer groups cannot emerge in the initial stages, in which Christians of different denominations and Churches also take part. At the same time special problems arise in regard to the celebration of the eucharist. The unity experienced in these prayer groups far transcends the solidarity of ecumenical services of the word. Many therefore do not understand why this very intense unity cannot be expressed also in receiving holy communion together. On the other hand the members of such prayer groups, in virtue of their spiritual experience, can also appreciate the fact that the human guilt of separation is not simply to be ignored (although not every one is personally responsible for the separation). Even the deliberate enduring of the schism is a spiritual contribution to the hoped for unity. What is the point of some individuals leaping over the wall if all the others remain separated? As a result of their very intense experience of the Spirit, out of love for the other person and in their awareness of their mandate for their respective Churches, charismatic prayer groups are enabled to bear spiritually any continuing eucharistic separation. They may keep therefore to the generally observed ecumenical practice. Among the separated Churches charismatic renewal is realized in the *foreground* of the eucharistic fellowship: that is, in the dimension of the Spirit and that experience of the Spirit which is presupposed for the celebration of the eucharist. But for this very reason it contains a powerful thrust towards this celebration.

The author is grateful to the many people who assisted by their prayers and corrections during the seminars from which this 'initiation' emerged. He is particularly grateful to Arnold Bittlinger, Erhard Griese and Manfred Kiessig for their collaboration and correction.

Paderborn, February 1976   *Heribert Mühlen*

First week: Meaning

No one can give a meaning to his own life

1. Everyone has plans and goals

2. What are you living for?
   a) Meaning is more than advantage
   b) You discover meaning in your relations with other human beings
   c) Who gives meaning to your life?

3. To live meaningfully, you must accept your life and your death
   a) You did not will your own existence
   b) Meaning must be able to withstand even death

4. Jesus Christ did not live for himself

5. God is self-surrender

1. Everyone has plans and goals[1]

What is the chief goal of your life? What are you living for, what attracts you, what fascinates you? What pictures do you carry around with you, in your wallet or in your heart? The picture of a friend, a girl, a film star, a pop singer, an Olympic victor, a political leader, a social revolutionary? Pause for a moment and think, what pictures you are carrying around with you.

And what do you expect from the *immediate* future, from the next weeks and months? Advancement in your calling? A better, more intimate, happier relationship with someone you love? To keep your job, to become wealthy? What plans have you for the next weeks and months? What do you dream about in your hours of leisure? Holidays? A house you want to build for yourself? The car you want to buy? And what do you expect for the *more distant* future? Further professional advancement? To be able to set up on your own or to become more independent in your work? Further advances in medicine to make your life easier and to prolong it (What is directly connected with sickness and death is not really all that bad)? To live on in your children? For these one day to become great and important? That one day all men may live in justice and peace, freed from oppression and war?

What then are you striving for? For more recognition, love and personal approval? For more wealth, power and influence? For more inward and outward independence, for more social justice?

If you have answered even one of these questions, it proves that you think your life has some kind of meaning. Or did you answer: I don't carry any pictures around with me. I have no plans for the next weeks and months, I don't expect anything at all from the future, I never dream of anything — neither of holidays nor of possessions — and I have no ideas about my future? It's all the same to me whether the money I've saved is eaten up or not by further inflation, whether my old age is assured or not, what will become of my children. I am not striving for anything at all, not for recognition, personal approval, professional advancement, influence or independence. For me *everything* is wholly irrelevant. This is not likely to be your answer, for then all your actions would be completely aimless, you would be letting yourself be driven from moment to moment, without in the least pursuing any kind of goal, your life would be without any orientation: it would be *pointless and planless.*

If we say that something is pointless, that it lacks meaning, we are saying that it has no direction, gets us nowhere, is not part of a plan. Can you seriously maintain that all you are thinking and feeling is 'pointless and planless', without any direction? Is your whole life only a journey into the unknown? You will certainly not put up with such a situation for long. You decide, for example, to take a really lazy holiday and to do 'nothing'; but even this is something you have already 'undertaken'. You are therefore pursuing an intention: that is, you want to be relieved of the burden of your ordinary work. You are in fact expressly aiming at a definite kind of holiday, at getting away from things and really doing 'nothing'. But is this true? You will certainly occupy yourself with something, reflect on your pet ideas, read a book: you will 'undertake' something. Even in your holiday you will 'plan' something, you will pursue your hobby, turn to your leisure-time occupation.

Since the questions raised are so important, a counter-check may be helpful. Suppose that nothing and no one interests you any more, that you are no longer busy with anything, no longer attracted by anything or anyone, that you have no plans. That would be a state of *boredom*. Did you ever go through such a state? During a dreary holiday, on a wet afternoon? Why is the feeling of boredom so unpleasant and depressing? Boredom is sadness at being no longer attracted by anything or anyone, no longer interested in anything, having no plans. This sadness is proof that we really do want to have definite objectives, to put plans into effect. In the long run it is *fatal* to go on living without any goal or plan. You are forced into some kind of purposive action and you also want to be certain that your whole life has some kind of purpose, that you are living *for* something.

It is certain however that you cannot plan everything in your life, that you will not reach all your goals, that you will meet with opposition and resistance. There are situations and conditions which you cannot change and which you must therefore somehow *accept*. We of the twentieth century live in a world where there is a multiplicity of plans: economic plans, social plans, political plans, plans for exploring outer space, and so on. There is certainly a great deal that we can produce, change and plan: nature, society; and even births — that is, human beings — are planned. But this does not mean that opposition and contradiction are thereby abolished. Far-seeing politicians tell us that, if the present evolutionary trends are extended into the future, then mankind is heading for a fourfold disaster: economic disaster, financial disaster, breakdown in food supplies, world-population explosion. Plans will be made to prevent these disasters, but economic wars, financial wars, cruelty and oppression cannot simply be abolished. The same holds for the plans we make for our own lives. You cannot — for example — plan another person's love for you; you cannot control it but must accept it. More especially, you did not plan yourself, your character, your abilities. But who then did plan you? Your parents? Are you quite sure that they loved you before you were born? Might you not have been an 'unplanned' child, a terrible accident?

This question of course probes very deeply. In the ordinary daily round we suppress it, but we simply cannot get rid of a certain feeling of mistrust and fear. We all live in a complicated and ultimately incomprehensible world and consequently there are those who say: I have plans and goals, but I don't know what *really* is the sense of it all, where it is all going to end. I cannot be certain that the plans which other people make and on which I am dependent really have any *meaning*. Why should I bring children into the world when I don't know what it will look like in thirty years time. I don't think there is much point in saving, since the economic future is uncertain. Even personal relations with another human being are often accompanied by a deep distrust: I don't know whether he or she really loves me.

From these indisputable experiences and facts some philosophers have drawn the conclusion that *everything is the result of chance*: that it is absurd to be born and it is absurd to die (Jean-Paul Sartre). This theory however cannot by any means be *proved*, but behind it there lies a *basic decision*, a basic reaction to the future. It is true of course that there is also no proof that there is possibly a hidden plan behind world-history and behind the life of the individual, a plan which does not become clear because human beings are continually frustrating it. Neither alternative can be strictly proved. But, whether you wanted to or not, you have always already made up your mind for one of the two possibilities. Either everything is the result of chance and even you yourself are an accident or behind everything there is in fact a meaning, some kind of plan. If you take the facts as they are, then you cannot escape this decision — or your whole life is a lie. We shall go over these questions once again step by step.

2. What are you living for?

(a)   Meaning is more than advantage

We raised the question about what pictures we carry around with us, what examples guide our lives. Such examples exercise power over us even when we are not aware of it. Most people do not normally reflect on the meaning of their lives, but come up against it for the first time when an important relationship is broken off. We shall speak of this later. But even at this stage anyone can see at a glance that his own action bears the stamp of the examples he follows, that he is pursuing definite goals. For example, when you go to your work in the morning, practise your profession or prepare yourself for it, what is the purpose of your action? One important aim is certainly to earn your *living*. But what further aims do you link with the exercise of your calling? Would you like to improve your living standard, make your life as pleasant as possible? In that case you yourself are giving a meaning to your action: *whatever benefits me is meaningful*. You are living entirely for your own advantage and judge everything in the light of this aim. You put your whole trust in your working powers, your abilities, your intelligence, and you are striving to make yourself as independent as possible.

What is certain however is that no one can live and act *only* for himself. When you work your action is always inevitably set within a larger context. You are working not only for yourself but also *for others*, and your calling is necessarily also a service to others. If you judge your calling only in the light of the advantage it brings to you, then you must allow for the fact that others will also judge you mainly according to your usefulness for society. You are certainly in somebody's personnel file and someone will judge you according to your abilities and the services you can render. You are part then of the disposable 'human material' and you are judged solely in the light of what you can do for society. But then the meaning of your life lies in the hands of those who decide your usefulness or your worthlessness. Your existence is justified essentially by the value of what you produce and the extent of your usefulness. *You are permitted to live if you accomplish something.*

But are you really satisfied with that? Animals and plants are also judged by their utility. Have you not also a value in yourself? Don't you expect people to acknowledge you as a person, even if — for instance — a factory accident has deprived you of your working power or if you are sick and old. Are you really only worth what you can accomplish? Can even your love for another person be judged solely from the standpoint of advantage? And what is supposed to be the advantage from the selfless action for which you don't expect any gratitude? What does it mean if you get involved with the underprivileged, the outcasts, those on the fringe of society, with the handicapped or with released prisoners: people who are only a burden on society? From the standpoint of pure advantage all this is pointless. The conclusion must be drawn that, if you are judged only by your achievement and usefulness, you are exchangeable and replaceable; that those who have power will fit you into their budget, involve you in their own plans, but also get rid of you when you are no longer useful. The principle of usefulness leads to a domination of men over men. Other human beings determine the meaning of your life and will eliminate you or leave you to perish when you have outlived your usefulness.

Every revolt against the principle of pure advantage is therefore simultaneously a criticism of the society which makes a total claim on you.

(b) You discover meaning in your relations with other human beings

Let us ask again more precisely: What has happened when a person says: 'Life no longer makes any sense to me' or 'I don't know any more *what I'm living for*', or '*it's all pointless*'? Behind such statements there is not only pain at seeing no advantage any longer is one's actions, but in most cases also a loss of prestige, recognition, acceptance, security, solicitude, love. The ageing person, eliminated from the work process and from the family group, no longer knows 'what he is living for', since a *relationship* has been broken off. When resilience and vitality begin to decline in middle age, the result is often a crisis of meaning. No further professional or social advancement is possible and there appears to be no sense in continuing to toil and drudge. There is no more prestige or recognition to be gained. 'My life no longer has any meaning': this terrible admission also occurs however when someone fails in his calling, when — for example, in an economic crisis — he has to give up his business. Even if the welfare state provides adequately for the necessities of life, abandonment of the business means a drastic loss of prestige, a loss of social credit. He no longer receives recognition, but — at most — sympathy. There is no longer the feeling of security that comes from the approval and recognition of others. We may be plunged into a crisis of meaning when someone close to us dies, when a marriage-partner has a fatal accident, a mother is taken from us, when a deep personal love suddenly breaks down. Here it is no longer a question of achievement or advantage, but of the loss of security, solicitude, love.

If we follow up all these observations, we come to the surprising conclusion that *acceptance and recognition by others are prior to achievement and usefulness.* Even the small child cannot grow in body or mind without the security and the continual attention of the mother, the father or some other person. It needs the wholly *personal*

personal acceptance of its existence by another individual human being. This is a fact clearly established by medical science. In all manifestations of its life the small child begs for this approval and attention, because it needs them as much as it needs air and food. Nor is it only the small child which has these needs. To be honest, we also continue to beg for this acceptance by our milieu. Even the ageing person needs approval and solicitude till his last breath. Doctors even tell us that if a person has not been really secure and approved *from the very beginning*, then he is incapable even in his later life of any real achievement for society. A happy, undisturbed relationship with other human beings is the precondition of our ability to pursue our goals, to act purposively, to serve society and be useful to it. Deeply concealed disappointments, distrust, inhibit our freedom of action and consequently our ability to create values.

I maintain then that the experience of meaning has primarily something to do with the experience of security, acceptance, recognition, by other people. This however is something that we cannot enforce or plan, but only receive. You cannot yourself produce and will the meaning of your life from your own resources, but you must *receive it from outside*.

This becomes still more clear as soon as you recall the fact that you are by no means content simply to authenticate yourself, to approve and love yourself. You need the love and the recognition of *others*. And this you can never enforce, but only receive. Have you ever been approached by someone who begged all too obviously for recognition and acceptance? Why is such an attempt so embarrassing? We cannot dispose of the freedom and love of others and therefore love, appreciation and recognition are refused as long as the attempt is made to *extort* them.

(c)   Who gives meaning to your life?
From what has been said up to now, we must conclude that the power which gives meaning to life will fulfil two conditions:
1. It must be at least *human*. You must be able to enter into a *personal relationship* with it and it must have the

ability and readiness to love and recognize you. Commodities or material things therefore cannot of themselves provide the meaning of your life.

2. The agency providing meaning must *outlive* you. It cannot end with you or before you, for you depend on it from your first to your last breath for approval and recognition which are reliable and given in absolute loyalty.

Consider then once more the different proposals which have been made to you for a meaningful life. In obituaries we frequently find expressions like 'He found the meaning of his life in caring for his dependents.' Of course you are responsible for your family, for the people entrusted to you. But the family as a caring unit does not outlive you. The first condition is fulfilled, but not the second. When your parents or other members of the family are dead, they can no longer give you this daily bread of approval. Consequently the loss of close relatives raises for many people the despairing question: 'What is the point of my life now?'

Or is the ultimate source of meaning for you society, the collectivity, an idea or a party-programme? The collectivity and the party programme certainly outlive you, but these agencies judge you mainly according to your usefulness. You are approved only as long as you are achieving something and are useful. An anonymous, bureaucratically-run society cannot accord you that measure of recognition of your unique, irreplaceable personality which you need. The second condition is fulfilled, but not the first.

Or is the meaning which sustains your life found in money, possessions, sexuality? Don't deceive yourself! These forces do not constitute a true partner for you and they do not outlive you. On the contrary, it is you yourself who attempts to give them a meaning, but they cannot really answer you. All you are doing is to try to authenticate yourself with their aid. You are living with an *illusion*.

3. To live meaningfully, you must accept your life and your death

(a) *You did not will your own existence*

The most profound reason why you cannot yourself produce

a meaning for your life lies in the fact that you did not will and plan *yourself*. You could not seek out for yourself your parents, your character, the century in which you wanted to live, the social conditions which were to determine your life. Certainly there is a great deal that you can produce for yourself and mankind in the twentieth century has made great advances in the production of synthetic materials, spacecraft, life-prolonging medicines. But, despite all progress in technology and medicine, it will never be possible for anyone to say: I brought myself into existence by my own decision; I willed, made, planned myself. I depend on no one but myself. Let us assume — for example — the horrible possibility of breeding human beings in a laboratory, of predetermining their character, the colour of their eyes and so on. Even then no one would ever be able to say that he had willed, outlined, planned *himself*. Under any circumstances you were willed and devised from *elsewhere*. Consequently you can *accept only from elsewhere* your existence, your life's plan. This is a perfectly simple, irrefutable fact. You can suppress it, but never deny it.

But who is my source? Where did I come from? Certainly my parents are my *immediate* source. Many can gratefully remember that they grew up in a good family, that they were loved and sheltered. But how do I know that my parents really wanted and loved me from the very beginning? I must allow for the worst possibility, that I was the consequence of a momentary whim. Perhaps I was originally an unwilled, unplanned child, a misfortune, a terrible accident. I might even assume in theory that my mother did not kill me in the womb only because it was still against the law and that she accepted me afterwards only half-heartedly. And in any case my parents did not will and plan me as I am. They could not determine my character, my abilities; they could not freely control the results of their action. I can thank them for the *fact* that I exist, but I cannot thank them for being *as I am and not otherwise*, with these abilities and with this character. The whole thing becomes more difficult if I possess qualities and dispositions which I cannot stand myself, bodily and mental defects. Is there anyone who would approve me just as I am?

When I raise this question, it immediately becomes clear that I cannot be satisfied with the information that society needs me, that it planned me because it needs my labour. This is a widespread view: society needs you and progress is the ultimate whence and whither of your existence. You are allowed to wear yourself out and sacrifice yourself for a rosier and happier future of mankind. We, society, planned you; we manipulate the population statistics with the aid of children's allowances, in the light of the economic necessities of the time. You will defend yourself tooth and nail against such a view, for you experience daily the fact that you have a value in yourself.

In any case however it remains true that you have to accept your existence and consequently also the meaning of your life from elsewhere.

(b) Meaning must be able to withstand even death
The question of the meaning of death becomes particularly hard when it is raised, not only in relation to our origin, but also in regard to our *goal*. There is no doubt that we carry our death within us even now, that our life is directed towards it. Perhaps you have not yet reflected on your own death or you have not yet faced it in all its harshness in your life-history. No one has a personal experience of his own death. We know indeed that we must die some time, but before death we have no real experience of it — not even of the fear of it. We see others die, but we do not know what they feel and therefore no one can say what death really is. Consequently we also suppress our thoughts about it. As soon as we return home after a funeral, we begin to talk about ordinary things, in order to prove that essentially everything will go on for us as before. But there can be no doubt that our death is in us even now and that we come closer to it every hour. If we cannot in some way accept this fact, there will remain a maddening pointlessness in our life. This is the reason for our attempts to make light of it.

We said a short time ago that meaning is linked with the approval of our person and that we enjoy this approval in personal relationships with other human beings. That is why we resist so vigorously the idea that this approval and the relationships it involves will one day cease. We suppress the thought of our death, we try to outmanoeuvre it with wishful thinking that our present life will somehow continue after death, that the relationships will not be broken off.

Two people who love one another very much do not want this relationship to come suddenly to an end under any circumstances — for instance, through the death of the other. Each one therefore cherishes the secret hope that the other will survive him. For the same reason we also look to other powers which can better resist transitoriness. We hope that something will survive us: our children, our own firm, our country, a social or political movement, the progress of mankind. We hope too that we shall always be honoured in people's memories, that we shall not be forgotten and that in this way we shall somehow live on after death. The idea of it however really amounts to a consoling thought with which we attempt to outmanoeuvre the harsh reality of our death. For in death we really do break off all relationships and this is the reason why we cannot accept it. Death is 'pointless'. What sense does it make if two parents are involved in a fatal accident on the motorway, while their small child alone remains alive? What is the point of the death of a mother of five children? Even when people die after a full life death remains a constraint imposed on them, a *breaking off of all relationships*.

But what happens when we face this fact? Can we gather any meaning from it? Let us try to answer this question as plainly as possible.

Observe how you breathe, how your chest heaves and sinks, how you breathe in and breathe out. Observe for a moment how your heart beats. Observe how *alive* you are and then consider quite coolly, without dramatization, that one day you will no longer be breathing, that you will breathe out your life. Consider also that you will be *forced* one day into your own death, some time, with absolute certainty. You cannot freely dispose of the end of your life. It is true that you can shoot a bullet through your head, but what comes *after* that moment is no longer under the control of your will. You can no longer say: 'Stop. I've had second thoughts.' Death comes upon you as an inescapable event.

Life is taken away from us without us. Whether we want to or not, we must *suffer* our own death. No one will ever succeed in ceasing to exist as a result of his own wholly personal decision. We spoke above of the fact that we have to accept our *existence* from elsewhere. Most people make no protest against this, at least as long as things go well and they feel secure. If on the other hand we take seriously the certain fact of our *death*, then we do register a *protest*, for death is degrading: we are surrendered, defenceless, to a power which relentlessly forces us into submission. The idea of certain death prevents us from accepting ourselves without reserve, it makes us aware of how *unimportant* we really are. Therefore we cannot simply accept our death, we cannot ourselves withdraw this thorn from our flesh. If however we want to be wholly ourselves, we must also attempt somehow to accept the fact of death as a part of us, of our death which is already in us. It is obvious that we cannot go further on this point. What answer does the Bible give us?

4. Jesus Christ did not live for himself

Up to now we have been asking about our own experiences, plans, aims. When we put these questions to the New Testament, we must allow from the outset for the fact that we shall receive answers which we did not at first expect. *Christian* basic experience is not simply to be identified with universal human basic experience. Jesus Christ was a human being who broke through all human standards and who turns our questions in a new direction. Jesus claims that he alone experienced God as he is in himself, so that we have access to God only *through him*: 'I am the *way*, and the *truth*, and the *life*: no one comes to the Father, but by me . . . . He who has seen me has seen the Father' (Jn 14. 6, 9). As we said above, 'meaning' has to do with direction, with getting somewhere, with planning. Meaning is always concerned with the way and the goal. Jesus therefore says that he is the way and consequently the meaning of our lives, the meaning of history and the world. This of course is an enormous claim. We shall have to consider it more closely during the fourth week.

From the first book to the last, the Bible shows us that our models, our goals, and the plans which correspond to these cannot be drawn solely from our human milieu. The Israelites were not allowed to venerate the objects which fascinated and provided meaning for the people of their milieu. They were not to look for a meaning in the powers of the earth, of nature, of blood, of Eros, of their ancestors. The powers which man sees in the form of gods are made by himself and are therefore *nothing*. The God of the Old Testament says through his prophet: 'Understand that I am He. Before me no god was formed, nor shall there be any after me. I, I am the Lord, and besides me there is no saviour' (Is 43. 10-11). *Gods represent man's attempt to provide a meaning for himself.*

The Bible therefore requires us to give up from the first our insistence on meaning. For God is quite different from what we expected. He gives our life a meaning which we could not work out for ourselves, a meaning which requires from us a *reversal* of our whole way of thinking, wishing and planning. The meaningful response which God gives us in Jesus Christ is the *cross* and this in fact is an answer which we cannot know and prove intellectually, which demands of us a *basic decision*. We have however already shown that even the assertion that everything is pointless and absurd implies a basic decision, a reaction to the future, which likewise cannot be proved right.

Let us ask now what meaning Jesus saw in his life. What were his goals, his plans, his models? What inspired him, *what* did he live *for*? Paul gives a summary answer in the letter to the Romans: 'Let each of us please his neighbour for his good, to edify him. *For Christ did not please himself*' (Rom 15.2f). In other words, he did not serve his own interest, did not draw his inspiration from himself; he was not self-centred in his action and thought. He lived for his fellow-men, committed himself for us who are living in separation from God. He did not proclaim himself, but the will of him from whom he had received everything, his existence and his meaning: 'My food is to do the will of him who sent me' (Jn 4.34). Jesus did not seek his own private advantage, nor did he sacrifice himself solely for the collective benefit of mankind. What he did achieve was to commit himself with the utmost determination for all who are rejected, excluded as sinners from fellowship with God, expelled as underprivileged from the society of their own time. In this action he knew that he was approved and authenticated by his Father. It was in his relation to his Father that he experienced the meaning of his life. He did not seek the recognition of other human beings, in order in this way to extort an experience of meaning. For him it was sufficient that *God* recognized him.

Even here it is clear that the answer of the Bible is different from what we expected. In ourselves we can find no incentive to exist primarily *for others* (that is why sacrifice for society and progress must be enforced in the collective, Marxist systems); nor have we in ourselves any tendency to await the approval and recognition of our person primarily from God.

There is another point. We said earlier that the relationship to one's own death is a test of the genuineness and truthfulness of what we call the meaning of life. We do not know whether Jesus' predictions of his death are 'historical' in the modern sense of the term. But, as a result of his confrontation with the ruling powers and with society at that time, he was bound to allow for a fatal outcome. The gospels in any case describe Jesus as someone who had a quite conscious relationship to his own death and accepted it from God.

This becomes very clear in Matthew 16.21-23. Jesus predicts that he will suffer greatly, be killed, but on the third day be raised up. Peter reproaches him on this account: 'God forbid, Lord! This shall never happen to you.' Jesus retorts harshly to Peter: 'Get behind me, Satan! You are a hindrance to me; for you are not on the side of God, but of men.' For Peter it is obviously 'pointless' that the Master should be killed and that he should even approve this himself. This is a very human way of thinking, so human that demonic forces can already be seen behind it. Consequently Jesus requires Peter and the disciples to state the question of meaning in a different form: 'If any man would come after me, let him *deny himself* and take up his *cross* and follow me. For whoever would save his life will lose it, and whoever loses his life for my sake *will find it.*' (Mt 16.24f). 'To deny oneself' means more or less not to consider oneself, to surrender oneself, to *exist for others*. Jesus then promises: anyone who exists — as I do — wholly for others and thinks of nothing else but serving others will gain his life in an unexpected way: that is, he will be given a new relationship with himself. On the other hand, anyone who wants to save himself, who asks in all his plans and actions what is their usefulness to *himself*, will lose his life: that is, will lose himself, will never find his way to himself.

Even during his life Jesus accepted his death in advance and, according to the interpretation of the evangelists, saw in his death the fulfilment of the deepest meaning of his life. On the cross he gave himself up to the Father and thereby — as his resurrection shows — also found himself to an incomprehensible extent. As man, like any other man, he felt fear in the presence of death; but he did not suppress or try to avoid this fear and even before he died, on the Mount of Olives, gave himself up with a great, primitive trust in God: 'Abba, Father' (Mk 14.36). No one knows what Jesus experienced at his death. Mark and Matthew interpret that experience with the aid of Psalm 22.1: 'My God, my God, why hast thou forsaken me?' (Mk 15.34; Mt 27.46). The one who saw the whole meaning of his life in existing for God and for others, the Son receiving meaning, here cries to God, the Father who gives meaning. Who can plumb the depths of this forsakenness? Jesus went through it for us, so that we may never again despair of finding a meaning in life and so that we are prepared also to accept our own death.

Like any other human being, Jesus in his death suffered the breaking off of all relationships and by that very fact the deepest sense of futility. This event is at the same time an event in God himself: for the one who cries to his Father on the cross is also the Son who exists from the beginning in *relation* to this Father (Jn 1.1). The Son took on himself this 'meaningless' death in order to conquer all meaninglessness, including the meaninglessness of our own death. This victory becomes evident in the fact that in his deepest forsakenness he continues to cry to *his* God. He does not give up hope that his suffering for us has a meaning in God's sight and that even he himself experiences this meaning in himself. He is ready to receive a new meaning from God and he really *experienced* this new meaning in himself in his resurrection. The resurrection is a *new* relationship to God, a ratification, recognition and approval of his person by God, a new acquisition of meaning.

Here then is the answer. In his own death Jesus also anticipated and accepted your death. If in virtue of Jesus' death you now approve and accept your own death, then even now a *new* relationship to God begins in you, your own resurrection begins. You no longer need shamefacedly to conceal from yourself the fact of your death or try to neutralize it by your insistence on living. The meaning of your life can no longer be rendered questionable by your death which is already present within you. It is certain that you cannot yourself conquer your own death, you cannot deprive it of its power. Consequently you are utterly *incapable* of affirming and accepting it of yourself. Permit then this Jesus Christ *himself* to conquer your death in you, *himself* to accept it now for you: Let him who anticipated this acceptance on the cross do this for you. Then you will be reconciled with · yourself, reconciled too with the indisputable fact of your death. This admittedly presupposes that you give Jesus dominion over your life, that the centre of your life is not you yourself but this Jesus Christ. Do not merely hand over to him your life, your vitality, your plans and goals, but leave to him also the fact of your death: give your death back to him. He lives in you and will accept your death *in you* and *for you*. In this way you will be given a *freedom* which no one else can give you, for no other human being can take your death on himself. But Jesus Christ has freed us from servitude to death: 'O death, where is thy victory? O death, where is thy sting?' (1 Cor 15.55).

5: God is self-surrender

Seeking the meaning of life, we were led to Jesus and Jesus

leads us to God as the absolutely final source of meaning. He gives us existence without us and takes it away again without us. What kind of a God is this? Jesus gives us the answer: God takes away our existence without us, but not *without himself*. 'God did not spare his own Son but gave him up for us all' (Rom 8.32). Since God did not spare his very own, his Son, neither does he spare himself; and, by surrendering his own Son for us, he also surrenders something *of himself*. The Son reveals this self-surrender of the Father by surrendering *himself* for us: 'Be imitators of God, as beloved children. And walk in love, as Christ loved us and *gave himself up for us*, a fragrant offering and sacrifice to God' (Eph 5.1f; cf. Eph 5.25; Gal 2.20). We might recapitulate the Christian message in one sentence: *God is self-surrender*. He is from himself and by himself, he has no origin outside himself, no God over himself from whom he receives his existence and his meaning. He has all that he could have; he is all that he could be; he has his meaning in himself. God however does not live wholly for himself, but has revealed his innermost nature by surrendering himself; God is love *as* self-surrender. The man Jesus Christ has shown us this God, for the whole meaning of his life was self-surrender. Christian *basic experience* therefore is nothing other than the imitation of that God who surrendered his very own Son for us; it is discipleship of his Son who surrendered himself for us. Initiation into the basic Christian experience therefore is initiation into being-there for others, self-surrender. In it an unexpected self-experience and self-discovery are added as a gift, an intensification of the whole person including his feelings and affections. What happens when a person wholly commits himself to God, is something unbelievable.

We shall show later that the exercise of God-given gifts of the Spirit (charisms) is also part of the basic Christian experience: that they are granted to each individual according to his abilities for service in the Church and in the world. These gifts of the Spirit are the expression of God's love for us, of his self-surrender and can therefore be exercised only in self-surrender to our fellow-men.[2] We shall show later that this process presupposes the acceptance of our own death, the 'baptism of death', and in this sense is anything but 'fanatical'. It has become customary to regard the 'charismatic renewal' as a phenomenon of 'enthusiasm.' It must however be emphasized that the word 'enthusiasm' (Greek *enthousiasmos*) does not occur at all in the New Testament. If it is thought impossible to avoid the word, it must be proved that the death of Christ is appropriately described as 'enthusiastic'. In modern usage the term has been linked with the idea of 'fanatical', 'effusive'. In view of this it is misleading to describe the exercise of the gifts of the Spirit as 'enthusiastic'.

Second week: God

Have you ever really experienced the presence of God in your life?

1. What makes a Christian?

2. Defective forms of Christianity
   a) Christianity from tradition
   b) Legal religion
   c) Good deeds

3. We must recover the initial Christian experience

4. What does 'experience' really mean here?
   a) A personal testimony
   b) Experience through personal encounter and personal relationships

5. Must we correct our ideas of God?
   a) Is God only 'Creator'?
   b) God as Holy Spirit
   c) The Holy Spirit is present among us in a way accessible to sense-experience

1. What makes a Christian?

If our life did not originate in blind chance, but in the love of that God who has revealed himself to us in the Bible, then it is of the greatest interest to get to know this God more closely. For then it is essential, not merely to *want* to find him, but also actually to find him, really to *experience* his guidance and presence in our life. From the first book to the last, the Bible continually tells us that God really makes himself known to us: in fact the Bible itself was not the product of scholarship, of desk-work, but describes living experiences with the living God.

Consequently the question arises first of all: how do you come to be a Christian? In the countries where Christianity is indigenous, more than 95 per cent of the inhabitants are Christians, mostly because they were first baptized as children and then given Christian education and instruction. What happened in your case? Probably you were baptized as a small child and then given a Christian education in the family and in school. You learnt certain dogmas, practised hymns and prayers, received sacraments. But, in addition to infant-baptism and education, did you take that decisive first step of a real personal *conversion* to God in the power of Christ which changes your life, the personal *decision* for Christ? Have there been days, weeks, months, in which you were so touched, overwhelmed, seized by the love of God as bride and bridegroom, wife and husband, touched and seized by one another? Love is not learned by instruction, but strikes the heart, often quite suddenly; and this is true of both love for another human being and love of God. Is your *baptismal bond* really as far-reaching for you as the *bond* between married people. According to the New Testament, in the last report, you became quite definitely a Christian only through your personal turning to Christ and the experience of his real *presence* in your life. Only in this way can you *experience* God's plan with you and with the world, only in this way can you really live meaningfully.

We must return to this question, but, before doing so, a prior question must be clarified: what did you really get out of your Christian education? Perhaps it's a long time since

you attended a religious service, perhaps you don't pray any
longer, perhaps you regard your Christian education with
indifference or even hostility. Perhaps you don't want to
have anything to do with the Church as an institution, with
its ministries, its precepts and its public acts. You would
possibly have nothing against all this if you really found you
had again something to do with God. In reality you are
always continuing to seek God and you would also like
actually to find him. If this is the case with you, then you
remain open to that experience of God of which I want to
speak. If you are a *convinced* Christian, regularly attend
worship, and get thoroughly involved in society, do you get
any joy out of being a Christian? Do you permit the Spirit
of God to guide you inwardly, without developing your own
plans and strategy from the very beginning? Did you make
your decision for Christ — as is envisaged in adult baptism —
before witnesses. Have you given back your life to him in a
wholly personal self-surrender. Perhaps you will recognize
yourself in one of the following defective forms of Christianity?

2. Defective forms of Christianity

(a) Christianity from tradition

In the ordinary course of our life as Christians we have to do
mainly with traditions, liturgical forms, dogmas, prayer-
formularies, institutions and ministries, which emerged *at
some time in the past* out of a deep experience of faith and
then became — so to speak — the form in which faith was
'preserved'. Our faith quite certainly lives *also* by the faith of
those who lived before us, but it cannot live *solely* and
exclusively at second-hand. If this were so, then we would
know of God, of Christ, of the Holy Spirit, only from *hearsay* and we would have to rely completely on the *experiences
of others*. Moreover, the still continuing decline in church-
attendance, the tacit apostasy of many Christians from their
traditional churches, shows that we are living at the
'beginning of a new epoch', as the Second Vatican Council
said, and much that actually sustained previous generations

will have to be filled today inwardly with new life. In fact, many time-conditioned forms of expression in the Church definitely need to be replaced by others (hymns, preaching style, etc.). In all this it becomes clear that we cannot be Christians solely on the basis of an essentially instilled tradition.

So-called 'good Christians' in particular, who are active in their parishes in associations and organizations as a result of an intensive education at home and at school, often seem least open to a life-transforming experience of God's presence. They trust far too much in what they have learned, in their own knowledge, plans and strategy. Such a Christianity, sustained by milieu and tradition, is really possible only against a wholly Christian background: government, laws, public opinion, prevailing norms of action. If you rely on these things, you must remember that even in the Christian West the milieu in which we live is no longer Christian and Christianity resting solely on tradition will not withstand a real crisis.

(b) Legal religion
Many devout Christians are restricted to a Christianity which has been instilled into them. Certainly Christian education is necessary, but education may be misleading, so that people simply fulfil their religious 'duties', say 'obligatory prayers' and so on. Christianity then easily becomes a *collection of unpleasant requirements* and God remains purely a sort of 'heavenly supervisor' for whom we are called to fulfil duties and produce achievements. If such a person is given a different offer of a meaningful life, containing fewer unpleasant requirements, he will turn his back on the Church or even God. The tacit apostasy of many Christians from their churches goes back to this defective form of Christianity. A lasting bond of faith is granted only on the basis of a personal decision for Christ, a personal encounter with the self-surrendering God.

(c) Good deeds
Many today do not attach importance either to tradition or to the fulfilment of religious duties, but insist so much the

more on active love of neighbour and involve themselves in society. They think that it is *sufficient* to be a good person, that they do not need any Church or commandments. They are involved in political and social life and are not interested in what people believe or how they believe. Many regard anything like experience of God as harmful. They think it would lead people to be satisfied with the existing structures in Church and society, prevent them from continuing to struggle, from continuing to protest. There are in fact Christians who talk a lot about experiences of one kind or another, but who wallow — so to speak — in their feelings, who want to enjoy their experience of God, to withdraw from responsibility for the world and to take refuge in an empty spiritualism. There are in fact groups which talk a lot about the Holy Spirit and a charismatic renewal of the Church, give an impression of exaggeration, of over-enthusiasm, and overlook the fact that Paul also envisages socio-critical charisms (we shall examine this more closely in the sixth week).

This lack of balance however should not give the impression that any renewal which makes a fresh discovery of the importance of worship of God is bound to draw people away from their social and political obligations. On the contrary, if social and political commitment do not flow from worship, the latter cannot be described as 'Christian' in the authentic sense of the term. For then we are forced to rely on ideologies which occasionally describe themselves as Christian, but which are not born of the experience of the Spirit and only serve political ends. For the Christian, social and political commitment is also charismatic: that is, sustained by personal experience of the Spirit. But anyone who takes the norms of his action solely from certain ideologies is living at second-hand.

Another form of 'Christianity of action' is restricted first of all to living and acting in a Christian way and then waiting for people to ask how we have come to live this sort of life. In a thoroughly Christian milieu, in which a personal testimony of the word is not expected of everybody, this may suffice. Sometimes it is in fact even better to commit oneself without words, to bear silent witness to the Christian hope.

But in a new missionary situation of the Church, even in countries where Christianity is indigenous, we can no longer dispense with the personal witness of the word. The Christian Church did not originally arise from the fact that the disciples first of all led a Christian life and waited to proclaim the word until people invited them to do so. Of course they were one in heart and mind, had everything in common and were loved by all the people (Acts 4.32-37; 5.12f). But this testimony of life was *founded* on the pentecostal experience of the Spirit which from the very beginning found expression in a *public*, hitherto unknown *praise* of God, in a proclamation of his great deeds (Acts 2.4, 11).

For the Christian, profession of faith on the lips is as important as the life he lives. Life and the proclamation of the word confirm each other mutually, each gives rise to the other: 'The word is near you, on your *lips* and in your heart (that is, the word of faith which we *preach*); because, if you confess with your *lips* that Jesus is Lord and believe in your heart that God raised him from the dead, you will be saved. For man believes with his heart and so is justified, and he confesses with his *lips* and so is saved' (Rom 10.8-10). Jesus himself began his proclamation with a *personal prayer in the presence of others* (Lk 3.21) and expressly required a personal profession of faith from his disciples: 'Every one who *acknowledges* me before men, the Son of man also will acknowledge before the angels of God' Lk 12.8). According to Paul, all Christians are called to the ministry of proclamation and not only the one 'cleric' or 'spiritual person' in the congregation. All Christians are 'spiritual men' (1 Cor 2.14f) and all are expected also in the word to be 'stewards of God's varied grace' (1 Pet 4.10f).

This testimony of the word is by no means a self-presentation, a boastful exhibition of oneself. For it is effected by the Spirit and fruitful when it comes from self-surrender, when the Christian 'dies' like the grain of wheat. Consequently at the very beginning of the proclamation of the word is self-surrender to Christ and this is anything but 'fanatical'.

3. We must recover the initial Christian experience

According to the statements of the New Testament, being a Christian begins with a very definite experience. What would be our answer to the question: 'Did you receive the Holy Spirit when you believed?' It was just this question which Paul put to the inhabitants of Ephesus when he came through their city (Acts 19.2). I would answer: 'When I became a believer? I can't link it with any particular time. I've always been a Christian, from birth onwards. When did I receive the Holy Spirit? I don't know, how could I decide that?' The people of Ephesus at that time even declared: 'We have never even heard that there is a Holy Spirit' (Acts 19.2). *We* perhaps did hear that there is supposed to be a Holy Spirit, we know about him from *hearsay*, but we can't get an idea of what he is like and we can scarcely say whether and when we received him. But Paul's question has a meaning if the experience of the Spirit was so far-reaching that we are able to recall it after many years.

In one of the earliest letters of the New Testament, the letter to the Galatians, we read: 'Did you receive the Spirit by works of the law, or by hearing with faith? Are you so foolish? Having begun with the Spirit, are you now ending with the flesh? Did you *experience* so many things in vain?' (Gal 3.2-4). There were people at the time who asserted that it was possible to merit the grace of God, to receive his Spirit, by observing the Old Testament law and certain rites (circumcision). Paul therefore reminds the Galatians that when they began to be Christians, they were granted a life-transforming *experience of the Spirit* which they can continually *recall* and which *permanently* determines their life. The servile fulfilment of precepts and laws on the other hand destroys freedom and ruins the initial experience. How can that experience be described more closely? In the light of the original Greek text, Galatians 3.4 should be literally translated: 'Did you then *suffer* so many things in vain?' The word used here is the same as that which is used to describe the sufferings of Jesus, his self-surrender on the cross. *The basic and initial Christian experience is a passive experience, of suffering, of being filled with the Holy Spirit.*

This occurrence presupposes that I allow myself to be utterly emptied, so that the Spirit of God can completely fill me. I must therefore be ready to surrender myself completely to this Holy Spirit. Luke describes this initial experience in these terms: they were *filled* with the Holy Spirit (Acts 2.4; 4.31; 9.17), they *received* him (Acts 2.38; 8.15, 17, 19; 10.47; 19.2), he *fell upon them* (Acts 8.16; 10.44; 11.15). In his introductory remarks at the beginning of the Acts of the Apostles, Luke summarily describes this occurrence as '*baptized with the Holy Spirit*' (1.5; cf. 11.16). This experience therefore comes at the beginning of being fully a Christian, since it was also the beginning of the Church (cf. Acts 11.15f).

Where this is mentioned in the New Testament the reference is always to *adults*. There is no absolutely clear reference to the practice of infant baptism in the New Testament. You were probably baptized as a small child. But at that time you were simply not capable of a personal self-surrender, of a conversion and personal decision for Christ. That is not to say anything against a Christian education in school and home. The requirement that the young person should first decide for Christ in adolescence in a milieu hostile or indifferent to Christianity is *utopian*. But a Christianity which rests *only* on education, *without decision or conversion*, is incomplete. No one can be converted in my place (not godparents, nor parents and teachers), no one can be baptized as my representative. I must then *take up again* the personal conversion and self-surrender which baptism presupposes. If I had been baptized as an adult, I would have rejected Satan publicly in the church: '*I reject Satan;*' I would have made a public profession of my faith: '*I believe;*' and I would have confessed before everyone: 'Yes, *I* will be baptized'. It is not sufficient therefore to repeat this confession in chorus with others (for instance, at the baptismal renewal in the Easter Vigil), since this means merely doing the customary thing. We cannot 'introduce' the personal self-surrender to Christ, we cannot prescribe it in liturgical renewals. Each one ought to ratify and repeat in a very *personal* way his baptismal promises which others made in his place.

Admittedly, this event is not primarily our own work, our own intention and our effort of will, God always takes the first step. He himself effects in us the beginning of faith, the beginning of conversion. In the fifth century there were people who asserted that we must approach God with good will on our part and then he does the rest. Against this view, the Church says: 'The *beginning* of faith and even the *readiness for faith*, which leads to faith in Christ and to baptism, is not in us by our own power, but by the inspiration of the Holy Spirit.[3] From this text it is also clear that the *beginning* of faith is not primarily the acceptance of the Church's teachings and theological truths, but the readiness to believe, the *emotion of faith* on the basis of which alone we are open to accept truths of faith. Faith draws on *all* our powers: mind, will and feeling. Since however faith was for so long regarded simply as the acceptance of statements as true and the part of the intellect over-emphasized, we must today stress the fact that the emotion of faith is also part of faith, the fact of being deeply *affected* (cf. Acts 2.37) by the testimony of faith rendered by others.

4. What does 'experience' really mean here?[4]

(a)   A personal testimony
Most Christians expect their clergy, not only to be good Christians, but in some sense also to be nearer to God (this holds not only for Catholics, but in much the same way for other Christians, even if in theory they adopt a different position). Consequently the account by a priest of a situation where the positions were reversed is important. It is at the same time typical of the renewal which came about in almost all the major Churches in the middle of the present century. This is the account, given by a Catholic priest:

On 16 May 1966 I attained an important goal in my life. I was ordained priest and indeed 'for ever'. I was convinced that the world would be waiting for me. There seemed to be no problem which would not have to yield to my passion for

for the gospel. I was convinced that my theological studies, my prayer-life and my modern psychological insights had prepared me to face up to any situation. I felt that I had the answer more or less to all problems and in retrospect I must say that I trusted myself, my psychology and my pastoral plans more than prayer and the guidance of the Holy Spirit.

After two years — it was the period after the Council — an increasing tension appeared in my life, I was dissatisfied with myself. I felt that I was no longer able to cope. New pastoral methods were continually recommended, fashionable theological trends set in; I became insecure and saw very clearly that my scanty psychological knowledge was by no means adequate for giving people really relevant advice. My prayer-life gradually disintegrated and finally completely collapsed. I noted that I was beginning to drink. In the evening I permitted myself one drink, or two or three. It helped me to relax. I had expected my priestly activity to secure recognition and acceptance of my person, but this was still denied me. Consequently I threw myself into a restless activism, which I took very seriously. I thought I was the only priest who was really working. I had also more money than I needed and began to indulge myself. I was unable to perceive my spiritual poverty and I attributed my dissatisfaction to the situation in my parish. All that I needed — so I thought — was a change in the locality of my work. My bishop agreed to my request and sent me to another parish. I threw myself again into wild activity, never having a moment free. I preached what others had written. It was clear to me that I was not speaking from experience when the words God, Jesus, Holy Spirit, came to my lips. I had certainly learned and studied a great deal, but I had now come to an end. I kept up the pretence of being an overworked priest and basked in the sympathy of the people around me.

It was at this time that I heard of a prayer-group in a neighbouring town and decided that I must make one more attempt. I came into a parochial hall in which about a hundred and forty men and women were assembled, all very ordinary people. I was greeted in a friendly way, but sat down cautiously in the last row. I wanted to be no more than an observer. After a hymn at the beginning, an elderly grey-haired man stood up and introduced himself as a taxi-driver. I was interested to hear what he had to say and I thought to myself: 'What will this man be able to tell me?' He uttered a brief, wholly personal prayer that God would give him the strength to bear witness. When he then began to talk quite spontaneously about Jesus, I immediately noticed that *he really knew the person about whom he was talking*. I had never before heard anyone speak of Jesus Christ in such a personal way, neither during my studies nor later. The words of this simple man touched me deeply.

During the following weeks I felt a restlessness in me, but it was different from what I had felt before. It was not the restlessness due to unceasing activity, but a disquiet because I might have blocked my own way to God. I continued to go frequently to the prayer-group and always returned feeling ashamed.

One evening it got so far that I began to pray again after a long interval: 'Come, Holy Spirit'. I knelt down and felt the tears running down my face. I have no idea now how long I prayed, but I recognized the immense pride which was at the root of my wrong attitudes. I knew that only God could liberate me from this pride. At one of the next prayer-meetings I asked the others to lay their hands on me. I remembered the words from the second letter to Timothy: 'Rekindle the gift of God that is within you through the laying on of my hands: for God did not give us a spirit of timidity but a spirit of power and love and self-control. Do not be ashamed then of testifying to our Lord' (2 Tim 1.4ff). In deep gratitude I said a personal prayer of surrender. The others laid hands on me, prayed for me and thanked God. Never in my life have I embraced people so heartily as I did after this service: with their help I had found my way back to God and so to my vocation.

(b) Experience through personal encounter and personal relationships

I shall cite further evidence later, but in the example given above important reference points can already be seen. The priest at his ordination had indeed accepted Christ, but he had not yet completely emptied himself for the Spirit of

Christ, had not yet died like the grain of seed, had trusted too much to his theological training and study. Anyone who has gone through a good Christian education can at the same time of course grow through his milieu into a deep experience of faith; but the real breakthrough is then granted only after a crisis. The conversion presupposed to baptism is conveyed not only through education, not *only* through *others'* experience of faith. There are certain basic experiences which we must go through ourselves. Christian faith is not merely the adoption of another person's experience, but also an experience entirely of *one's own*. The decisive thing is that it does not come from ourselves, but *begins* when we *see and hear* the faith of others. The highly trained priest saw and heard in the simple taxi-driver something which he could in no circumstances have produced for himself. Faith comes from hearing. This principle of Paul (cf. Rom 10.14) is essential for a renewal of the Church. The more anyone has set himself apart from God, so much the more intense is the regaining of the first experience. It begins with the senses — that is, with seeing and hearing — and it is expressed again also through the senses — in the above account is the gift of tears (incidentally, a special prayer for this is provided in the Roman missal).

The conversions reported in the Acts of the Apostles take a similar course. The Pentecostal experience as Luke describes it is wholly a conversion-experience, for it enables the apostles to bear witness to their faith in face of the threat of death by the Jewish authorities (Acts 4.20), although previously they had not had an interior relationship either to the death of Jesus or to their own death (they had fled at the death of Jesus, Mt 26.56), nor had they followed Jesus to the foot of the cross. The Pentecost experience must have been manifested in them also in utterances perceptible to sense, for the 'devout men from every nation', who were present there, were amazed. Some even ridiculed them: 'They are filled with new wine' (Acts 2.13). Peter explains this event in his Pentecost sermon: 'Jesus being therefore exalted at the right hand of the Holy Spirit, he has poured out this *which you see and hear*' (Acts 2.33). This testimony of Peter, which at the same time was a testimony of his own experience of faith, evidently shook the hearers deeply, for Luke reports: 'When they heard this *they were cut to the heart*' (Acts 2.37). The perceptible experience of faith, *coming from outside*, affected them deeply *inwardly* and led them to ask the question: 'Brethren, what shall we do?' Peter answered: 'Repent, and be baptized every one of you in the name of Jesus Christ for the forgiveness of your sins; and you shall receive the gift of the Holy Spirit' (Acts 2.38). This gift of the Spirit is again completely perceptible to others, through the senses, frequently in the gift of tongues, as can be seen from later accounts in the Acts of the Apostles (cf. Acts 10.46; 19.6; 8.18). *All gifts of the Spirit are such sensibly perceptible signs of the presence of the Holy Spirit* (1 Cor 12.7).

In concluding, we must insist that the experience of conversion, presupposed to baptism and to be repeated in view of the practice of infant-baptism, is roused in us by the testimony of faith on the part of others and leads to a self-surrender to Christ, seizing on the whole person down to the very depths. It must clearly be distinguished from mere book-knowledge or knowledge acquired by study, but also from experiences simply taken over from others through education. This self-surrender *grows* in intercourse with God and in the many experiences with him again a *certainty* is granted which can neither be produced nor refuted through rational arguments (cf. Acts 2.36).

An example may clarify our meaning. There is quite a considerable difference between going on a journey, where we can 'experience' a landscape, and simply reading an account of a journey. There is a difference between having the appearance and the character of a person described to me and meeting him face to face, seeing and hearing the man himself. The first encounter can at the same time make a deep impression: 'It was about the tenth hour' (Jn 1.39). With this first personal encounter began the history of a life-long association with Jesus and out of the experiences so collected grew the gospel of John.

The experience understood here results therefore from *immediate contact*, it is *knowledge on the basis of personal encounter*. In this sense we say: 'I have had experience of this person', that is, of our parents and friends, of people in our profession or whom we meet at work.

After Job had had his experiences of God, he recognized: 'I had heard of thee by the *hearing of the ear*, but now my eye sees thee' (Job 42.5). What is your position? Do you know God only from hearsay or did you once see and hear him or something of him? Nowhere in the Bible is it said that we are to wander in the desert our whole life long, that we may never experience the presence of God in our life. Perhaps we have made too much of a virtue out of our lack of experience.

5. Must we correct our ideas of God?

Experience is never completely blind, but is always accompanied by ideas, for the whole person is involved in the experience of faith: not only the emotions, but also the will and the mind. The result is that we may well construct mental barriers, may regard a thoroughgoing experience of faith as quite impossible, because we have a one-sided idea of God. Consequently it would be helpful to write down now, without much reflection, all the ideas which we generally associate with the word 'God'. This is a really important step in our 'initiation' into that basic experience which is so strikingly described in the New Testament.

(a)   Is God only 'Creator'?

Among the terms on the list are probably 'father', 'creator', 'supreme being', 'cause of the world', 'omnipotence', perhaps also 'love'. The enumeration will scarcely contain the name 'Jesus Christ' and certainly not 'Holy Spirit'. These findings reveal a widely held, very one-sided attitude to God. We see him primarily as the *almighty Creator*. At the beginning of the creed common to all Christians we also read: I believe in God, the almighty Father, Creator of heaven and earth. We are so accustomed to associate the ideas of 'God' and 'almighty Father' with one another that the mystery of the divine Trinity plays almost no part in our practical Christian

life. For we overlook the fact that the creed speaks not only
of one, but of three divine persons. The word 'God' means in
fact these three persons equal in dignity, as the twofold 'and'
in the structure of the creed makes clear: 'I believe in God:
(that is, in) the Father *and* the Son *and* the Holy Spirit. This
Holy Spirit is *'at the same time* worshipped and glorified
with the Father and the Son'. He is no less God than the
Father and Jesus Christ, but scarcely anyone is aware of this.
This is a disaster. For we believe in the Holy Spirit 'who is
Lord and *giver of life'*. Why is this not said of the Father and
of Christ? Because it is the Holy Spirit who is the power of
God and of Jesus Christ, the power that will raise us up
(cf. Rom 8.11) and even now raises us to live a Christian life.
You will never really *experience* the presence of God in your
life, you will not be able to be an alert, convinced Christian,
if you do not believe in the Holy Spirit who gives you life, if
you are not *open* to his activity in you.

(b)   God as Holy Spirit
At this point we must raise a further question. What occurs
to us spontaneously when we hear the word 'Holy Spirit'?
Dove? Tongues of fire? Pentecost? We see at once how feeble
are these ideas of the Holy Spirit. Jesus Christ is a human
being and we know what a human being is. The Holy Spirit
did not become man; unlike the Son, he did not 'appear' in
a single human person. But neither did he become a dove or
tongues of fire, for these terms are merely *metaphors and
analogies*. It is dangerous to attempt to depict the Holy
Spirit, for the metaphors give scarcely any indication of the
form of his presence. And what occurs to us when we hear
the word 'Pentecost'. If we do not think immediately of a
holiday, perhaps it is the word 'Church' which occurs to us.
But is the feast of Pentecost really a specially vital *experience*
of the Church for us? Is there not something wrong here and
must we not *thoroughly* correct all our ideas of God?
    'Holy Spirit' in the New Testament is *the power and
dynamism* (dynamis) *of the 'Father' and the 'Son', with
which these two divine persons are present and active in us
and among us*. He is present in all of us as one and the same
power and makes possible a 'we-experience' going far beyond

any other human solidarity.[5] 'By *one* Spirit *we* were *all* baptized into one body and *all* were made to drink of *one* Spirit' (1 Cor 12.13). The Holy Spirit appears as a person only in a very few texts of the New Testament, as — for example — when he is called 'helper' and 'counsellor'. We *experience* this helper and counsellor in our relations with God, however, only in so far as we help others, support others, promote the faith of others in his power. There is no point in putting up a statue in church with the title of 'Helper' (on the other hand it is very appropriate to depict the man Jesus Christ as a human being). Unlike Christ and ultimately the Father, the Holy Spirit is not a person who *confronts* us; but he enables us from the very beginning to enter into a relationship with Christ and with the Father and he wants also to organize, purify and liberate our relations with one another.

Let us ask again therefore more precisely: *Where* then is the one whom we commonly understand as God? The answer usually given is: He is in heaven, or even, he is everywhere. But is not this a somewhat theoretical statement, something we have learnt, which has been instilled into us? Have we at any time really *experienced* God everywhere? We said at an earlier stage that experience has something to do with seeing and hearing. Have you then ever seen or heard this God the Creator? Certainly not. The Bible teaches us that God the Creator is not a part of creation, not a star, not a tree or an animal, or any other sort of thing. But how then is he present in his creation? Certainly by his omnipotence. God is everywhere because he keeps all things in existence. But we cannot see and hear *God himself*. We can only *conclude* from creatures to the Creator (if we do not decide that everything has come about by chance).

In education and instruction therefore it has been brought home to us (rightly) that God lives in himself and independently, outside the world; but then he easily becomes a heavenly supervisor, watching over the world from outside. Children are frequently told to remember: 'What I am and what I do, God my Father sees me too'. This of course can be meant wholly in the biblical sense that God is my loving father who cares for me and is always with me. A more threatening note is struck in another reminder: 'An eye that sees whatever happens, in light or darkest night'. Is not our freedom, our joy in life, somehow threatened by this God, this heavenly spy? It can be proved that this idea of God was one of the causes of modern atheism. Towards the end of the last century, the philosopher Nietzsche said: 'I can't bear anyone to be continually watching me and so depriving me of my freedom'. He drew the conclusion: 'Away with such a God. Better no God, better place our fate in our own hands, better be God ourselves'.

Is not Nietzsche here making a protest which we also feel? If God is supposed to be present as an observer, wholly from outside, then we are really not interested in getting to know him more closely. We keep him as far away from us as possible. Then again, what sort of a God is it who permits wars, world-wide hunger, concentration-camps? Who has been constantly demanding something of us even in our own life-history? Perhaps we admit that he has created the world, but basically we still think that he does not bother very much about it afterwards.

(c)   The Holy Spirit is present among us in a way accessible to sense-experience

At first it seems as if the Bible confirms the idea of God as remote from the world. For in the Old Testament it is repeatedly stressed that we cannot and may not make for ourselves any image of God, that we cannot see and hear God himself. Moses, we are told, was in contact with God, for they spoke together 'face to face, as a man speaks to his friend' (Exod 33.11; cf. Deut 34.10). And yet Moses cannot and may not see God's countenance, 'for man shall not see me and live' (Exod 33.20). This is also continually stressed in the New Testament. God the Father has no voice that we can hear, no form that we can see (Jn 5.37). He dwells in inaccessible light: 'whom no man has ever seen or can see' (1 Tim 6.16; cf. 1 Jn 4.12). It is clear then that we have no experience of God conveyed through our senses.

The statements of the New Testament on the man Jesus of Nazareth take us a step further. In him there *appeared* physically the God who is invisible and cannot be experienced in himself (Tit 3.4). Jesus' contemporaries, who had personal contact with him, speak of themselves when they say: 'That which we have *heard*, which we have *seen* with our eyes, which we have looked upon and *touched* with our hands, concerning the word of life — we proclaim' (1 Jn 1.1f). Anyone who saw and heard the man Jesus of Nazareth really *saw and heard* something of the eternal 'Word' and thus of God himself. Jesus' contemporaries *experienced* God himself in the man Jesus of Nazareth. But what is our position?

After Jesus' departure, we can no longer see, hear and touch him, but that does not mean at all that we are deprived of any opportunity of an experience of God conveyed through our senses. Jesus left us his Holy Spirit who 'brings to remembrance' (Jn 14.26) all that he did and said. The Holy Spirit does not bring us any *new* revelation, but he keeps alive in history Jesus' testimony and experience of himself. The Pentecost event in Luke really amounts to a proof[6] that Jesus is risen: the risen Lord has poured out the Holy Spirit, *which you see and hear* (Acts 2.33). In other words, *when we see and hear how other people give themselves to God, eulogizing and thanking him, then we see and hear something of the Spirit himself of God and of Christ.* This becomes especially clear at the assembly for worship, as Paul explains when he speaks of someone who is uninformed or an unbeliever (for instance, one of our religiously indifferent contemporaries) entering such a gathering, where all speak to his conscience and reveal the godlessness hidden in his heart, so that,'falling on his face, he will worship God and declare *that God is really among you*' (1 Cor 14.25). This God, who is among us and in our midst, the New Testament also calls 'Holy Spirit'. God then is not only 'above us' and 'outside his creation' as the almighty Creator, but *present among us and in our midst* accessible to sense-experience as the Spirit of Jesus Christ. This will become still more clear in the fifth and sixth weeks when we speak of the Church and of the charisms. Here first of all it should be pointed out that in the creed we profess our faith in the Holy Spirit who 'has spoken through the prophets' and that biblical studies show that the origin of the experience of the Spirit in the Old Testament lay in prophecy. In the New

Testament also, after the charism of the apostle, the most important gift of the Spirit is that of the prophet (1 Cor 12.28). It is of their function that the words are used: 'God making his appeal through us' (2 Cor 5.20). God is present therefore accessible to sense-experience in the gifts of the Spirit, in the charisms. That is why we read in 1 Corinthians 12.7; 'To each is given the manifestation of the Spirit for the common good'. *In the gifts of the Spirit the Holy Spirit himself is manifested.* As the eternal Son of God therefore was 'manifested' in the man Jesus of Nazareth, so the Spirit of Christ is similarly 'manifested' in the gifts of the Spirit, particularly in the assembly for worship.[7]

In conclusion then we must once again raise the questions: When the word 'God' is mentioned, why do we not think in the first place of 'worship of God'? Is the assembly for worship for us an event in which we can *see and hear* something of the Spirit of the Father and of Christ? If this is not so, then we must also correct our ideas of God.

Third week: Separation

Distrust of God is the origin of separation from him

1. Renewal of the baptismal promises as the recovery of salvation
   a) God's salvation is healing
   b) Sin and distrust do not arise solely from ourselves

2. We are distrustful of God
   a) 'I believe you'
   b) Basic trust
   c) The conquest of fear

3. We have insured ourselves against God
   a) Begging for recognition — supercilious dissociation
   b) Power — submissiveness
   c) Pleasure — self-contempt

4. The celebration of reconciliation (confession)
   a) Confession — Catholic
   b) Confession — Protestant

1. Renewal of the baptismal promises as the recovery of conversion

(a) God's salvation is healing

In the second week we said that, in view of the practice of infant-baptism, the adult Christian must recall his baptismal promises and the conversion-experience which these presuppose. Even for someone who has been baptized as an adult it is not sufficient frequently to 'recall' his initial experience purely in thought: he must constantly *renew* it in himself. Luther once said that the whole Christian life was a 'crawling into baptism'. The renewal of the baptismal promises therefore is an event that is central to the Christian life. This very personal step is not possible without the assistance of others, since it is a step of faith; but it affects the individual in his wholly *personal* relationship to God. We shall show later that Christian 'initiation' or 'introduction' has several aspects: in baptism God orients me to *himself*, in confirmation to the salvation of *others*.

Baptism takes place 'for the forgiveness of your sins' (Acts 2.38). The external sign of baptism especially points to this: 'You were *washed*, you were sanctified, you were justified in the name of the Lord Jesus Christ and in the Spirit of our God' (1 Cor 6.11). 'Be baptized, and *wash away your sins*, calling on his name' (Acts 22.16; cf. Heb 10.22). External washing signifies and effects internal purification from sin. The Holy Spirit is given in baptism as that divine power and dynamism which takes away our sins, orients us to God and gives a start to our own resurrection (cf. Rom 6.1-14). Baptism is therefore a *rebirth* (1 Pet 1.3, 23; Tit 3.5; Jn 3.3-8). In what was known as 'Baptism of the Spirit' (in some Churches confirmation is the outward sign and offer of this) it was not then primarily a question of my own salvation before God, but of the salvation of *others*. In it we are made witnesses to Christ and equipped with the charisms (gifts of the Spirit) enabling us to be such. In baptism we are first of all made members of the Church, at the second stage we become witnesses in the Church and for the Church (Diagram 1).

Baptism has two aspects: God orients us to *himself*

(justification) and he orients us to the *salvation of others* (testimony). The two aspects are not in every respect the same (we shall have something to say on this later). The first three weeks of this 'initiation' prepare for the renewal of the baptismal promises and the rest prepare for personal receptivity to the gifts of the Spirit which serve for the salvation of others.

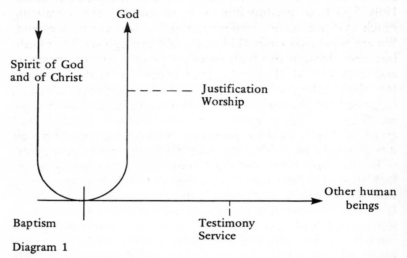

Diagram 1

Justification or 'forgiveness of sins' in the New Testament means two things: God forgives me those sins for which I am wholly *personally* responsible in his sight, but he also cures those faults of mine which have arisen in me through the sins of *others* and made me distrustful of him. The personal sins of others, which determine my life from the very beginning and which arouse and strengthen the inclination to sin coming from myself, are also recapitulated under the designation of 'original sin.'[8] In this third week we shall pay special attention to this second aspect, since many people are separated from God without really knowing why. The mere intention of returning to God is not sufficient: we must permit him to penetrate into our depths, for everyone of us has certain negative experiences, painful memories driven into the depths of his unconscious life. In our relations with God we must learn not to dwell on these internal wounds, we must permit God to make good much that we have suffered and to heal us. Such a healing is a long process and can be said to have really begun only when we can recall these wounds and painful experiences without sadness, indignation or shame, without reproaching God because of them. We must learn — to express it for once in a wholly human way — to be reconciled with God in the power of the Holy Spirit, to pardon him — so to speak — for permitting much that we do not understand and will never understand. We are separated from God, not only through our own fault, but also through the fault of other people, of our ancestors and in fact of all those who lived before us. With the prayer for the healing of memories and expectations, which is suggested for the end of the third week (fifth and sixth day), we shall — if God leads us so far — *learn* that baptismal grace is God's *healing presence.* Sanctifying grace, which was promised us in baptism, is at the same time *healing* grace.

In the third week we shall appreciate more precisely the fact that the very first beginning of sin (including original sin) is not our vast pride in relation to God, but *distrust.* Each of us is distrustful of God, each of us has secured himself against God and each of us must therefore permit God himself to give him a new *basic trust.* The history of mankind, and therefore our own pre-history, is more or less stamped with an *inherited distrust* which is of demonic origin.

The candidate for baptism is asked: 'Do you reject Satan?' But the question could also run: '*Do you reject distrust of God?*' From the depths of our consciousness premonitions, rooted in negative experiences with other human beings, continually arise: 'Trust no one, not even God'. Are you then prepared to rely on the power of the Holy Spirit, resist these premonitions and once more put your trust in God? In the last resort only God himself can cure our distrust, for which we are not wholly ourselves to blame, and that is why in the third week we want to lay bare our deeper self to him. *His salvation is healing.* The renewal of the baptismal promises therefore includes bringing before God our personal sins, for which we ourselves are responsible, in whatever way is customary in the Church to which we belong.

(b) Sin and distrust do not arise solely from ourselves
What has been said up to now needs further clarification.
Man's mind can be compared with an iceberg the visible tip
of which is above the surface of the sea, while the greater
part remains immersed below. With each of us the tip of the
iceberg is the conscious, rational mind, but this is only a
small part of our whole person. Most of what we do, think,
feel, will, comes from the depths of what the Bible calls 'the
heart'. The heart is the innermost part of man. From it
emerge feelings, impulses and resolutions, but also fear,
suffering, love and desire. God wants to seize us in this innermost part, he wants to open these depths, as with the
disciples on the way to Emmaus: 'Did not our hearts burn
within us while he talked to us on the road, while he opened
to us the scriptures?' (Lk 24.32). The Spirit of God is poured
out and sent into these depths of ours (Rom 5.5; 2 Cor 1.22;
Gal. 4.6). But how does it come about that from these depths
of ours there arises also resistance to God: doubt, distrust
and even impenitence (cf. Mt 13.15; Rom 1.21; 2 Cor 3.15)?
We know today better than formerly that much of this
resistance to God depends not only on our free will, our
clear consciousness, but also on attitudes and habits conveyed to us by our *milieu*. We cannot properly control them,
but grow into them from birth onwards. The grace of God
then offered to us cannot be fully developed, because the
milieu constantly provokes us to sin, because the sin and
guilt *of others* prevents us from growing in the grace of
God. Sin is never something wholly private, not even when
no one else knows about it, but it has consequences for our
fellow-men, for those around us: it has a *social* character.
If — for example — I yell angrily at someone, the latter will
probably react in the same way. My own anger then returns
to me in the anger of the other person and provokes me to a
further outburst of anger. *Through my own sin I create a sinful environment for myself.*

The Bible teaches us that this was the state of things from
the very beginning, so that all those who lived before us share
responsibility for the basic sinful attitudes in the world.
Through the sin of the first human beings 'sin *came into the
world*' (Rom 5.12). 'All that is *in the world*, the lust of the

flesh and the lust of the eyes and the pride of life, is not of the Father but is *of the world*' (1 Jn 2.16). That is why 'the world did not know Jesus' (Jn 1.10). 'Original sin' therefore does not merely go back to the first human couple, but everyone has a share in it and each of us is responsible for the fact that future generations in turn grow up in situations which provoke them to sin. Our milieu is a constant appeal to evil, which becomes so much stronger the more it is coupled with social pressures. If — for example — a child grows up in surroundings in which people make their living from stealing, he will find it very difficult not to steal. The value of honesty is simply not appreciated in his milieu and so will be unintelligible to the child from the very beginning. There is thus a *situation* preceding the personal decision of the child for which he is not himself responsible.

The sin of the world — or original sin — cannot however be restricted to this sinful situation which comes upon us from outside and which we have to endure. From ourselves too there arise instincts and impulses as a result of which we are *inclined* to give a sinful response to a sinful situation. In each of us there is at work an inexplicable and mysterious inclination to evil which has its ultimate origin in distrust of God. We can be so deeply marked by it that we are scarcely capable any longer of hoping in God. For, if we give way to distrust, the result is fear and this itself increases to the extent that we try to fight against it. Jesus Christ does not want only to assume our own death in ourselves and so deprive it of power, but also to liberate us from any exaggerated distrust, from unjustified fear. We must not only suffer our own death, but we suffer also the sins of other human beings and our own inclination to sin. Jesus does not promise to liberate us at a stroke from these consequences of hereditary distrust (we shall have to cope with them to our very last breath), but he tells us: 'In the world you have tribulation; but be of good cheer, *I have overcome the world*' (Jn 16.33).

2. We are distrustful of God

(a) 'I believe you'

It is only against the background of faith that the meaning
of sin really becomes clear. Faith first begins in the confidence that the God who has revealed himself to us is
truthful. This confidence finds expression in the statement:
'I believe *you*'. This faith must be distinguished from that
which is expressed in the statement: 'I believe *what* you
say'. By this is meant: I believe in the *content* of your
statement. I regard it as true. I believe you in this respect.
If, for example, someone tells me about a traffic accident of
which I was not a witness, I believe this report, since the
person who told me is worthy of belief. Only when I believe
the other *as a person* and trust him, when I regard him as
worthy of belief, am I also prepared to believe the *content*
of what he tells me. Faith then is not purely an intellectual
act in which we accept as true what the Church teaches us,
nor is it a pure act of the will (faith is not merely a declaration
of the intention to love God), nor is it pure feeling isolated
from intellect and will. Faith grasps the human person in his
innermost core and in all his depths, it lays claim to all his
resources. At the same time however it must be observed that
this faith in a person, confidence in the credibility of God,
includes faith in the content of his message, that is, in what I
can perceive with the intellect.

It is particularly important to emphasize this in connection
with the initiation into the basic Christian experience. In
these seven weeks we are not speaking primarily about the
content of faith, we are not giving preliminary information
on faith. This is either presupposed (with those who still
describe themselves as Christians) or it can be accepted only
when the original readiness for faith, the basic trust, is roused.

(b) Basic trust

'Whoever does not receive the kingdom of God *like a child*
shall not enter it', says Jesus in Luke 18.18. By this he means
that we should entrust ourselves to God as guilelessly and
confidently as a child entrusts itself to its parents or to
others who care for it. Anyone who does not adopt this

approach to God will never know him by experience. Let us therefore attempt to reawaken the earliest memories of our childhood. We wanted in any circumstances to be close to our parents and we looked to them for security and a home. We would not be separated from them for anything in the world. Our basic attitude towards them was primarily the very opposite of distrust: it was in fact the great *primitive trust* of a child which expects everything from its parents. In the history of our own lives we cannot get back behind these first memories. We can learn from the relationship of the very small child to the people in its circle, to its mother, what is spontaneous, basic trust. For the small child the mother is — so to speak — that beyond which nothing greater is expected: it lives in a kind of paradise of trust. The small child lives with its mother in a quite elementary and close unity, in physical proximity, and is oriented to its mother with all its powers, in all its still completely unconscious depths. Modern psychology naturally recognizes also that even in this very first initial phase not all the child's expectations are fulfilled. The child already experiences (quite unconsciously, of course) its first disappointments; and a distrust of other human beings and of God — later often seen to be unjustified — is established even at this early age.

As adults, more fully conscious and aware of our freedom, we cannot turn to God with the still completely *unconscious* trust of a child. We are told, however, in the second chapter of Genesis that God originally created man for a paradise of close familiarity with himself. The biblical writer depicts paradise as the background for his description of original sin, which consists in the last resort in distrust: the fear that God might be very different from what he had shown himself to be.[9]

He created man for a paradise of close familiarity with himself and issued only one commandment: 'You may freely eat of every tree in the garden; but of the tree of the knowledge of good and evil you shall not eat' (Gen 2.16f). This means that the sole commandment which God gave to man is: *Never give way to distrust of me.* The serpent however, the prototype of evil, knows how to seduce the woman, to lead her precisely into this distrust with the shrewd question: 'Did God say, "You shall not eat of *any* tree of the garden"?' (Gen 3.1). This of course is *not* what God said (only: you shall not eat of *one* tree), but the woman now begins to feel distrust, to suspect that God is perhaps a tyrant, wanting to suppress her freedom and not even permitting her to be distrustful towards him. This, she thinks, is an interference with her freedom and she sees no reason why she should not put it to the test. But in this way the trap is already locked, the step has been taken from a distrust that remains *possible* to a real distrust. The history of evil in the world is the history of a single attempt to free ourselves again from this trap by our own powers. But the more man struggles to get out of it, so much the more firmly does it close.

You must already have noticed something like this in yourself. Another person has promised you something — assistance, support — depending solely on his free choice. Your trust in this person is always inevitably accompanied by the *possibility* of distrust. You are not quite certain whether the other person will fulfil his promise, for you cannot control his freedom. Perhaps he will behave quite differently from what he promises at the present moment. If however you do trust him, this means that you have conquered the possibility of distrust: if you had not done so, you would not be free to trust him. Trust cannot be enforced, it is an act of freedom. If you wanted to, you could also distrust him. If you now give way to this distrust — which is always possible — and keep up this attitude, it very soon turns to fear. Fear that the other will perhaps not *really* keep his promise. The more you are preoccupied with this fear of yours, the more intense it becomes.

Every deep human love — especially at the beginning — is accompanied by this sort of distrust. When — for example — two people assure one another, 'I love you', there always lurks in the background the suspicion that the love might not be genuine, that one person would like to dominate and so oppress the other. Who keeps the upper hand? Will the other person help me to become aware of myself or will he only use me to strengthen his own self-consciousness? However justified such distrust may be, anyone who gives way to it will destroy the trust which alone can secure enduring love. Moreover, *excessive* distrust leads to the *fear* that the other is not really what he claims to be. Anyone who gives way without reason to this fear must share the blame if love breaks down. *Excessive fear is culpable.*

This sort of thing can be seen also in the social, economic and political relationships of individuals and nations with each other. In the industrial countries today we are no longer in fear mainly of natural disasters, but we are anxious about our savings, our employment, our provision for old age. The competitive struggle in the efficiency-oriented society is accompanied by continual distrust, the fear that one party will overreach the other and a constant terror of losing prestige. Peoples and nations too have this fear of one another. Excessive fear is the beginning of wars, oppression and exploitation.

(c) The conquest of fear

The question thus arises as to whether our relationship to God may be similarly conditioned? Can I really say: 'My God, I love you with *all* my heart?' Have we not already been too often disappointed by this God? Has he not expected too much of us in the course of our lives: suffering, for instance, which was certainly not due to our own fault? And is this God not really terribly cruel, when he permits social injustice, when he permits Auschwitz or the incomprehensible starvation of young children? Must we not be distrustful of such a God, when he tells each of us quite personally: 'I am with you, you are in my hands'? Or when he tells all mankind: 'I am your God'? Why must the innocent suffer? Is not this God really a tyrant who acts quite differently from what he has promised, who demands subjection from us, a child-like spontaneous trust, who even *forbids* us to distrust him? Does not this very requirement, to trust God in a childlike way, make us distrustful? Does he not want us to grow up, to approach him as adults?

We find this kind of fear also in reverse — so to speak — on the part of parents. They fear that their own child will break off its child-like relationship to them, that it will stand on its own feet, become their equal and no longer belong

completely to them. Parents often tend to keep their
children at the infantile stage as long as possible, for fear that
they might become their equals. Every small step of the
young person is supervised, restricted by precepts and
prohibitions. The parents are afraid that the child will no
longer remain in a state of childish dependence, but will
confront them freely and autonomously, that they will no
longer be able to control him. Precepts and prohibitions for
their part produce fear in the child. The concealed wish to
transgress the prohibition produces feelings of guilt and these
in turn lead to fear. Is it not similar with the relationship
between God and ourselves? Nietzsche once said: 'I can't
bear anyone to be continually watching me and suppressing
my freedom'. The origin of modern atheism is rooted in the
fact that people really gave way to the suspicion that God
can and will suppress our freedom.

In the relationship between parents and children only one
thing can get us out of this twofold vicious circle: calm,
relaxed trust of one another. It is the same with our
relationship to God. The *possibility* of distrusting God,
which is part of the nature of freedom, must never become
reality. This very short step from possible to real distrust is
the beginning of sin and evil in us. But once we have given
way to this distrust, once we become afraid of God (even if it
is not the Christian God, but perhaps society, the party or
some other divinity), we can no longer free ourselves from
this fear by our own resources. The more we fight against
fear, the more invincible it becomes; the more we try to get
absorbed in the daily cares and other activities, each one of
us becomes so much less of a person, so much the more are
we abandoned to the seductive powers and forces of this
world.

In our relationship to God also only one thing will help us:
calm, relaxed trust, spontaneous trust, which in the last
resort cannot be sustained with rational arguments, but
which we can accept as a gift from the Spirit of God who
elicits the *beginning* of faith in us.

The same is true also of social and political fears. Let us
assume for a moment that all human beings in the world,
including the politicians and statesmen, were at this moment

to surrender their lives quite personally to Christ, to accept him into their life with a complete trust which is his own gift. Political, social and economic activities would not decline, but would be intensified; and all this would result, not mainly from fear, but from a spontaneous trust in *God's plan* for mankind. Without God, fear drives nations and peoples into increasing isolation and selfishness, into further estrangement from one another, and the final result is the fragmentation of mankind.

'Be reconciled to God' (2 Cor 5.20): This is the permanent, prophetic message of the New Testament. If we cannot remove basic fear from the world at a stroke, at least we can begin to discover our own fear and permit it to be cured by the power of God. That alone would be a major contribution to reconciliation with our own life-history and with our fellow-men, and a contribution to social progress which only Christians can achieve.

3. We have insured ourselves against God

We saw that distrust of God turns into fear and — since all men have given way to this distrust — there is also in all of them a secret fear of God at work. Modern atheism too is a fear-reaction, the result of seeing God mainly as a tyrant, continually watching us. But abolishing this God is by no means the same thing as removing fear, which again is manifested between individuals and nations in a variety of forms. In the long run this fear leads us to hostility and the latter in turn creates a need to secure our own existence. In our modern civilization the need becomes all the greater because of the vague sense of menace in a hostile world beyond our comprehension: a world whose development we ourselves cannot directly and immediately control. Out of this situation every individual acquires a feeling of isolation and this again results in both insecurity and an incapacity for human fellowship.

The security measures which we adopt towards other

human beings react on our relationship to God and prevent a radical conversion to him. The more we insure ourselves against other human beings, the more reserved we are also towards God: for we cannot love God whom we do not see, if we do not love our fellow-men with whom we are in contact (1 Jn 4.20). Fear in regard to God however is mostly due to a one-sided idea of God, as we showed in the second week. According to the New Testament, 'There is no fear in love, but perfect love casts out fear' (1 Jn 4.18). The more we entrust ourselves to the powerful *presence* of God among and in the midst of men, to that dynamism of God which we also call the 'Holy Spirit', the more will unjustified distrust and excessive security measures be broken down, the more our love for our fellow-men and for God will grow. Here again then we are faced with a decision. Either we suppress our distrust and our fear and attempt at the same time also (mostly unconsciously) to protect ourselves by every means from being hurt and disappointed; or we surrender ourselves to God completely, give back to him the story of our life in a spontaneous trust which is his own gift, permitting ourselves to be healed in depth by him.

In this 'initiation' we cannot discuss all security measures towards our fellow-men and towards God; we can mention only those which arise from man's most important basic instincts, that is, from man's need for prestige, power and pleasure (cf. 1 Jn 2.16). At the same time it will become clear that even the apparent reversals of these three attitudes — that is, supercilious dissociation, submissiveness and gloomy, joyless, combative abstemiousness — are security measures.

(a) Begging for recognition — supercilious dissociation
Everyone longs for happy and pleasant relationships with other human beings, for it is in these that he experiences the meaning of his life, as we saw in the first week. This aspiration is insatiable and is shown in a longing for in-creasing love, finding expression in a variety of forms. A very widespread and also obvious form is begging for recognition. We see that we are dependent on this recognition by our milieu in order to be able to give a meaning to our actions

and our lives. But what happens if this love in the form of recognition remains denied to us? Then we use every means to get it for ourselves, we beg for it. Even as children, any signs of life were dependent for their effect on the attention of parents and others belonging to our circle. If this attention was persistently denied us, hurt and disappointment became deeply rooted and remained in adult life. In our later life therefore we try to gain for ourselves the recognition then withheld from us. Thus we insure ourselves at the same time against being hurt again and act according to the principle: *If the others recognize me, they cannot do me any more harm.*

Perhaps this is the sore point in your life. Have you not already been too often disappointed? Have you been given that degree of recognition and love for which you long? Did your parents prefer your brother or sister to you, did they not recognize you and take you as seriously as you in your spontaneous childish trust had expected? Perhaps they discriminated against you in school, treated you unfairly? Has your professional advancement been all that you could have wished? Perhaps you blame God for all these inner wounds, for in the last resort he at least permitted them. In order to insure yourself against further disappointments, you now live according to the principle: *I no longer trust any-one, not even God.* I'll get the love and recognition of other people as best I can and then I need not bother about God's recognition and acceptance of me.

Or did you take refuge in supercilious *dissociation*? Did you look for protection by withdrawing from other human beings and even from God, making yourself independent of them? You are acting then according to the principle: *If I withdraw into myself, nothing can hurt me any more.* I remain protected against disappointments if I no longer take myself, other human beings or even God so seriously. You avoid people who are unsympathetic to you, get out of the way of controversies and avoid even God since you distrust his promises. You keep a safe distance from God and secretly maintain that he is a God who in reality does not bother about you at all. Perhaps you still hold firmly that not everything is the result of chance, that a 'supreme being' created the world, but you protect yourself against an all-too-immediate relationship with this supreme being. Such an attitude is very widespread among so-called 'intellectuals'.

Jesus described begging for recognition as a decisive obstacle to gaining access to God: 'When you pray, you must not be like the hypocrites; for they love to stand and pray in the synagogues and at the street corners, *that they may be seen by men*. Truly, I say to you, they have received their reward' (Mt 6.5). In the shrewd advice of Gamaliel, the teacher of the law, we have an example of supercilious dissociation: if what is happening among the Christians is from men, it will be destroyed; if from God, then you can't destroy it (Acts 5.38f). The distinguished teacher does not simply leave open the question as to whether God has intervened anew in the history of his people, he regards it as highly improbable.

(b) Power — submissiveness

The second great basic instinct of man is to strive after power, possessions, superiority (here we can combine these three ways of repressing basic fear). *Each* of us acts in some way according to the motto: *If I am powerful, no one can touch me*. It is part of man's nature to be his own master and master of his material surroundings, but in a greedy, excessive striving for power he tries to disguise his inward insecurity, to insure himself. The modern efficiency oriented society lives by the competitive struggle which is at the same time a power-struggle. I must prevail and my advantage is necessarily another's disadvantage. I feel secure only when I've eliminated all my competitors. But this struggle for power is at the same time also a struggle for respect and prestige. That is why professional and business failure also means severe loss of prestige. Even in personal relationships between one human being and another — for instance, in marriage — power-struggles are involved: who is the stronger, who is superior?

Don't you also get satisfaction out of exercising power over others? Do you perhaps misuse the authority given to you, in order to show your superiority and to oppress others? Because of your striving for power, are you not continually forced to compare yourself with others? And where do you stand in regard to political parties? Do you regard them mainly as means of exercising power, of suppressing other opinions? Do you feel pleased with the thought that you have joined a powerful party, trusting completely in its power? Of course there are circumstances in which we should, can and must exercise power: but by excessive striving for power and precedence we are trying to make ourselves like God, to be as he is. In this case the exercise of power is a *security-measure in regard to God* and we shall then tend at the same time to oppress others. Excessive striving for power results in tyranny. On this point Jesus' warning is clear: 'You know that those who are supposed to rule over the Gentiles lord it over them, and their great men exercise authority over them' (Mk 10.42).

And where do you stand in regard to your personal possessions? Do you see in them an excuse for leading a private existence, *private even from God*? If this is the case then you will scarcely be hungry for God, for trust in possessions is one of the best security-measures in regard to him. You will scarcely notice your need of inward healing: 'Woe to you that are rich, for you have received your consolation' (Lk 6.24). 'It is easier for a camel to go through the eye of a needle than for a rich man to enter the kingdom of God' (Mk 10.25). Jesus' message is not a cheap consolation for the poor, merely promising them a better life hereafter (I shall have to speak later about socio-critical charisms), but an appeal to entrust everything to God, even one's own possessions. 'The love of money is the root of all evils: it is through this craving that some have wandered away from the faith and pierced their hearts with many pangs' (1 Tim 6.10).

In our relationship with God, the apparent contrary of excessive striving for power — that is, *submissiveness* — is equally disastrous. Excessive submission to a superior authority, an idol, a leader, a fascinating personality, is also a security-measure in regard to God, an attempt to gain a feeling of safety. We act then according to the motto: *If I submit, no one can touch me.* Perhaps you were educated very strictly and never really given a chance to enjoy your freedom. You always wait for 'instructions from above', never risk a decision of your own. You have a need to receive and carry out orders. You place your whole trust in persons and institutions superior to yourself, venerate them in such a way that — for you — God himself recedes into the remote distance.

Such an attitude towards the specific traditions and authorities of their Churches is widely spread among Christians. People insist on keeping to the traditional views and rules and are not in the least prepared to commit themselves to anything new. But anyone who thinks in this way is not open to God's offer to intervene in the history of his life and in the history of the Church. He simply does not see what ought to be changed in his life, for he does his religious duties and submits himself in every respect. Submission of course is necessary in the Church, but *submissiveness* is a *security-measure in regard to God*. If I surrender myself to him without reserve, if I entrust myself to his unforeseeable guidance, then he might perhaps require of me more than I can accomplish from my own resources. I might perhaps have to change my life radically overnight, give up certain habits and entrust myself to a renewal of my life and that of the Church which I cannot comprehend. There is a great deal in the Church which is defended by every means only because the *fear of what is new* is stronger than trust in God's guidance. Jesus condemned sharply a similar attitude on the part of the Pharisees. They observed the many laws and precepts in a scrupulously exact and exaggerated way, but for that very reason were not open to the originality of his message, not ready for conversion (cf. the great speech against the scribes and Pharisees, Mt 23.1-33).

(c)   Pleasure — self-contempt
The third great basic urge in man, pleasure-seeking, can likewise be used to insure oneself in regard to God. 'I want to get something out of life'. This does not mean merely eating and drinking in a superficial sense or the use of stimulants (cf. Lk 12.19: 'Take your ease, eat, drink, be merry'), but also the *enjoyment of life* in all its fulness and wealth. The motto for this attitude to life runs: *If I'm enjoying myself, nothing can upset me*. The loss of prestige, recognition,

personal acceptance, is frequently 'compensated' by excessive eating, drinking, use of stimulants. Even sophisticated enjoyment of life may conceal the fear that we might not be getting the best out of it. We can take pleasure in possessions, prestige, power, works of art and even in ourselves or in the love of another person, to such an extent that we can no longer pray sincerely to God: 'Thou art my Lord; I have no good apart from thee' (Ps 16.2). Augustine, himself an epicurean in his youth, warns us therefore against any desire to enjoy created realities. We may 'use' them only in order to find the way through them to a personal encounter with God himself. In the Letter to the Hebrews we are told that even in this life we may 'taste' the heavenly gift, the powers of the age to come (Heb 6.4f).

Anyone who seeks his whole happiness, his final bliss, in savouring created realities is protecting himself against the liberating hope of the future world (which is by no means an empty consolation). He is no longer open to a proffered experience of God's presence even now. Anyone enjoying life in this way is no longer detached from things or from human beings: he surrenders himself to them without reserve and trusts that such pleasure is sufficient to secure his human existence, to make possible his full personal development. On the second day of the first week we asked: 'What is it that fascinates, attracts, inspires me'? Fascinating things or persons radiate the promise of happiness once we possess them. What an illusion! That which fascinates us loses its attractive force when we possess it, use it and thus use it up. The novelty of fascinating experiences wears off, they become ordinary, so that one might even speak of the 'melancholy of fulfilment'. Who is there who is not openly or secretly pleasure-seeking and attempting to insure himself against the necessity of having to *accept* God's love, the sole source of happiness in his life.

The apparent contrary of enjoyment of life is contempt for the world and for oneself. This occurs when someone is disappointed and withdraws into himself, preoccupied — even though in self-depreciation — only with himself. Someone who does not succeed in enjoying life proudly dissociates himself from all that for which he strove: he dissociates himself even from himself in unjustified self-criticism and reproaches. He cannot reach the grapes, so he claims that they are sour. He protects himself against a further loss of prestige with the aid of the motto: *What I cannot enjoy I despise*. The self-denial demanded by Christ has nothing to do with self-contempt. Christ wants to show us that it is just the person who surrenders himself who will find himself: he will respect himself in a new way as someone through whom God wills to reach others human beings.

There are almost as many attempts, arising from distrust of God, to insure ourselves in regard to him as there are human beings. Everyone tries to do this in his own way and the attempts hitherto mentioned are only a few typical examples. *Every* sin is a dissociation and an insurance in regard to God. We need not explain more precisely how the activity of the basic sexual forces in man has also something to do with 'pleasure' (and correspondingly the contempt of these forces with 'self-contempt'). An inordinate striving after sexuality for its own sake, detached from any personal relationship and no longer an expression of personal love, has become today a widely spread security measure in regard to God and frequently a reason for internal resistance to a complete surrender of ourselves to God.

4. The celebration of reconciliation (confession)

The charismatic renewal of the Churches has within itself the power to break through encrusted traditions, liberate them from one-sidedness and open them up to the future of a newly reconciled Christendom. This is true also of confession. The end of the third week is a kind of turning point in the internal dynamism of the seminar. The prayer for internal healing on the fifth and sixth day of the week is itself an incentive to bringing before God the sins also for which each is *personally* responsible to him, to make us accept his reconciling grace. At the time of the Reformation the conception and practice of the sacrament of penance were the object of controversy. In what follows we give some

brief pointers to the present practice in the Protestant and
Catholic Churches. The prophetic call applies in the same
way to both: 'Be reconciled to God' (2 Cor 5.20).

(a) Confession — Catholic

In the Catholic Church in recent decades the understanding
of the sacrament of penance has changed considerably. In
1973 the Congregation for Divine Worship published
suggestions for the 'celebration of reconciliation' (see CTS/
Do 464 and 471, *Penance: Introduction to the New Rite* and
Penance: the New Rites). In the *communal* celebration of
reconciliation the members of the congregation help one
another to lay themselves open to the reconciling grace of
God and to permit him to rouse them to repentance. 'The
priest himself, or a deacon or other minister' may offer brief
suggestions for this (n.26). At this point the *universal priesthood of all the faithful* is recalled. Everyone should be
prepared to undertake the prophetic ministry, 'on behalf of
Christ' (2 Cor 5.20), admonishing and exhorting (cf. 1 Cor
14.3). In the charismatic prayer-services, of which we shall
speak later, this gift is often granted in a surprising way (lay-
preaching, for instance). Such a communal celebration of
penance (at the end of the third week) can become an
important aid to the 'initiation into the basic Christian
experience'.

In connection with this service, the opportunity of private
confession (general confession being the renewal of baptismal
conversion) may be offered (n.28). In the light of the new
suggestions this is an action *shared* between priest and
penitent and a form of *social experience of God*: it is
suggested that the two pray together at the beginning
(n.15). Then the priest *or* the penitent reads a text of
Scripture (n.17). The faith of the one rouses and strengthens
the faith of the other. Not only does the priest help the
penitent, but the latter also by reading Scripture and by his
own faith can and should prepare the priest for his sacramental ministry of reconciliation.

After confession, the penitent can express his contrition
and resolution in an extempore prayer. At the sacramental
words of reconciliation (absolution) the priest extends his

hand over the head of the penitent (n.19). The laying on of
hands here is the sign and expression of the healing, reconciling power of God, the sign of peace with God and the
Church. (As a result of the charismatic renewal the express-
iveness of this sign is being rediscovered, as I shall show in
connection with the renewal of confirmation.) The priest's
laying on of hands in confession is a form of *renewal of the
Spirit*, that is, a renewal of the promise of God which was
given to us at baptism. The celebration of reconciliation
closes with praise of God which again the penitent can
express in his own way (n.20). It is obvious that such a form
of the celebration of the sacrament of penance cannot simply
be 'introduced'. Here the 'charismatic' renewal will be able
to provide new incentives.

(b)   Confession — Protestant[10]
Is there confession also in the Protestant Church?

What was said in our exposition for the third week applies
both to Protestants and to Catholics. Some other Christians
will feel less certain about confession. First of all, therefore,
a number of points should be noted.

In Protestant services, especially when they include the
eucharistic celebration, there is a 'general confession'. Anyone who takes it seriously or is accustomed to examine
himself at home before receiving Holy Communion, to search
his conscience and to pray to God for the forgiveness of his
concrete sins, will have felt the blessing of this practice.

Many Christians admittedly think that confession in the
sense of acknowledging real sins to a 'confessor' is not
'evangelical'. This is not correct.

Martin Luther certainly turned very sharply against abuses
of 'auricular confession' and against the Church's enforce-
ment of confession. But he himself esteemed it highly
all his life. He says:

> 'I do not want to take away secret confession from
> anyone and would not give it up for the treasures of the
> whole world, for I know what strength and consolation
> it has given me. I would long ago have been defeated
> by the devil, if this confession had not preserved me'.

And in the Greater Catechism:
'If you are a Christian, then you need neither pressure
from me nor a precept of the Pope, but you will force
yourself to it ... If then I exhort you to go to
confession, I am doing no more than exhorting you to
be a Christian'.

Private confession should simply be proposed, not compul-
sory. It is of course clear from the history also of the
Reformed Churches how difficult it is — on the one hand —
not to exert pressure and — on the other — not to permit the
institution of confession to become a mere habit or to
despise and neglect it in the course of time. In the eighteenth
century, under the influence of the Enlightenment, private
confession was attacked and abolished. Since in many places
it had become interrogation by rote, it met with rejection
also in the revival movement of Pietism.

There have been many incentives for a revival of confession in the Protestant Churches. In the communities
stemming from the revival movement people speak of
'personal ministry' when one Christian confesses his sin to
another and receives from the latter the assurance of
forgiveness. Such a form of what is called 'confession' elsewhere in Christendom is often part of a life-transforming
decision for Jesus Christ for which the person gained
courage at evangelization meetings.

In the newer Protestant communities and the groups and
brotherhoods closely linked with them confession is part of
the obligatory form of the Christian life. The Taizé community have produced a guide to the examination of conscience
before confession which has been widely distributed and
frequently used.

There are two ways in which the practice of confession
can be helpful in a Christian's life. The one is regular,
personal confession to a pastor, who should be the same over
a long period of time and who can also make suggestions for
the spiritual life in confession and after the assurance of
forgiveness. This way is not absolutely necessary, nor —
according to Protestant understanding — is it necessary in
order to obtain God's forgiveness for sin. But it can be

necessary for *you*, to enable you to believe that you are forgiven. It is conceivable that a Christian who is involved in a community and wants to contribute to the proclamation of the gospel could find this way an aid to an examination of his life in all its concrete details and to offer it to God.

At the same time there are no rules as to how often pastoral guidance should be sought in confession. Any legalism is out of place here.

The other way is deliberate repentance and a turning to God to be realized only once — or only a few times — in the course of life. It is with this conversion, marking a clear break with all that hitherto meant separation from God in our life, that we are concerned at this stage of the initiation into the basic Christian experience. We receive what is new from God only if we give up the old and deliberately and concretely repudiate distrust of God.

Here too it should be noted that God does not need it, but *we* need such a step. It is helpful if this kind of conversion occurs at least once in your life. We want to encourage you also later to see and experience this confession, which you are now making, as the turning point in your life which you do not need to repeat.

None of this is law. There are many ways and all sorts of possibilities by which a human being may find his way to God.

If you are already familiar with confession and have practised it in a Christian congregation, then there will be nothing unusual for you in having forgiveness of your sin assured to you by your pastor at this point.

Can any Christian hear confessions?

In the Catholic Church the priest has authority to give absolution (declaration of freedom from sins). In the Orthodox Church the *startsy* (monks who are not ordained, but regarded as endowed by the Spirit for the ministry) also are expected to hear confessions. Protestant teaching on the subject is not uniform, mainly in fact because the question is not generally raised.

From the Protestant standpoint it ought to be said first of all that any Christian is able and permitted to hear confessions and to console anyone who expresses his guilt with the proclamation of God's grace and forgiveness of sins.

But this does not mean that it is possible to get round the problem so easily or that the Catholic and Orthodox view has no spiritual significance. This ruling stems from early Christendom, when Christians lived together in a close community and it was necessary for someone clearly to give expression to the decision of this community. He had to be authorized to do this. Not just any individual can act for the whole community.

Hence at the present time too, where there is a community of committed Christians, it is clearly of spiritual value that at least those sins which are also offences against the community should be brought before that community or its leader. Here an individual who heard confessions would be over-taxed. Moreover, an individual layman can always refuse to hear a confession. He has the right to feel that he has no vocation for it.

This does not mean that one can confess only to an ordained minister. There are spiritually minded people with experience of pastoral care in confession and who are obviously called to this ministry even though they are not ordained. But even this still does not mean that anyone can simply take it for granted that he has this vocation. Anyone who hears confessions must know what he is doing. He will have authority only if he goes to confession himself. And he will need the exhortation and intercession of other Christians who assure him that this is his ministry and his vocation.

'Hearing a confession is an important service which one Christian can perform for another. But it involves also a temptation to exalt oneself above the other person. We should never forget that it is always one sinner who is speaking to another' (German Protestant Adult Catechism, p.1198).

This may also give you the courage to seek out a minister for confession. A Protestant pastor, Wilhelm Löhe, who directed the spiritual life of his congregation in the last century, said:

'A person's honour begins with his repentance and his readiness for penance. I can assure you in the sight of

God that I never felt deeper respect for a human being than I did before my penitents acknowledging their misdeeds with shame and repentance. I bowed before them, I served them gladly'.

What has confession to do with the community?

It is a good thing also to make a statement and an acknowledgment of sins in front of two or more Christians. It can be helpful if several individuals use their specific gifts to make their contribution to the assurance of forgiveness, the consolation of faith and to guidance in a new life. Sometimes God may even grant a new beginning to a group or community in their communal and reciprocal confession. But we should beware of demanding or planning anything of this kind. Generally confession will be a private affair between two people.

Even then however it is related to the Christian community. We can explain this aspect in the words of Dietrich Bonhoeffer, words which should be read, considered and applied in ourselves particularly before a confession:

'Despite sharing in worship, praying together and despite all communal service, Christians can often remain isolated; the final breakthrough to real fellowship is not achieved, because they form a community as believers, as devout Christians, but not as irreligious people, as sinners. The devout community just does not permit anyone to be a sinner. Consequently each must conceal his sin from himself and from the community .... It is in confession that the breakthrough to fellowship occurs. Sin seeks to be alone with the person involved in it, it draws him away from the community. The more solitary a person becomes, the more destructive does the power of sin over him become; and the deeper the entanglement, the more hopeless his solitude. In confession the light of the gospel breaks into the darkness and stubbornness of the heart'.

Fourth week: Jesus Christ

Jesus' basic experience: testimony for God

1. Who was Jesus Christ?

2. Jesus' baptism of the Spirit — Prototype of our renewal in the Spirit
   a) The primitive Church's experience of the Spirit: key to the understanding of the accounts of Jesus' baptism
   b) Beginning of prophetic-charismatic activity
   c) God's intervention in Jesus' life-history

3. Jesus, the original charismatic
   a) Charism as gift of the Spirit
   b) Jesus, the prophet

1. Who was Jesus Christ?

At the beginning of the third week it was pointed out that the 'introduction' to the Christian life had several aspects from the earliest times. In baptism of water it is mainly a question of my personal salvation before God, of the 'forgiveness of sins', while the Pentecost event and its continuation in the Church orient us to the salvation of *others*. The eucharist is then *full* incorporation in the Church.

The Pentecost event is described as being 'baptized with the Holy Spirit' (Acts 1.5; 11.16). The view of the primitive Church was that Jesus experienced this happening in himself at his baptism in the Jordan and therefore it is to be discussed at greater length in the fourth week. The historical investigation of the New Testament has shown that Jesus' baptism in the Jordan is an indubitable historical fact, no less so than his death on the cross in Jerusalem. Even though it is impossible to write a life of Christ, since this was not the intention of the evangelists, nevertheless the beginning and the end of Jesus' public activity, his baptism and the cross, the turning points in his life, are described with historical fidelity in the New Testament. For this reason too the accounts of the baptism of Jesus acquire a heightened significance today, for in their light it becomes possible to obtain a more *original* picture of the man Jesus of Nazareth and to get rid of the accretions of later times. The accounts of Jesus' baptism, of the beginning of his public activity, show us Jesus as the *new*, the *last prophet*, *bearing witness to God* in a unique and unsurpassable way. We shall see later how important is this observation with reference to the present situation of the Churches.

Consequently we must ask first of all: What is your wholly personal image of this Jesus of Nazareth? What kind of a person was he? Merely someone who preached and practised love of one's neighbour? A noble, pure person who never harmed anyone? The social revolutionary and reformer to whom we can appeal when we defend class-struggle slogans, when we seek the redistribution of property and agrarian reform? Or was he simply someone who set himself against the political and social trends of his time? Was he perhaps a fanatic who wanted what was good but was not understood? Or a super-star to whom people streamed in crowds, by whom they were inspired, fascinated?

It is important to have a wholly *personal* relationship to Jesus, to the Jesus whom the gospels describe for us. The latter however are more than descriptions of his life. In the light of the Pentecost experience continuing in the primitive Church, they seek to show us — without making it transparent — the innermost nature of this man Jesus of Nazareth. Every human person is a unique mystery and this is true to an inconceivable extent of this Jesus of Nazareth, for he cannot be fitted into any psychological pattern. He acts, lives and speaks with an originality which is and will always remain incomprehensibly new. But for that very reason we have a keen interest in the basic experiences by which Jesus' life was determined, in the way he himself experienced his relationship to God.

Fortunately the New Testament provides an important pointer to this, for we are told there how Jesus addressed God in Aramaic, his mother-tongue. He used the word *Abba*. New Testament scholarship has shown that this form of address is one of the most historically certain of Jesus' sayings (cf. Mk 14.36). *Nothing is more typical of the man Jesus than this form of address in prayer.*[11] The first Christians adopted it (cf. Gal 4.6; Rom 8.15) and at the same time experienced in themselves the strength and power of the Spirit of Jesus. Moreover there are twelve passages in the gospels where it is said that Jesus turned in prayer 'to the Father': a clear recollection of Jesus' basic attitude to God. The word 'Abba' is difficult for us to translate. In Jesus' time it was a trustful form of address rooted in family life, used by children to their natural father more or less as we say 'Daddy' or 'Dad'; but it was also used by adults. When Jesus addresses God in this way he shows a spontaneous, natural simplicity which is clearly opposed to the aloof veneration of the remote, unapproachable God at the time of Jesus.

The form of address, 'Abba', goes back to the *original experience of Jesus*, to his extraordinarily intimate relation-ship to God, from which all other human beings are excluded. Never at any point in the gospels does Jesus combine with other human beings when he prays to his father. Jesus taught his disciples to pray: *'Our* Father' (Mt 6.9; cf. Lk 11.2), but he does not include himself in this 'we' of the disciples as they address the Father. John expressed this very clearly: 'I am ascending to *my* Father and to *your* Father, to *my* God and *your* God' (Jn 20.17). If on the other hand Jesus includes the Father in a 'we', then all other human beings are excluded: 'If a man loves me, he will keep my word, and my Father will love him, and *we* will come to him and make our home with him' (Jn 14.23). John 17.11 is equally clear: '. . . . that they may be one, even as *we* are one', and John 17.21f: 'That they may all be one; even as thou, Father, art in *me*, and *I* in *thee*, that they also may be in *us*, . . . that they may be one even as *we* are one'.

This 'we' also describes only the I-thou relationship between Father and Son: that is, Father and Son are set as a 'we' *over against* all other human beings. This and similar formulations bring out the first Christians' recollection of the basic Abba-experience of Jesus which found expression in his whole life, up to his death. Looking back over his life, the first Christians could put into Jesus' mouth the words: 'My food is to do the will of him who sent me' (Jn 4.34). 'I seek not my own will but the will of him who sent me' (Jn 5.30; cf. 6.38; Heb 10.9).

We are inclined to associate the word 'father' with the idea of implacable authority, of precepts and prohibitions. On the other hand, in Jesus' life and proclamation the word 'Father' means a benevolent God who liberates and loves human beings, who seeks to establish a rule of peace, justice and joy, in opposition to the inexorable human history of suffering, disaster, discord, injustice, sickening, enslaving oppression. This is the *basic religious experience* of the man Jesus of Nazareth, in virtue of which he is the sole witness of God to reveal and exemplify who God is and what he is like. We do not know when, where and how Jesus experienced this relationship to God in himself and in regard to himself. Luke maintains that the twelve year old Jesus was already given the charism of wisdom (Lk 2.40, 52), a God-given insight into his will. This 'increased' (Lk 2.52) and at about the age of thirty Jesus then appeared publicly as the new prophet, filled with the Holy Spirit. The New Testament tells us nothing about a 'vocation-experience' of Jesus, but the accounts of his baptism can be regarded as a recollection of the suddenness of his public appearance (his fellow-townsmen at Nazareth consequently ask in astonishment: 'Is not this Joseph's son?, Lk 4.22). We may assume that the prophetic-charismatic endowment of Jesus made its complete breakthrough at his baptism in the Jordan, for it is from that point that he came on the scene as the Spirit-filled prophet, bearing witness publicly to his unique Abba-experience. If we want to know how the primitive Church interpreted and reconstructed the self-experience of Jesus, we must therefore keep to the accounts of Jesus' baptism.

2. Jesus' baptism of the Spirit — Prototype of our renewal in the Spirit

(a)   The primitive Church's experience of the Spirit: key to the understanding of the accounts of Jesus' baptism
The earliest books of the New Testament were written about twenty years after the Pentecost-event (the letter to the Thessalonians about 52, to the Galatians about 54) and the gospels of Mark, Matthew and Luke emerged about 20-30 years later; John's gospel between 90 and 100. For a long time then the memory of what Jesus said and did was attested and transmitted almost exclusively in the primitive Church's missionary preaching and instruction. It is understandable therefore that the experiences bestowed on the first Christians after the death of Jesus (personal contact with the risen Christ, Pentecost event) entered into the accounts of Jesus. This is true also of the accounts of Jesus' baptism. The key to their understanding is found in both the charismatic-missionary experience of the primitive Church and its baptismal practice. Recent studies have brought out the fact that baptism of water for the forgiveness of sins was clearly distinguished in the earliest times from laying on of hands as a sign of the continuation of the Pentecost experience)[12]. The record of this is found in the following passages:

'When the apostles at Jerusalem heard that Samaria had received the word of God, they sent to them Peter and John, who came down and prayed for them that they might receive the Holy Spirit; *for it had not yet fallen on any of them, but they had only been baptized in the name of the Lord Jesus*. Then they laid their hands on them and they received the Holy Spitit' (Acts 8.14-17).

'On hearing this, they were baptized in the name of the Lord Jesus. And when Paul had laid his hands upon them, *the Holy Spirit came on them*; and they spoke with tongues and prophesied' (Acts 19.5f; cf.2.38).

In these texts it is not disputed that the Holy Spirit is given also at baptism, but at that stage his effects in the person are forgiveness of sin and the first incorporation into the Church. The laying on of hands by the apostles is meant to signify and effect the baptized person's contact with the initial charismatic-missionary experience of the Church, with the Pentecost event. Through this external sign the gifts of the Spirit (charisms) for testimony and mission are offered and granted by God to the baptized person. With the laying on of hands (Acts 8.15ff and 19.5f) it is a question, not of the candidate's personal salvation, but of his orientation to the *salvation of others*. As distinct from the baptism of water the New Testament calls this procedure also 'being baptized with the Holy Spirit' (Acts 1.5; 11.16). 'Baptism of the Spirit' therefore is Luke's title for his account of the charismatic-missionary propagation of the Church (Acts 1.5). He described how it takes place in Acts 2.1-13 (Pentecost-event). It can also be bestowed even before baptism of water (Acts 10.44-48) and this possibility again shows that these two events and experiences are completely *distinct:* initiation into the basic Christian experience has several aspects which do not completely coincide. We shall mention later that the Orthodox and the Catholic Churches see in the accounts given above of the laying on of hands by the apostles the origins of the sacrament of confirmation. The latter may therefore be described as *sacramental baptism of the Spirit.* Since sacraments are God's *offers* and are effective in us only to the extent that we accept the offer, the graces promised in the sacrament of confirmation must be continually freshly welcomed and accepted in the course of our life-history. This acceptance we call *renewal of the baptism of the Spirit (renewal of confirmation)* or *renewal of the Spirit.* The same holds for Confirmation and other forms of baptismal renewal in the reformed Churches.

Experts in New Testament interpretation tell us now that the accounts of the baptism of Jesus are composed in such a way that Christians can understand it as the proto-type of their own 'introduction' to faith and testimony.[13] They formed part of the primitive Church's baptismal instruction. John the Baptist's preaching on penance, which precedes the accounts of Jesus' baptism, had therefore also the character of a 'baptismal address' and for the Christians already baptized it was a reminder of their own preparation for baptism and the instruction which had been part of it. We can therefore understand why there is a clear distinction in the baptism-accounts between Jesus' baptism by water and his baptism by the Spirit: *'And when Jesus was bap-tized,* he went up immediately from the water, and behold, the heavens were opened and he saw the *Spirit of God* descending like a dove, and alighting on him' (Mt 3.16; cf. Mk 1.10). Luke in addition emphasizes the fact that Jesus' baptism of the Spirit took place *while he was praying* (3.21). This too corresponds to the experience of the prim-itive Church, for the Holy Spirit is given when God is addressed in prayer (Acts 1.14; 4.31; 8.15ff; 13.3; Lk 11.13).

Before I go more closely into the matter, I must first say something about the expression 'baptism of the Spirit'.[14] The experience of the primitive Church which it describes has today been bestowed in an historically new and surprising way to many Christians in all Churches: a sign that the Lord of the Church himself has begun to renew his Church. The primitive Church put into the mouth of John the Baptist the words: 'I have baptized you with water, but he will *baptize you with the Holy Spirit'* (Mk 1.8; Mt 3.11; Lk 3.16). What is the more exact meaning of this? The word 'baptism' in Greek meant 'dipping' or 'immersing' in water. In baptism of water for forgiveness of sins we are plunged into the water (baptism was originally conferred by complete immersion). It is water *with which* we are baptized in baptism of water. In baptism of the Holy Spirit on the other hand it is not water which is poured on us, but this divine power and dynamism which is also called Holy Spirit and which enables us to bear witness. This is the meaning of Acts, 2.33 where we are told that the risen Lord 'poured out' the Holy Spirit (cf. Acts 10.45; Tit 3.6; Rom 5.5). The same metaphor is found in 1 Corinthians 12.13: 'By one Spirit we are all baptized' (embraced by one Spirit, made to drink with one Spirit). The same thing is meant when we are told that we are *filled* with the Holy Spirit (Acts 2.4; 4.31; 9.17), we *receive* him (Acts 2.38; 8.15-19; 10.47; 19.2), he comes down upon us (Acts 8.16; 10.44; 11.15), we are anointed with him (2 Cor 1.21; cf. Acts 10.38). In the expression 'baptism of the Spirit' the word 'baptism' is used in a *metaphorical* sense. We are plunged — so to speak — into the Holy Spirit as into a vital element; we move in him like a fish in water; breathe him in as we breathe in the air around us; are filled with him, filled to repletion, as a vessel is filled up. Consequently the event of baptism of the Spirit is *distinguished* from that of water and is in no way a substitute for the latter. In baptism of the Spirit we are plunged into the divine *power for testimony*, for self-renunciation and self-surrender to others. We could call this event 'baptism for witnesses' as distinct from baptism for sinners by water.

The difference between the two events arises not least from the fact that, after encountering in baptism for the first time the pardoning and reconciling love of God and becoming initially a member of the Church, it is not possible on the very next day to bear witness of this love. Remission of sins must be shown to be effective in a life which bears the signs of it, experience must grow and ripen before we can give an account of that remission as witnesses. Even in Jesus insight into the will of God and experience of his presence 'increased' (cf. Lk 2.52), and his own baptism of the Spirit was then the complete breakthrough to his charismatic-prophetic activity.

(b)   Beginning of prophetic-charismatic activity
The three accounts of Jesus' baptism complement each other
(that of Matthew corresponds in essentials to that of Mark).
Following the usage of the primitive Church, we may read
them as preparation for our baptism of the Spirit:

> 'Then Jesus came from Galilee to the Jordan to John, to
> be baptized by him. John would have prevented him,
> saying. "I need to be baptized by you, and do you come
> to me?" But Jesus answered him, "Let it be so now; for
> thus it is fitting for us *to fulfil all righteousness."* Then
> he consented. *And when Jesus was baptized*, he went up
> immediately from the water, and behold, the heavens
> were opened and *he saw* the Spirit of God descending
> like a dove, and alighting on him; and lo, a voice from
> heaven, saying, *"This is my beloved Son*, with whom I
> am well pleased" ' (Mt 3.13-17).
>
> 'Now when all the people were baptized, and when
> Jesus also had been baptized and *was praying*, the
> heaven was opened, and the Holy Spirit descended upon
> him *in bodily form*, as a dove, and *a voice came* from
> heaven, "Thou art my beloved Son; with thee I am
> well pleased" ' (Lk 3.21f).

Luke stresses the fact that Jesus was baptized *together
with others*. This itself is quite surprising. Did Jesus need to
be baptized, to have something happen to him, and moreover
at the hands of a person whose status was so much lower
than his own? Could he not have begun his public activity in
virtue of his own fulness of authority? Was such an 'abase-
ment' necessary, a 'rite' which he permits to be carried out
on him? Matthew gives us the answer? 'Thus it is fitting for
us to fulfil all righteousness.' Grace-given wisdom, insight
into God's will, which — according to Luke — was given
already to the twelve-year old Jesus, here reaches its complete
breakthrough. Jesus does *nothing of his own will*, but has
received everything from the Father, including particularly
prophetic testimony to the Father. At the beginning of his
public activity he wanted to make clear in a sign that his
testimony for God did not come about by his own will, his

own effort, but is a vocation and gift. Jesus lets John's baptism happen to him as something he *endures and accepts,* in order to testify that he is proclaiming, not himself, but the Father. The first public appearance of Jesus was therefore already a *prophetic action.* It is important to keep this in mind, for the primitive Church saw in Jesus from the very beginning the new and also the last, unsurpassable prophet, revealing in his person, his words and works, who God is and what he is like.

As the Old Testament saw him, a prophet is a 'caller', a 'herald', and as such at the same time one who 'is called'. A prophet is a person who acts for someone, in his place and by his mandate, communicating and attesting something to others.[15] This communication and attestation can occur in words or even in *deeds.* The Old Testament prophets themselves linked their proclamation with striking, significant actions. Jeremiah, for example, carried an ox-yoke on his shoulders to exhort people to be obedient to God (to put up with the political domination of the Babylonians). Similarly Jesus at his first public appearance accepted baptism, in order through this sign to draw attention to the fact that all men — as the Baptist had preached — need to repent and must again be converted to God. In this way Jesus needs it clear that the people were living remote from God. At the same time he identified himself with them. John the evangelist puts into the mouth of the Baptist words which express the mind of Jesus: 'Behold, the lamb of God, who *takes away the sin of the world'* (Jn 1.29). Jesus identifies himself with those who express their need of conversion by receiving John's baptism of penance.[16] Baptism as understood by the primitive Church always had something to do with repentance and remission of sin. With Jesus this does not hold for himself personally, but refers to the sins of others.

When at the end of the sixth week (or later) you come forward to ask for the baptism of the Spirit and renewal of the Spirit (renewal of confirmation) by the laying on of hands on the part of those present, this event also includes a renewal of the baptismal promise: 'I reject distrust of God.' Without such an inward conversion, without a confession also of personal sins, no one can accept the gift of baptism of the Spirit, the gift of testimony. At the same time for you this event will also be a *prophetic action*. Simply by coming forward you are bearing witness to the fact that you again need repentance, forgiveness of sins and the assistance of others. A prayer-gathering is always packed when someone is asking for renewal of the Spirit, for this event is also a service to the faith of others. Baptism of the Spirit will also enable you to share the burden and the sin of other people in a way you had not anticipated. For weeks or months after this step you will observe certain changes in your life. You are not concentrated on yourself as you were formerly, you have more time for others, you are more open to their problems and needs. You are aware from your own experience that you are no longer living for your personal advantage, but equipped for service, that — without having yourself really willed or aimed at it — you are oriented in a new way to others.

Matthew attaches special importance to the fact that it was *after his baptism* (after he emerged from the water) that Jesus was given an experience of the Spirit which affected him deeply. He *saw* the Spirit of God descending upon him like a dove and he *heard* a voice. The expressions 'see' and 'hear' in the New Testament refer to the *experience* of God's presence, which begins in the senses. The evangelists do not mean to say that Jesus saw a bird after his baptism. The dove is merely a very ancient symbol for the Spirit of God, not the Spirit himself. Neither do the accounts assert that Jesus heard a mysterious voice from heaven, as it were, from a loud-speaker hidden in the trees. What the expression means is that Jesus at that moment and in the presence of others experienced in a very profound way the *presence of God*, making his choice. If someone speaks audibly, he is present here and now.

We should note that Jesus himself *saw* and *heard*, and that the bystanders *also saw and heard*,[17] for in Matthew the voice from heaven announces: '*This* is my beloved Son, with whom I am well pleased.' Jesus' experience of the Spirit has a *public character* from the very beginning. That is what is meant when the evangelist John makes the Baptist also say: 'I *saw* the Spirit descend as a dove from heaven and it remained on him' (Jn 1.32). From the very beginning Jesus did not guard his experience of the Spirit as a personal secret, but allowed people to share in it; he divested himself of it and made it public. *This is the origin of the Church.* The Church lives by the fact that Christ made public his own experience of the Spirit and that Christians 'bequeath' it — so to speak — in their testimony before one another. Hereditary distrust is thus overcome by the bequest and transmission of Jesus' experience of the Spirit. Everyone is called upon, by his personal testimony of faith, by the publication of *his* experience of the Spirit, to keep alive Jesus' own experience of the Spirit.

Luke goes a step further and describes for us in the light of the primitive Church's experience of the Spirit *how* those present took part in Jesus' experience of the Spirit at the Jordan: '*When Jesus was praying*, the Holy Spirit descended upon him in bodily form.' The primitive Church had learned by its own experience that the experience of the Spirit is the fruit of prayer and that its first expression is again prayer (cf. Acts 1.14; 4.31; 8.15ff; Lk 11.13). For the Church this experience was the *key* to the understanding of the person of Jesus. The first Christians were convinced that the Spirit, whose efficacy they had learned in the confident address, 'Abba, Father', is the *Spirit of Jesus*; for them in fact the experience of the Spirit was the ultimate *proof* of the resurrection of Jesus (cf Acts 2.33). It is in this light that we can interpret also Luke's account of the baptism. Luke does not tell us expressly what was the view of the primitive Church on the *content* of Jesus' first public prayer. The 'voice' which Jesus and the bystanders 'heard' could however give us a hint: 'You are my *son*' (Ps 2.7). In the Old Testament the king was regarded as 'Son of God' and therefore we cannot immediately conclude from this quotation that Jesus at his baptism of the Spirit experienced himself as 'Son of God' in the sense of the later teaching on the mystery of the Holy Trinity. The Abba-call of Jesus as we have received it, which certainly goes back to Jesus himself and describes his own original, intimate experience of God, could however clarify for us the basic charismatic-prophetic experience of Jesus which he made public for the first time during his baptism of the Spirit.

John the evangelist made that experience his own when he described Jesus praying in his farewell discourses: 'Father, the hour has come; glorify thy Son that the Son may glorify thee, since thou hast given him power over all flesh, to give eternal life to all whom thou hast given him' (Jn 17.1f). Perhaps Jesus' prayer at his baptism of the Spirit was something like this. In any case Luke does not mean to describe a purely mental prayer of Jesus, which would not have been perceived by the bystanders. *Jesus' first proclamation of the word was a public prayer.* Jesus did not pray to his Father only in solitude, but also in a very personal way in front of others. We have an example in Matthew 11.25: 'I thank thee, Father, Lord of heaven and earth, that thou hast hidden these things from the wise and understanding and revealed them to babes; yes Father, for such was thy gracious will.' Matthew certainly did not invent this prayer, but most probably took it from the tradition coming from Jesus' earthly life.[18]

For many Christians today their first personal testimony before others is the prayer before and during their baptism of the Spirit (renewal of the Spirit, renewal of confirmation). Perhaps you too in these weeks will be led by God to proclaim your faith in a personal prayer in front of others. Perhaps you too will hear the 'voice' at the same time saying: 'You are my beloved son (my beloved daughter).' All are sons and daughters of God 'who are led by the Spirit of God' (Rom 8.14). Perhaps you will be so deeply affected at that moment that you will be unable to say anything or at best only: 'Lord, here I am.' Others will lay hands on you, address to you prophetic words which come from God, will pray for you, praise God and thank him. When you see and hear how others pray with you and for you, you are seeing and hearing something of the Spirit of God himself, you are *experiencing* his presence, even though you 'feel' nothing at that moment. It is not a question of yourself, of your own inward emotion as something with which you could rest content, which you could — so to speak — enjoy. *Baptism of the Spirit is a baptism of witnesses.* Almost all who go through it say that after this event their lives are perceptibly changed. Of course this change may come about at an earlier stage. Many people are awakened by God today without the laying on of hands and prayer. But external, material signs help us on the way to God.

To recapitulate: we must regard as certain a number of aspects of Jesus' prophetic-charismatic activity. The first public *act* of Jesus was to place himself at the side of sinners. Later he supported still more clearly those who were aware of their sinfulness in the sight of God and also those who were outcasts from society at that time, those on the fringe, the underprivileged, the despised. His first public *utterance* was a prayer. It is certainly not accidental that in some manuscripts of Luke's gospel the very first verse of the Our Father — 'Hallowed be thy name. Thy kingdom come' — has been replaced by: 'Thy Holy Spirit come upon us and make us holy' (cf. the footnotes to Luke 11.2).

The first of the petitions Jesus taught us is the petition for the Holy Spirit and this request the Father will in any case fulfil in us (cf. Lk 11.13). The basic proclamation of Jesus, 'The kingdom of God is at hand' (Mk 1.15), as understood by the primitive Church, means therefore, the final outpouring of the Spirit, the baptism of the Spirit is imminent.

(c)   God's intervention in Jesus' life-history
'Jesus, when he began his ministry, was about *thirty years of age*' (Lk 3.23). This indication of his age must not be taken too strictly, since it goes back to Old Testament models (age of priests: Num 4.3; Joseph's at the beginning of his service of Pharaoh: Gen 41.46; David's at his anointing as king: 2 Sam 5.4 etc.). But what is certain is that Jesus did not appear on the scene at the age of fifteen like a boy wonder, nor was he like one of the modern gurus. Why did he lead the completely normal life of a craftsman up to ripe manhood? Today we would like to know how his day was spent, when he got up, how often and how long he prayed each day, what occupied him otherwise. We do not know what the situation was in Jesus' twentieth year, or in his twenty-fifth year, but evidently up to then he had not publicly acknowledged his vocation and election. It must have dawned upon him at about the age of thirty that he

had to make his public appearance, to bear witness in public. This *sudden* appearance of Jesus has about it all the marks of a *personal breakthrough*, even though the evangelists do not describe it as a 'vocation-experience' after the model of the Old Testament prophets.

Their intention is not by any means to say that Jesus experienced the presence of the Holy Spirit *for the first time* at his baptism. The point of the narrative is that God acknowledged Jesus at his baptism, recognized him and publicly authenticated him as the promised Messiah. That too is what the Baptist means when he says: 'And I have seen and have borne witness that this is the *Chosen One of God*' (Jn 1.34). The Church's magisterium in the first centuries then brought out clearly the fact that Jesus was 'Son of God' from the very first moment of existence and that from then onwards the Spirit in his fulness was already present in him. But this does not exclude an increase in his self-awareness as man of the fact that he was Son of God (although we have no explicit statements to this effect) and that the fulness of the Holy Spirit only gradually became effective in him. This is clear, not only in his fear of death on the Mount of Olives, but also at the crucifixion itself: according to Hebrews 9.14 Jesus offered himself on the cross to his Father 'through the eternal Spirit'. The resurrection of Jesus is therefore a further stage in his experience of the Spirit: 'The Spirit of God raised Jesus from the dead' (Rom 8.11), and in the event of Pentecost Jesus makes it clear finally that he is the one who himself baptizes with the Spirit and who leaves to the Church his own experience of the Spirit. But even the Pentecost event is not the close of the history of Jesus: it continues up to the present time, up to this very moment.

Jesus wants to inundate, fill, baptize you also with the power of the Holy Spirit, and this event will also mark a decisive stage in your life history, a turning point in your life, just as it was to those present at the first Pentecost. When Jesus was arrested, the disciples had fled (Mt 26.56), leaving him alone (Jn 16.32). Evidently they were not mentally oriented to Jesus' death as saving death, nor to their own death (cf. Mk 8.33). Even after the Easter events they still assembled behind closed doors for fear of the Jews

(Jn 20.19). But after their baptism of the Spirit at the feast of Pentecost, undaunted by the prospect of death, they made their profession of faith before the Jewish authorities: 'We cannot but speak of what we have seen and heard' (Acts 4.20). Between Easter and Pentecost then their experience must have become more intense and made its full impact in the event of Pentecost. Paul describes this experience in the words: 'becoming like him in his death' (Phil 3.10). The acceptance of one's own death is the beginning of the Pentecostal turning point in life, not only for the disciples, but for everyone who allows himself to be led by the Spirit of God and of Jesus to a full Christian existence.

Something of what has been said up to now can be made clear in a diagram — although, of course, a diagram cannot even remotely indicate the mystery of the person of Jesus (Diagram 2).

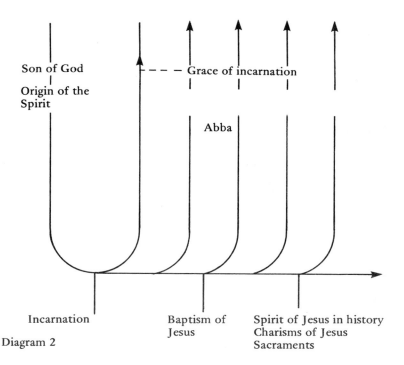

Son of God

Origin of the Spirit

Grace of incarnation

Abba

Incarnation

Baptism of Jesus

Spirit of Jesus in history
Charisms of Jesus
Sacraments

Diagram 2

The incarnation of the 'Word', of the 'Son' (cf. Jn 1.14; Phil 2.5-11; Gal 4.4-6) is a *unique historical event* which is not repeated. The grace of the incarnation is granted *only* to the man Jesus of Nazareth: he alone is 'of one being with the Father', as we read in the creed of the first ecumenical council of Nicea, which all Christians even today still regard as binding and use in the liturgy. All Christian Churches further confess that the Son made man sends and gives the Holy Spirit in the sense indicated in John 7.39; 15.26; Acts 2.33.[19] With the incarnation of the Son of God, therefore, the source of the Holy Spirit has entered history. This forms an ineradicable difference between Jesus of Nazareth and the Old Testament prophets, who were also filled with the Spirit of God.[20] The Spirit of God therefore was present in the man Jesus even from his birth. But this became completely evident only at his baptism.

The New Testament and the ancient councils teach us that Jesus' incarnation and his experience of the Spirit are closely linked but are *not the same thing*. Through the incarnation the man Jesus of Nazareth becomes 'Son of God' in a unique way and as excluding all other human beings. The grace of the incarnation relates him to the Father and Jesus' Abba-prayer is the expression of that relationship. The divine sonship of Jesus does not rest solely on the fact that the Holy Spirit dwells in him, nor is he a kind of 'incarnation' of the Holy Spirit, but incarnation and experience of the Spirit on the part of Jesus are distinct *in themselves*.[21]

According to the texts of the New Testament, the point of Jesus' experience of the Spirit is the salvation of others (cf. Acts 10.38; Lk 4.18 etc.). It has a thoroughly prophetic-charismatic character. His experience of the Spirit makes him a witness for God and not Son of God. On the contrary, his divine sonship is the presupposition of his testimony to God.

It is extraordinarily important to note these two distinct orientations of meaning in Jesus' basic experience: to the Father and to us. We shall see later that the distinction between the grace of *justification* (in virtue of which we may cry 'Abba' in the Spirit of Jesus) and *charismatic grace* for the sake of the salvation of others (consecratory grace, ministerial grace) is based on this dual orientation of meaning of Jesus' basic experience. Moreover, it must be firmly maintained that under no circumstances do we share in the grace of the incarnation, for we are not 'sons of God' in the sense that Jesus was Son. As 'anointed ones' (this is the literal translation of 'Christians') we share in the anointing of Jesus with the Holy Spirit at his baptism of the Spirit, his experience of the Spirit, his being filled with the Spirit. Consequently the Church is not the continuation of the incarnation, since this was realized once and for all in the man Jesus of Nazareth, but the historical continuation of his experience of the Spirit, of his charisms, the latter in turn being very closely connected with the sacraments, as we shall see later. For that reason we may bring out once again here how Jesus' gifts of the Spirit were made public at the same time as his baptism of the Spirit.

3. Jesus, the original charismatic

(a) Charism as gift of the Spirit

The results of New Testament scholarship show that the earliest and most important idea held about Jesus was of the eschatological *prophet, filled with the Spirit of God, 'anointed' with his Spirit.*[22] 'Christ' literally means 'anointed'. Unlike the Old Testament kings and priests however, Jesus was not anointed with oil, but 'with the Holy Spirit and with power' (Acts 10.38). The word 'anointed' therefore is used here in a metaphorical sense, as it had been earlier used of the Old Testament prophets. A typical example of this understanding which permeates all the New Testament writings is found in Luke 4.16-24. In the synagogue of his home-town, Nazareth, Jesus has the scroll of the prophet Isaiah brought to him and he reads aloud from it: 'The Spirit of the Lord is upon me, because he has *anointed* me to preach the good news to the poor. He has sent me to proclaim release to the captives and recovering of sight to the blind, to set at liberty those who are oppressed, to proclaim the acceptable year of the Lord' (vv 18f). According to Luke's account Jesus applies this quotation from Isaiah 61.1f to himself and thus defines himself as the prophet promised for the endtime (cf. Lk 4.24, 27). We cannot say for certain whether Jesus actually considered himself a 'prophet', but his whole demeanour and his fate show the same characteristics as those of the Old Testament prophets. In the eye of his contemporaries anyway he was certainly not a priest.

The quotation from Isaiah 61.1f itself contains a list of 'gifts of the Spirit', the effects in Jesus of his baptism of the Spirit. They were given him by the Father, not for his own personal use, but so that through him the Father could make his salvific missionary will effective in the world. They were for the benefit of the poor, the captives, the oppressed. Paul, the greatest missionary of all time, describes these gifts of the Spirit also as 'charisms'. As often elsewhere, he chooses here an unusual word in order to bring out the peculiarity of the basic Christian experience. The primitive Church transferred to Jesus many titles and designations. They can all be summed up in the proposition: Jesus is the *original charismatic*. He is the prophet, teacher, healer, lord over the demons and the powers of nature, the Son of God: in a word, 'the anointed one'.

Jesus' gifts of the Spirit cannot all be enumerated, for in him there is the 'fulness' of graces (Jn 1.16). In what follows we shall name only a few of them.

(b)   Jesus, the prophet
Jesus' contemporaries regarded him primarily as a prophet (cf. Mk 6.15; 8.28; Lk 24.19). The evangelists took the view that Jesus also saw himself as a prophet (Mk 6.4; Lk 4.24; 13.33; Mt 13.57; 23.31-39). Jesus however is not one in the series of Old Testament prophets: he is 'greater than Jonah', 'greater than Solomon' (Mt 12.41f).

John in particular brings out this unsurpassable 'greater'. Jesus, the charismatic prophet, appears as 'God's messenger' here, who himself has seen and heard — that is, experienced — what he proclaims from God: an experience that is utterly unique, excluding all other human beings. He is the absolutely unique 'witness of God.' The words 'witness' and 'testimony' are used in the New Testament very much as we use them at the present time in everyday speech. For example, anyone cited before the courts as a witness is expected to make a statement about what he has *seen and heard*, perceived with his senses. At the same time it is assumed that the facts are not known to everyone and that the witness must therefore be trusted. A witness's statement then is not one that can be completely demonstrated by reason. He demands trust in himself, he expects people to trust him — all the more so, the less they can test his statements. In this sense Jesus of Nazareth is the original witness of God. In the light of the character of the testimony, we cannot read the following texts in a 'neutral' spirit, but must submit to their unparalleled claim:

> 'No one has even *seen* God, the only Son, who is in the bosom of the Father, has made him known' (Jn 1.18).
>
> 'He *bears witness* to what he has *seen and heard*, yet no one receives his testimony; he who receives his testimony sets his seal to this, that God is true. For he whom God has sent utters the words of God, for it is not by measure that he gives the Spirit' (Jn 3.32f).
>
> 'Not that any one has *seen* the Father except him who is from God: he has *seen* the Father, Truly, truly, I say to you, he who believes has eternal life (Jn 6.46f).
>
> 'I declare to the world what I have *heard* from him . . . I speak of what I have *seen* with my Father . . . You have not known him; I know him' (Jn 8.26, 38, 55).
>
> 'The words that I say to you I do not speak on my own authority; but the Father who dwells in me does his works' (Jn 14.10).

This man Jesus of Nazareth, whom John describes for us, therefore claims that he alone has really seen and heard God. As we saw already in the second week, in the New Testament 'seeing and hearing' is an expression meaning immediate contact with someone, *immediate experience*. Jesus then asserts that he alone knows God, he has experience of God in an exclusive way. He tells us quite squarely:

'You do not know him' (Jn 8.19, 55). Jesus' experience of God then is absolutely unique and indeed it is in itself divine. That is why we declare in the Creed: 'God from God, Light from Light, *true God from true God*'. Do you believe that? Can we really learn only from Jesus who God is and what he is like? Have not other great men and founders of religions borne witness to God? Is not at least the God of the Old Testament, whom the Jews and Muslims also worship, the true God? Is not Jesus then essentially someone who brings home to us only one particular aspect of this God. Jesus' claim, excluding all other human beings, is in fact provocative, for he submits to *no human examination*, permits no comparison with other religious men. Even the testimony of John the Baptist is not authoritative for him: 'The testimony which I receive is not from man' (Jn 5.34). Jesus thus requires of us an *unqualified* trust of faith in his own testimony of himself.

Nevertheless he does not leave his contemporaries or ourselves without any opportunity of testing what he says of himself: 'If I bear witness to myself, my testimony is not true ... The works which my Father has granted me to accomplish, these very works which I am doing, bear me witness that the Father has sent me. And the Father who sent me has himself borne witness to me' (Jn 5.31, 36f). The prophetic works which Jesus does, his whole life and demeanour, are God's testimony to the truth of his claim. He takes the side of the sinners, the underprivileged, the oppressed, and so lets us know who God is and what he is like: 'If you know me, you would know my Father also' (Jn 8.19; cf. 14.7-9). If then someone has contact with Jesus, knows him from direct encounter, he thus knows and experiences at the same time who God is and what he is like.

In the fifth week we shall show that the Christian Church is basically nothing other than the continuation of this unique, prophetic, charismatic testimony of Jesus. In virtue of our 'baptism of the Spirit' we are all expected to share in it, so that we too attest and proclaim what we have *seen* and *heard* (1 Jn 1. 1-3).

In this charism of Jesus, to be the legate, witness, prophet of God, his other charisms are also involved (there is no question in the New Testament of listing the full number). The charism of wisdom is seen in the adult Jesus (cf. Lk 2.40), not only in his shrewd answers to catch questions (cf. Lk 20. 20-26) or on other occasions (cf. Lk 13.17; 14.6; 20.39), but more particularly in his 'insight' into the nature of God, which he did not possess from his own resources, but which was given him by God (cf. Jn 14.10; 12.49). We shall return again to the distinction between human shrewdness and charismatic inspiration. Jesus possessed also to a high degree the charism of a *knowledge of men* which was not based on psychological studies: 'Jesus needed no one to bear witness of man: for he himself knew what was in man' (Jn 2.25; cf. 4.18; 11.14; 13.11, 27).

In performing his prophetic deeds Jesus also shows a *faith* beyond all measure in God's power to conquer sickness and anti-divine powers, a faith which 'moves mountains' (cf. Mt 17.20; Jn 11.41f). That is why also the charism of *healing* was granted to him more than to any other human being (there is no need to give detailed examples here) and the charism of *distinguishing* from each other in their effectiveness divine, human and anti-divine powers. To give one example of the latter. Jesus describes Peter as 'Satan' because he has in mind, not what God wills, but what men will (Mt 16.23).[23] Jesus' basic charism is his *self-surrender* (cf. Section 5 of the first week) and out of this all his charisms and therefore ours also flow.

Fifth week: Church

The continuation of Jesus' experience of the Spirit in history

1. Jesus' experience of the Spirit: Origin of the Church
   a) Yes to Jesus — No to the Church
   b) The Holy Spirit and the history of the Church
   c) Schism does not come from the Holy Spirit

2. The Church is active in the charisms and in the sacraments
   a) The prophetic-charismatic origin of the Church
   b) What is a charism?
   c) The relationship between charismatic and sacramental signs

3. Renewal of the Spirit
   a) The permanent reality of baptism (Protestant)
   b) The sacrament of confirmation: historical continuation of the Pentecost event (Catholic)

1. Jesus' experience of the Spirit: Origin of the Church

(a)   Yes to Jesus — No to the Church

In the fifth week we cannot avoid discussion of questions and problems which are difficult and even to some extent painful. A part of the 'initiation' into the basic Christian experience is the *teaching* which corresponds to that experience. Jesus was not only a prophet, but also a teacher (Mt 23.10; Jn 3.2); he imparted not only experience, but also doctrine. Experience is broader and deeper than the intellect can grasp and convey by teaching, but teaching is nevertheless an indispensable part of the Church's work. The gift of teaching too is a charism (cf. 1 Cor 12.28; Rom 12.7; Eph 4.11). At all times in the Church spiritual and charismatic revivals involved the special danger of wanting to replace teaching by experience (mostly as a reaction to the equally disastrous tendency to replace and suppress experience by teaching).

If we are to speak of the Church in the fifth week, then we cannot appeal only to *verbal* statements of the New Testament. The structures, forms of expression, usages and doctrines of the new separated Churches have emerged only in the course of history, although each Church appeals to statements of the New Testament to justify its specific character. In this 'initiation' we cannot discuss all the difficult questions which still divide the Churches from one another even today, but we must examine some basic elements of the teaching of the Church. Baptism of water and renewal of the Spirit can be carried out only within a concrete congregation and Church and their effect is incorporation into that congregation. Consequently a decision for Christ is always at the same time a decision for the Church (or, provisionally, for a particular Church). The world-wide spiritual awakening and in particular the renewal of the gifts of the Spirit, granted by the Lord of the Church himself, may be seen also as the hopeful beginning of a *common* tradition of the now separated Churches.

Consequently the question arises: Are you really mentally oriented to your Church? What is the first thing that occurs to you when you hear the word 'Church'? Do you see it primarily as an organization, a power-structure, an institution which is represented by its officials? A sociological group which has always looked for support to the wealthy and powerful? Or do you associate with the word the idea of observance of religious duties, precepts, requirements, prohibitions. For many today the word goes round: 'Yes to Jesus — No to the Church'.

If you have not yet turned your back on your Church, do you still like to attend its services? For the original and essential meaning of 'Church' is 'assembly'; and if Christians no longer assemble for worship, the congregation can no longer be alive, the Church dissolves.

Opinion polls have shown that attendance at worship has declined in all the Christian Churches, mainly for two reasons: 1. *The participants at worship are in no way linked with one another.* People sit next to and behind each other and are oriented to the one 'spiritual leader' in the pulpit or at the altar. There is scarcely a hint of any real solidarity in the congregation. Even the presence of friends or neighbours is scarcely noticed, since that would be a distraction, would show a 'lack of devotion'. Nor is there much trace of a spiritual communion with one another. Only the hymn gives us a greater sense of fellowship. If people next to me, in front of me and behind me are singing with deep faith, then my own faith is strengthened and sustained. Nevertheless, it is difficult to see that the Church is an 'assembly', to which each person makes his own contribution (cf. 1 Cor 14.26) according to his particular gift of the Spirit. Worship remains essentially individualistic, each individual remains isolated. This is very different from the process of community-formation, of the socialization required in modern life. The deeper reason for this is the one-sided image of God of which we spoke in the second week. God is seen almost exclusively as the almighty Father whom we cannot see and hear, while the Holy Spirit as the divine reality among us and in our midst has fallen into oblivion. Fundamentally, it is assumed as a principle that there is only *one* God and only *one* man who can represent him on earth: the one spiritual leader. There is little evidence of the fact that every Christian is a 'spiritual man' (cf. 1 Cor 2.14f). At the Reformation of the sixteenth century the fact was stressed that every Christian is a priest and also has a mandate to preach, but this largely remained no more than a demand. The awakening of the gifts of the Spirit in all the major Churches in the midst of the present century, the gift of a *social experience of God*, could bring about a decisive historical turning point in this respect:[24] the transition from 'I' to 'we' also in worship.

2. *The language and rites of worship are outlandish*, they are no longer in harmony with our experience of life and faith. The linguistic expression, the hymns, date from past centuries. At that time, in a particular historical situation, they were the expression of a profound experience of faith; but feelings have changed now, the world has become different. Many prayers are derived from a rural way of life which is utterly remote from most people today. Some rites and forms of expression in Catholic worship date from the fourth or fifth century. These forms of expression amount to what might be called 'frozen' faith and can scarcely rouse faith today.

What the faith of past centuries has bequeathed to us is not all obsolete, but renewal is just as much a part of the essence of the Church as is the preservation of what has been handed down. On the other hand, renewal is not purely human work, it does not depend on strategy and planning, but can only be sought from God. Consequently the petition for the gifts of the Spirit and their acceptance is the presupposition for a spiritual renewal in the Church. Anyone who acts only according to the principle of 'Yes to the Church, No to the *traditional* Church' is evading the call to place himself at God's disposal for the renewal of his Church.

In any case, *no one comes to Jesus without the Church*. We can no longer see and hear Jesus himself and are therefore thrown back on the *historical tradition* of the testimony of the witnesses of Jesus' life. This tradition is not found mainly in the transmission of a book, the Bible, but in living proclamation. The Church — as the Reformers of the sixteenth century said — is the 'living voice of the gospel'; it is and remains such despite all sin and disfigurement.

Today there are well-meant attempts at new missionary methods. Young people go on to the main shopping streets of the great cities or to the beaches, and begin conversations on the meaning of life, on God's plan and about

Jesus. As a result, real conversions often take place, people frequently pray for the first time again after many years. But since they have been approached only as individuals, the seed of the word and the first flickering of a conversion-experience are very soon overgrown by weeds. A decision for Christ can be enduring only in an actual Church community. Even many 'revival movements' growing out of the major Churches have often failed to produce the expected fruits. In the first generation many parishes, whole regions, were gripped by a spirit of deep faith, but scarcely anything of this has remained in the second and third generation. Structure, order, discipline were lacking.

Such 'movements' also tend to get away from their Churches, to form Churches of their own and thus to speed up the division of Christendom. In a number of districts some 'awakened' families simply combine together. They reject any sort of relationship with other 'Churches', but neither do they regard themselves as a 'Church'. At this point we have the beginning of a new 'sect' and thus of further divisions.

Certainly the Holy Spirit is at work wherever people come to believe in Jesus Christ, but this Spirit does not come simply *on one occasion after another*, not only from 'above', upon men, but he is also the Spirit of the man Jesus of Nazareth and became effective in the latter at his baptism of the Spirit. Jesus 'committed' this Spirit of his to the Church, so that he comes to us also *throughout the history of the Church*. 'Being baptized with the Holy Spirit' is always at the same time a sharing in the initial historical experience of the Church (cf. Acts 11.16) and therefore we must consider this experience a little more closely.

(b)   The Holy Spirit and the history of the Church
The Holy Spirit is God's power and dynamism among and in the midst of men. With Jesus of Nazareth this power entered definitively into history, for the incarnation of the Son means that the source of the Holy Spirit has also become man. The Holy Spirit has entered history in order to remain continually present there: 'I will pray the Father, and he will give you another Counselor, to *be with you for ever*' (Jn 14.16). In the Old Testament the Spirit of God descended

only on individuals and for a very definite task: he was not yet definitively present in the history of the people as a whole. Experts in biblical interpretation tell us that the first experience of the Spirit was the sudden appearance and activity of men who accomplished unusual deeds in times of need as charismatic leaders and deliverers. The Spirit of the Lord came upon Othniel, so that he could help Israel to regain its freedom (Jg 3.10). 'The Spirit of the Lord took possession of Gideon' (Jg 6.34; cf.14.6). The Spirit of Yahweh came also as a charismatic endowment upon Saul (1 Sam 11.6) and David (1 Sam 16.13). The same thing happened also to Joshua (Num 27.18; Deut 34.9) and to the great prophets (cf. Is 61.1; Ezek 37. 1-14).

The Jewish view is that, after the death of the last great prophets (Haggai, Zechariah, Malachi), the Spirit of Yahweh was no longer found in Israel and would be alive again only in the great new prophet of the expected end-time. But the Spirit does not descend on Jesus merely as he descended on one of the Old Testament leaders and prophets: Jesus has the authority and power to transmit his own experience of the Spirit to the people of God in such a way that it remains *permanently* present among them.

Even before his resurrection, by his words and miracles, he gave his disciples a share in his own experience of the Spirit: 'For he whom God has sent utters the words of God, *for it is not by measure that he gives the Spirit*' (Jn 3.34). In witnessing to what he had 'seen and heard' (v. 32), he did not convey merely a doctrine, but his own experience with God, his experience of the Spirit. We said already in the second week that the Holy Spirit is the dynamism, the strength and power of God, his *experience of himself* (cf. 1 Cor 2.10). Through Jesus' testimony this self-experience of God becomes definitively present in history. Jesus transmits it to us by 'committing' (according to the original Greek text of John 19.30) it on the cross to those present, remaining there as representing the future Church.

At the feast of Pentecost it then becomes completely clear that the Church is the *historical continuation of Jesus' experience of the Spirit*. The one who baptizes with the Holy Spirit is the one who was himself baptized with the Holy Spirit in the Jordan. The power to testify, which the disciples experience in themselves at the feast of Pentecost, is nothing other than that of the pre-paschal Jesus. In an ending to Mark's gospel, added in the first half of the second century, we read: 'And these *signs* will accompany those who believe: in my name they will cast out demons; they will speak in new tongues; they will lay their hands on the sick, and they will recover' (Mk 16.17f). If then Jesus' gifts of the Spirit continue in the Church, he must also be alive himself as the source of all gifts of the Spirit. This is the primitive Church's *proof from experience* of the resurrection of Jesus. Paul is firmly convinced that Christ himself acts through him in word and deed. In his proclamation 'signs and wonders' occur in the power of the Spirit of God and of Jesus (Rom 15.18f). When people are converted to Christ through the proclamation of the apostle, this is a 'sign' of the presence of God's Spirit in his word and work (2 Cor 12.12; 1 Thess 1.5; 1 Cor 2.4f; Gal 2.8f). The Church arose out of the participation of the disciples in Jesus' experience of God and of himself, and this initial experience remains *binding for all time*. It is out of this initial experience that the New Testament emerged, although it must be remembered that experience cannot be entirely embodied in words but has a much wider range.

In view of the Church's renewal, which God himself continually offers throughout its history, it is extremely important to reflect a little on the transmission of this experience. Experience can be conveyed in words and expressed in signs.

Transmission of experience by words

If someone introduces his parents to another person with the words, 'These are my parents', his whole experience with these two people vibrates in this sentence, and the other perceives the nature of his experiences in the way he says it. He conveys in these words something of his love for his parents. He is not merely giving objective information which does not affect him personally — as he might explain a mathematical problem — but he is bearing witness to his love. Similarly Jesus conveyed to us through his testimony his love

for his Father, but human words cannot capture and en-
compass this love. That is why John says that Jesus in his
word gives us at the same time his Holy Spirit. This same
Holy Spirit is then present in the word of proclamation after
the resurrection of Jesus: he 'reminds' us of all that Jesus said
and did, keeps alive the experience of the Spirit (Jn 14.26;
16.13f). The Church lives on this Spirit-filled word, and
consequently the uninterrupted chain of those who proclaim
the word in the power of the Spirit is necessary for its
continued existence. It lives from the tradition of the original
witnesses.

Transmission of experience by signs
Since words are not adequate, we express our attachment and
love by signs. If — for example — I shake hands with someone
while wishing him 'Good morning', this is a comparatively
superficial sign of attachment. If on the other hand I give
something to the other person, I am already expressing a
deeper, more personal relationship. Parents give something to
their children, children to their parents, friends and engaged
couples give presents to one another. The present, the gift, is
an *expression of personal love*. That is why the New Testament describes the Holy Spirit himself as the first of all
God's gifts to us, as the 'heavenly gift' (Heb 6.4; cf. Acts
2.38; 8.20). In this gift God bestows on us, not merely
'something' but *himself*, his own experience of himself. What
is meant by this we see in the love between married people:
in bodily intercourse they give themselves to one another,
not only something, but themselves, their whole persons.
For this reason marriage is an imitation of God's bestowal
of himself on us: 'Husbands, love your wives, as Christ
loved the Church and gave himself up for her, that he might
sanctify her, having cleansed her by the washing of water
with the word' (Eph 5.25f; cf. 5.5). The 'sign' of baptism is
therefore a sign of Christ's self-surrender to us.

   This is true also and more especially of the eucharistic
gifts. In these Jesus gives us not only something — bread and
wine — but *himself*. The eucharistic gifts are 'signs' of what
he said of himself: 'I am the living bread' (Jn 6.51). In this
'spiritual' food and this 'spiritual' drink Jesus gives us at the

same time his own Holy Spirit, for it is only by the power of the latter that the gifts are transformed, that we experience Jesus' presence in them. 'Do this in remembrance of me' therefore means, not simply, 'Recall this event of the Last Supper as you recall any sort of historical event,' but 'Open yourselves to my Holy Spirit who will "remind" you of everything.' Without the abiding presence of the Holy Spirit in the Church the eucharistic celebration would not be possible. In this respect it is important to notice that Jesus held the Last Supper only with the *twelve* (cf. Mk 14.17; Mt 26.20) and that it was in fact only through these twelve that the experience of the Supper entered into the history of the Church. Hence, when we celebrate the eucharist, we are sharing in the experience of the twelve at the Last Supper. That is why Paul gives us the eucharistic words and thus also the twelve disciples' experience of the Supper without introducing his own suggestions (1 Cor 11.23).

In the light of this evidence some Churches — especially the Catholic and the Orthodox — insist that the office-holders as successors of the apostles are responsible in a special way for the continuation of the experience of the Last Supper, and this requires order and discipline. The office-holders are to *maintain* the mystery of the faith with a clear conscience (1 Tim 3.9) and therefore also the teaching and tradition entrusted to them (2 Tim 1.13f). This mandate holds despite all sin and disfigurement and we are thus confronted with the painful questions of schism by which the history of the initial experience of the Church has been darkened.

(c)   Schism does not come from the Holy Spirit
We cannot examine in detail here the complexity of the events which led to the divisions of Christendom. It is not the work of the Holy Spirit, but — as Vatican II says — 'men on both sides were to blame' *(Decree on Ecumenism*, art.3.1). What did their fault consist in? We can assume from the beginning that what was involved were not merely human whims, but that many divisions emerged out of real *experience of the Spirit*. The fault then lay in the fact that the Church at the time did not perceive and did not recognize these experiences of the Spirit, while those to whom the

experience had been granted over-emphasized particular aspects of it. The Church has its origin in the prophetic-charismatic proclamation of Jesus. The *continuation* of Jesus' gifts of the Spirit in history is not possible without a certain order (cf. 1 Cor 14.40; 11.34). Those who are responsible for order in the Church (the office-holders), however, are always in danger of regarding the system as more important than the gifts of grace themselves. Consequently it is part of the nature of the Church that prophetic incentives and corrections should be necessary from time to time.

In particular historical situations the Spirit of God has continually chosen men and women for this prophetic ministry, especially when certain charisms and effects of the Spirit were no longer active. Luther, Calvin and Zwingli must be mentioned here, as well as others after them who again took up this prophetic ministry within the Reformed Churches (Spencer, Wesley and many others). Such prophetic criticism of the Church was not produced in the study, but by individuals deeply affected by their experience of the Spirit. When this criticism was not accepted, it was the fault of individuals on both sides that new Churches and ecclesial communities were formed where certain gifts of the spirit were isolated and over-emphasized in the life of those communities. Luther's discovery of the experience of justification was as necessary to the Catholic Church as the protest against a preaching appealing predominantly to the intellect was within the Reformed Churches.

The fault of human beings on both sides then lies frequently in the *exaggeration of what is good and true*. In the course of its history the Catholic Church exaggerated order and discipline (the sense of order refined by the Holy Spirit is certainly also a gift of the Spirit) and thus became blind to other gifts of the Spirit. The same can be said also of the reformational experience of justification and other experiences of the Spirit (we need only recall the over-emphasis on the gift of tongues in the free Pentecostal Churches). Thus it comes about that there is *not one* of the now separated Churches where *all* the charisms of Jesus are active. The Catholic Church therefore expressly recognizes that the effects of the Spirit active in other Churches and ecclesial communities contribute to its own edification and that schism has made it difficult 'to express in actual life in all its aspects' the fulness of what Christ has bequeathed to us *(Decree on Ecumenism*, art.4.9f).

On the other hand this means that, if the one Holy Spirit has awakened in other Churches and ecclesial communities gifts of the Spirit which are not prominent in one's own Church, none of the still separated Churches *can be permitted* simply to abandon its spiritual heritage. Every Church *must* bring its experience of the Spirit in its own specific form into a hoped for, freshly reconciled Christendom. In the light of these reflections Catholics and Protestants in Europe, aware of their responsibility for charismatic renewal in their specific Churches, have drawn up certain principles which are re-produced in the appendix to this book. From them it emerges that the charismatic renewal must be Lutheran, Reformed, Orthodox, Catholic and so on, before it can be truly ecumenical. *The dynamism of this renewal is not directed to a new charismatic super-Church (Church of the Spirit), but to the one charismatically renewed Church.* We cannot simply leap back into the situation of the primitive Church and then start out again from the beginning. This would contradict the fact that the Spirit of Christ has indeed been effective also in *history*, even in the separated spiritual traditions: not to recognize this would amount to a 'sin against the Holy Spirit.' Every Church therefore must be allowed to profit from the other Churches' gifts of the Spirit. Nothing that really comes from the Holy Spirit can be divisive of the Churches. Thus in the interplay of the different charisms, which are especially prominent in the individual ecclesial communities, a *common tradition* begins to emerge from all the still separated traditions. For each individual Christian this could be a fresh occasion for rediscovering the charisms which are particularly active in his own Church. Anyone who has been baptized with the Holy Spirit, for that very reason, will gain a new orientation also to *his own* Church. (Cf. the ecumenical theses and theological guidelines in the appendix to this volume.)

In this respect it must be remembered that neither Martin Luther nor John Calvin wanted to found a new Church:

they retained the essential forms of the Church's life, the structure of the eucharistic service, the system of congregational leadership and the ordination of pastors, etc., to say nothing of preaching and sacraments. It is true of course that the Protestant Churches attach greater importance to the continuity of the gospel and its proclamation than to the rites and forms in which the gospel is conveyed. But for them too the testimony of the Fathers counts (see the *Catalogus Testimoniorum* in the Lutheran Confessions of Faith) as a sign of the historical continuity which belongs to the nature of the Church.

The Reformers had no intention of dividing the Church, but sought its spiritual renewal through penance and faith. The fact that a schism did take place is obviously due both to historical circumstances and to partiality and human faults on both sides. The same holds also for the emergence of the Free Churches or of the Pentecostal congregations which at the beginning sought a renewal of Christendom, revival and reconciliation and became separate ecclesial communities as a result of human deficiencies.

All examples from Church history show that original experiences of the Spirit are always affected by the human-historical circumstances which accompany them. Today more than ever we see that God is summoning us to contribute in our Churches to a renewal which can lead in the future to concrete reconciliation and unity.

2. The Church is active in the charisms and in the sacraments

(a)   The prophetic-charismatic origin of the Church

The 'assembly', which we call 'Church' today, was visibly manifested for the first time at the baptism of Jesus, 'when all the people were baptized' (Lk 3.21). In the power of his baptism of the Spirit Jesus then came forward in the manner of a prophet and gathered disciples around him. Mark summarizes the content of his proclamation in the words: 'The time is fulfilled, and the kingdom of God is at hand; repent and believe in the gospel' (Mk 1.15). As we showed in the fourth week, this proclamation was accompanied by the exercise of other charisms (curing the sick, teaching, etc.). It should be observed that Jesus himself did not baptize (Jn 4.2). It was only at the end of his life that he established a sign which we designate today by the collective noun 'sacrament'. This he did at the Last Supper. Although it is the supreme expression of his self-surrender, this sign did not appear at the beginning of his activity. The historical origin of the Church is the prophetic-charismatic *proclamation* of Jesus, and the *nature* of the Church can also be seen in this beginning. Jesus' message must continually be given fresh expression, adapted to the situation at the time, before sacraments can become meaningful. Giving effect to the sacramental sign is subordinated to proclamation and is at the same time the particularly compact expression of the latter. Thus, for example, Paul says of the eucharist: 'As often as you eat this bread and drink the cup, you *proclaim* the Lord's death until he comes' (1 Cor 11.26). Jesus commanded the twelve to hold this meal after his death, so that his original charism, his self-surrender, his experience of the Spirit, should remain present throughout history. Jesus' basic charismatic experience is 'deposited' — so to speak — in the eucharist, so that people in all ages can take part in it: indeed, he is himself present in the eucharistic gifts as the one who surrenders himself for us to the Father.

In order to understand the relationship between charisms and sacraments, it is important to be able to see the rest of the sacraments also as expressions of the one charismatic self-surrender of Jesus. The evidence for this in regard to *baptism* is found in the letter to the Ephesians: 'Christ loved the Church and gave himself up for her, that he might sanctify her, having cleansed her by the washing of water with the word' (Eph 5.25f). We showed already in the fourth week that each of the individual charisms of Jesus is a different expression of his experience of the Spirit, of his love and self-surrender to us. The Catholic, the Orthodox and other Churches are convinced that certain charisms of Jesus are 'deposited' in the other sacraments and remain throughout history. The *sacrament of penance* is basically nothing other than the repetition of the repentance presupposed to baptism.

In it the 'spiritual' authority of Jesus is present to remit or not to remit sin (Jn 20.22f) and at the same time the charism of mercy, forgiving not only once but continually (Mt 18.21f; Lk 17.3f). In the *anointing of the sick* Jesus' charism of healing is present and preserved (cf. Jas 5. 14-16); in *confirmation* we have Jesus' prophetic charism, in so far as the whole Church and each individual shares in it (cf. Acts 2.17; 8. 14-17; 19.5f). All are called to priestly ministry to one another, to be stewards of the manifold grace of God, each according to the specific gift of the Spirit granted to him (1 Pet 4.10). What lives on in the *sacrament of holy order* is Jesus' charism for awakening the charisms of others (Lk 10. 1-12), for leading all men as the Good Shepherd (Jn 10. 1-18) and, as 'apostle' and sole high priest of the New Covenant (Heb 3.1), to offer himself for them to the Father in the power of his Holy Spirit (Heb 9.14). *Marriage* too is an 'imitation' of Jesus' self-surrender for us (Eph 5.1f, 25, 32).

In the linguistic usage of the Protestant Churches baptism and the eucharist are generally described as 'sacraments'. Some of the Free Churches do not use the word 'sacrament' at all, since it does not appear in the Bible. But in all Protestant Churches baptism and the eucharist exist in fact; we also find confirmation, Christian marriage, ordination of pastors and preachers, words of forgiveness after confession of sins (absolution) and in individual cases even anointing of the sick (following Jas 5. 14-16). But for the last five the term 'sacrament' is rarely used. (The Lutheran confessions of faith describe absolution and ordination in each case as sacraments, since they contain God's promise.)

> 'No prudent man will argue about the number of sacraments or the word itself, as long as those rites alone are retained which bear God's command and his promises'
> (Apology of the Augsburg Confession, art. 13).
>
> 'For centuries the question of the number of the sacraments was regarded as a classical theme of denominational controversy: seven on one side, two on the other. Today a change is impending. Roman Catholic

theology, which formerly attempted more or less by force to find or at least to claim Christ's words of institution for all the sacraments, has recognized that this is no longer possible. But, as a result of modern New Testament studies, Protestant theology too has become less certain on this point. Today it is impossible to distinguish so clearly between the words of Jesus and those of the primitive community. Theologians on both sides therefore have again begun to reflect on the New Testament term, *musterion*. Jesus Christ as God's Son made man and the Church as his body form the primordial mystery, the primordial sacrament, which is explicated and brought home to men in the word of proclamation and in a variety of ecclesial actions. Despite the many differences in detail, all denominations regard baptism and the eucharist as having special significance among ecclesial actions' (Protestant Adult Catechism, Gütersloh 1975, p.1125).

(b)   What is a charism?[25]

If long-forgotten gifts of the Spirit are granted by God now in a surprising way to many people in all Churches, we cannot avoid further reflection on the relationship between sacramental and charismatic signs. We must therefore try again to define more closely the meaning of 'charism'. Literally it means a gift of grace. Paul also calls the charisms 'services' or 'workings' (1 Cor 12. 4-6). The Holy Spirit appears in these gifts of grace in a similarly obvious and sensibly perceptible manner as that in which the Son of God appeared in the man Jesus of Nazareth (cf. 1 Jn 1.1-3 with 1 Cor 12.7).

The word 'gift' indicates that God does not force his charisms upon us and that we can also really make use of them. When I give something to another person, it is after considering whether he can do anything with it. So God too does not give someone the gift of teaching others unless this is something he is able to do from his own resources. He does not give to an unmusical person the gift of leading the singing at worship. A charism is a capacity and endowment given at birth, *but later refined, strengthened and made to serve by the Spirit of God for the building up of Church and society.*

Gifts of the Spirit are not given us for our own salvation, but so that we can promote the salvation and healing of *others*. They are given 'for the common good' (1 Cor 12.7), *they orient us to others*.

In a wider sense any aptitude for a particular *calling* or a particular ministry may form the basis for a gift of the Spirit. If, for instance, we see our own calling — which in fact presupposes certain abilities — as a *service* to our fellow-men in society, if we have not used our abilities solely for our own private advantage, then the exercise of our calling is in a board sense 'charismatic'.

In a narrower ecclesial sense all ministries which serve to build up the community are charisms. Among them are first of all 'positions', to which people are appointed: the congregational leader (pastor, parish priest), parish assistant, sacristan/verger, organist and so on. In addition there are unpaid, honorary offices: reader, server, social worker, etc. All these charisms have always been active in the Church, while others have almost completely died out. Among the latter are especially the 'more luminous' *(clarissima)* charisms (Second Vatican Council, *Constitution on the Church*, art. 12), the gifts of prophecy, of tongues, of healing and also the social-critical charisms of which we shall speak later. Today the Church is being given in an unexpected way a renewal of these forgotten or missing charisms. The charismatic renewal however does not attach importance solely to these 'more luminous' charisms but involves in its inner dynamism a renewal of the *whole* Church in *all* its expressions of life. But the exercise of the 'more luminous' charisms demands a very profound and total surrender to the Lord of the Church and distributor of all the gifts of the Spirit.

The harmonious interplay of the charisms is essential to their exercise. Paul elucidates this in terms of a body which consists of many members.[26] To each is given a gift of grace by God: by no means the same gift to each and still less all gifts to one person, but to *each his own*, adapted to his particular character (1 Cor 12.11). According to 1 Corinthians 12.4 the one Holy Spirit produces the very *diversity* of the gifts and thus also their inequality. The equality of all consists solely in the fact that his own gift of grace is given to absolutely everyone and for that very reason not in the possibility that everyone might exercise any function in the community. The metaphor of the diverse functions of the members of the human body means that every function is necessary and none is interchangeable with the others. God has fitted each member into the body in the way which corresponded to his plan (1 Cor 12.18). The ear is not the eye and the eye is not the hand, and so on. All members should care for one another in harmony and so complement one another to form the whole body (1 Cor 12.25). In the same way the gifts of the Spirit should be related to one another, should complement one another and each contribute in the light of its specific task to the building up of the community. We shall deal more closely in the sixth week with individual gifts of the Spirit.

(c)   The relationship between charismatic and sacramental signs

By 'sign' the Bible means an occurrence perceptible to the senses or a feature by which we recognize someone or something.[27] We are accustomed to speak of sacramental signs (although the term 'sacrament' does not occur in this sense in the New Testament). The external sign of baptism consists in pouring water and in the words explaining this action: 'I baptize you in the name of the Father, and of the Son, and of the Holy Spirit.' Baptism takes place 'by the washing of water with the word' (Eph 5.26). The external sacramental sign of the eucharist consists in bread and wine and the words from the account of its institution spoken over them. It is highly significant that Paul also uses the word 'sign' to describe the gift of prophecy and the gift of tongues (1 Cor 14.22; cf. Mk 16.17) and therefore also all other charisms. The charisms indicate the presence of the Holy Spirit, for he is 'manifested' in them, they make him evident (1 Cor 12.7). So — for example — the prophetic word in itself is a *sign* for the presence of the Holy Spirit. In the sentence, 'be reconciled to God' (cf. 2 Cor 5.20), the Spirit of God and of Jesus is *manifested*, in it he is himself present in power. In a similar way the Spirit of God and of Jesus is *manifested* in spoken prayer, for the Spirit himself prays in us 'with signs too deep for words' (Rom 8.26). The same is true also of the other charisms. Between sacramental and charismatic signs there are certain similarities, but also important differences. While the sacramental signs hold a greater *certainty* of the presence in them of the Holy Spirit, it is only the charismatic occurrences (prophetic rebukes, exhortation and so on) which make the sacramental signs *fruitful*, for they alone make possible the acceptance of the sacramental offer. We may clarify this in the light of the relationship between the gift of prophecy and baptism of water.

1. Common to both is the fact that Christ is and remains their source. The gift of prophecy is exercised as by 'ambassadors for Christ' (2 Cor 5.20), and the minister of baptism also acts on behalf of Christ, for it is in fact Christ himself who baptizes.

2. The exercise of the prophetic ministry is the *presupposition* for administering baptism. The faith presupposed by baptism comes from hearing. The gift of prophecy and the other charisms *awaken* faith and serve the Church's mission. On the other hand, the administration of the sacraments presupposes faith.

3. The charismatic signs emerge out of our *innermost being*, from the graciously granted *love for others* (1 Cor 13). On the other hand, when the human minister pours water on the head of the baptismal candidate, saying at the same time, 'I baptize you in the name of the Father, and of the Son, and of the Holy Spirit,' this action is not primarily an expression of the minister's personal love for the recipient, but the *direct* expression of *God's love* for the candidate. At the same time the human minister largely fades into the background.

4. The prophet can really exhort, console and so on only if in this procedure he surrenders himself *quite personally* to God. The more he himself is affected by the message he has to deliver, the more his words will affect the listeners (cf. Acts 2.37). On the other hand, the remission of sins and justifiaation offered in the sacramental sign of baptism is *not* strictly dependent on the personal holiness and involvement of the human minister, as long as he intends to do what the Church does. Of course the personal involvement of the

minister of baptism is not without any influence on the faith of the candidate, but the grace of baptism is also offered by God to the candidate infallibly and with *absolute certainty* even if the minister of baptism himself is not personally affected by this event.

This last aspect is particularly important. The minister of baptism does not act in virtue of a charismatic impulse; he does and says what the Church does and says. He does not invent the sacramental sign, but is bound to keep closely to the Church's rulings. This becomes very clear in the celebration of the eucharist. The person who presides at this celebration and repeats the eucharistic words of Jesus does not himself act in the strict sense as a prophet. He does not speak words he has himself formulated under divine influence, but repeats exactly word for word what Jesus — according to the New Testament tradition — said in the supper room. All Churches see to it that the person presiding at the eucharistic celebration does not change anything in the institution account and for that reason, by comparison with the prophetic ministry, the *certainty* that Jesus himself is really present is greater. A prophetic utterance must be *tested* as to whether it comes from God or not, for there are also false prophets (1 Jn 4.1; cf. 1 Cor 14.19-32). It is then by no means absolutely certain that God himself is acting in a prophetic message. But, if we assume that the human minister really says and does exactly what the Church says and does, we cannot speak in the same way of 'false sacraments'. Sacraments do not have to be *tested* in every case as to whether they come from God or not.

At the same time however it must be observed that the sacramental signs do not work automatically: they represent an *offer of God* which is effective only to the degree that the recipient of the sacrament accepts it. We can therefore describe this offer also as *infallible*. God stands by his offer even when the recipient at the moment of reception is not yet capable of a full personal response. He can take up this response later (here lies the problem of infant baptism). The charismatic signs on the other hand are *never an absolutely certain 'proof'* of the presence of the Holy Spirit, so as to leave no possible doubt. They must always be tested and for this purpose above all the Church is granted the charism of discernment (cf. 1 Cor 12.10). This is true also with reference to the gift of tongues, which is regarded in the Pentecostal Churches up to a point as an irrefutable proof of the presence of the Holy Spirit, of baptism of the Spirit.

For an understanding of the charismatic renewal in the Catholic Church it is then of the greatest importance to note that some sacraments orient the recipient predominantly to God himself (baptism, penance, anointing of the sick), while others are mainly intended to confer on the recipient the ability to minister to the salvation of others (confirmation, holy orders, matrimony). These sacraments are thus more akin to charisms.

The sacramental sign of *baptism* is a washing with the words pertaining to this. Through this sign God offers the baptismal candidate the remission of all sins and also healing of the wounds caused by the sins of other human beings. By baptism God makes us just and holy (cf. 1 Cor 6.11) and thus orients us to himself. Baptism therefore is at the same time the beginning of *my* eternal life, of *my* resurrection. Here I am involved with God in a wholly personal way, in my eternal life, for no one can receive remission of sin in my place, no one can rise in my place. In baptism then the Holy Spirit is given to us in the sense that he overcomes my hostility to God and orients me to my eternal life (Rom 8. 7-11). The expression of this new relationship to God is the cry 'Abba, Father!'. We do not use it in exactly the same way as Jesus, for he was Son of God in an absolutely unique fashion: our cry is made in the power of his Spirit (Rom 8.15; Gal 4.6). The gift of tongues — about which we shall speak in detail later — is in a similar way an expression of our personal relationship to God: 'One who speaks in a tongue speaks not to men but to God' (1 Cor 14.2).

Penance and *anointing of the sick*, in the Churches where they are regarded as sacraments, are similarly predominantly oriented to God. Here too it is a question specifically of my personal salvation in the sight of God. Of course the sacraments mentioned up to now have also something to do with the Church. Through baptism I am incorporated into the Church and also receive the promise of being able at later stages of growth to work for the salvation of others. Penance is peace with the Church and for that very reason also peace with God; and in anointing of the sick the gift of healing promised to the whole Church is present.

By contrast, confirmation, holy order and matrimony can be described as *'charismatic sacraments'*. By laying on of hands and anointing at *confirmation* the baptized person is given the opportunity of coming into an historical contact with the initial experience of the Church (cf. Acts 8.15-17; 19.5). Confirmation is *sacramental baptism of the Spirit* (we shall return to this question). Through the laying on of hands in the *sacrament of holy order* the confirmed person then comes into historical contact with the special commissioning and authorization of the twelve, with their experience of the Last Supper. The parties also receive (and administer to one another) the sacrament of *matrimony*, not in view of either party's personal salvation, but to enable each to work for the salvation of the other and of the children.

Paul therefore describes marriage (and also celibacy) expressly as a 'charism' (1 Cor 7.7). The Catholic (and Orthodox) view then is that *charismatic graces are sacramentally offered* in confirmation, holy orders and marriage. It is not necessary to stress the fact that, by accepting this offer, the Christian is also brought into a deeper relationship with God himself. For it is God himself who admonishes, builds up, consoles, exhorts, heals, *through us* (2 Cor 5.20).

3. Renewal of the Spirit

The mystery of faith and participation in Jesus' experience of the Spirit cannot be adequately exressed in words, still less in a single word. We can never warn people sufficiently against detaching certain aspects from the totality of the one Christian basic experience, against turning *one* aspect into Christianity as a whole. That is why in this 'initiation' we have been careful not to pin ourselves down to any one particular expression to describe the world-wide spiritual awakening. The term 'charismatic renewal' has come into general use, but it can lead to misunderstandings. The term 'renewal of the Spirit' could perhaps give expression to the most diverse elements of the basic Christian experience and therefore — with all due reservations — I shall briefly elucidate it at this point.

From the most ancient times the introduction of the candidate for baptism into the Christian life has taken place in several steps all of which are made possible and effected in us by the Holy Spirit.

1. *Conversion.* In Ephesians 4.22f we read: 'Change your former life and *renew your spirit* and mind. Put on the new man who is created according to God's image, so that you may live in true righteousness and holiness'. The word 'spirit' here means our *human* spirit which is renewed by the Holy Spirit, so that we become new human beings. Similarly in Colossians 3.9f we find: 'You have put off the old man with his actions and put on the *new man* who is *renewed* according to the image of his creator in order to recognize him'. In Romans 12.2 also we read: 'Do not be conformed to this world but be transformed by the *renewal of your mind*, that you may prove what is the will of God'. In this sense renewal of the Spirit is the renewal of our *human* spirit effected in us by the Holy Spirit: the renewal of our feeling, willing, thinking, of our *whole* person. It begins with our surrender to the will and plan of God, with seeking the meaning of *my* life (first week). In the sense of Hebrews 6.6 such a conversion is a radical and unique act in our life which can never be repeated with the same intensity and yet must be continually renewed.

2. *Baptism of water for forgiveness of sins.* According to Titus 3.5f baptism is 'the washing of regeneration and *renewal in the Holy Spirit*, which he (God) poured out upon us richly through Jesus Christ our Saviour, so that we might be justified by his grace and become heirs in hope of eternal life'. Renewal of the Spirit therefore is also the renewed acceptance of what happened to us in baptism (third week).

3. *Baptism of the Spirit.* In the New Testament being qualified to bear witness is also described as 'being baptized with the Holy Spirit' (Acts 1.5, 8; 11.16; Lk 3.16 par), as we showed in the fourth week. Renewal of the Spirit is a renewed

acceptance of the gifts of the Spirit and a renewed 'baptism of death' (cf., in the second part of this 'initiation', the sixth day of the fourth week).

4. *Guidance by the Holy Spirit*. Someone who has become a new man is no longer afraid either of God or of the future and allows himself to be guided by the Spirit of God (Rom 8.14). He trusts then, not so much the plans he has made for his own life or for the future of the Church, but the plans and the ever new, surprising originality of God. This receptivity to the guidance of the Spirit is necessary particularly in times of upheaval. No one knows what the Church of the future will look like. So much the more important is receptivity for the promptings of the Holy Spirit, as we shall show again in the seventh week.

5. *Eucharist*. In the eucharistic gifts the living Lord of the Church is present. He transforms these gifts in the power of the Spirit and we receive them in the power of the same Spirit. The step of a renewal of the Spirit and the daily surrender to the Spirit of Christ is therefore linked with a deepened understanding of the eucharist (and also of the other sacraments).

Renewal of the Spirit is a life-long process. But, since this life of ours goes on in space and time, it is good and helpful to accomplish this renewal from time to time at a definite place: that is, in the assembly of the faithful and with their help. But it is then not *only* regained conversion and decision for Christ, not *only* renewal of the baptismal promises, not *only* acceptance of the gifts of the Spirit, not *only* receptivity to the guidance of the Spirit, detached from the Church, its ministry and its sacraments, not *only* a new spiritual admission to the sacraments, but all of this in one single, indivisible event.

In this respect differences between Catholic or Orthodox on the one hand and Protestants on the other exist mainly with reference to the sacramental offer of 'baptism of the Spirit' and also to the understanding and exercise of the Church's ministry. What follows then is a contribution from Protestant colleagues on their standpoint.

(a)   *The permanent reality of baptism (Protestant)*
Infant baptism and conversion
There are variations in the baptismal practice of the Protestant Churches. The established Lutheran, United and Reformed Churches as well as some — for example, the Methodists — of the Free Churches practise 'infant baptism'. They baptize newly born children if the parents want this and if parents and godparents promise a Christian education. Some of the Free Churches on the other hand reject infant baptism and baptize only those who have themselves professed their faith (from about the twelfth year). Logically therefore they generally expect a Christian from an established Church, if he joins a Free Church congregation, to get himself baptized. In such a case Catholics, Protestants belonging to an established Church and Methodists say that the person has been baptized *again*. They reject this 'rebaptism'. For them baptism, however and wherever carried out, is a permanent reality. It is God's turning to man in which the whole fulness of the salvation won for us in Jesus Christ is offered and promised to us. Baptism contains the promise of our salvation. It is for us to accept it, so that the power of this promise may be unfolded in our life.

Infant baptism of course is a sore point in a number of respects. Those Free Churches which do not recognize it see the baptism of someone who has come to believe, after being baptized as an infant, not as 'rebaptism', but wholly and entirely as his one and only baptism which they can likewise recognize as an effective sign of the promise of God.

Another criticism of infant baptism, which is also heard within the established Churches, is based on the fact that the parents scarcely know the significance of baptism and thus are hardly capable of giving their children an education in accordance with it. Some attempt is being made to solve this problem with the aid of discussions before baptism, to be followed up by pastoral care.

What is certain is that baptism can and may be administered only where it is *desired*. This means also: where Christian baptism is really desired in its spiritual significance (that is not to say that the parents must express all this with theological exactitude). Generally speaking the desire for baptism should be on the part of the person who is being baptized. In this sense adult or believer's baptism is the basic form of baptism. (The Anglican Church has recently stressed this in its new baptism ritual.) There is of course also the opportunity for a desire which is representative and intercessory on the part of parents for their young child. Such representation too can be based on the certainty that God will stand by his sign and his promise. But, particularly at a time when parents in a pluralistic world have far less power than formerly to decide the way their children will go, the established Churches must be prepared to face the question of the critics of infant baptism as to whether and how far this opportunity should be claimed.

Again however Christians belonging to the established Churches will have to ask the Baptists if they are not aware of other instances in which they would expect a representative and intercessory desire to find a response. Experience shows too that even the baptism of someone who already believes is not always the result of a really free and mature decision of faith: it may be brought about by education and especially by the expectation of parents and the rest of the congregation. Nor can this be entirely avoided, any more than the unfortunate fact that people baptized as 'believers' sometimes leave the community and are unfaithful to their decision.

We shall have to allow for the fact that Catholics, Protestants belonging to the established Churches and members of Free Church Protestant congregations are praying and living with each other. When therefore the question of infant baptism arises in a concrete case in these circles, all involved will have to show great understanding for one another. It is not our task here (nor will it be the task of a charismatic prayer group) to settle the theological questions which divide the Churches on this point. Even a Christian belonging to one of the Free Churches, baptized after his conversion, will continually have to renew his faith. In this respect he will perhaps describe some things differently; but in that situation we are all equal. Every renewal of faith in confession and in a new promise to Jesus Christ is what Martin Luther called 'creeping back into baptism'. Christians of both the established and the Free Churches can perceive in their own particular baptism the sign of the enduring reality of God's grace, which continually seeks to be freshly active in our life.

Renewed acceptance of the baptismal reality

How many people know exactly what is the procedure at a baptism? The Lutheran Church includes a rejection of evil as part of the baptismal liturgy. But this rejection is also part of each and every confession, whether public or private. This amounts on each occasion to a 'renewal' of that part of the baptismal action. But at baptism also there is *always* a prayer for the Holy Spirit. The prayer is brought before God with laying on of hands and linked to the pouring of the water which, together with the baptismal formula, constitutes the nucleus of the action. This laying on of hands expresses the fact that someone is becoming a member of the body of Christ, of the community. This comes from God in such a way that baptism with water, linked with the prayer for his Spirit, is unrepeatable. And the Protestant view is that it is not completed at a later stage. For Protestants therefore renewal of baptism means two things:

1. personal acceptance of the baptismal reality in faith and in confessing Jesus and

2. the continually new actualization (renewal) of the operation of the Holy Spirit.

In the light of biblical usage the first of these is called 'conversion'. It can be said that baptism, including conversion, is 'rebirth' as a new man. For a number of those who have grown up in the ambiance of the Christian community and who now turn personally in faith to Jesus, this step together with the prayer to be filled with the Holy Spirit can lead immediately into the life of a committed Christian, using his gifts for the propagation of the kingdom of God, for other human beings and for their salvation.

In this respect however it is often pastorally advisable to proceed cautiously and gradually. Since the prayer for the Holy Spirit in baptism first of all incorporates the candidate into the community, it is a good thing for someone coming for the first time to the faith to spend some time in trying to strike roots in the group or congregation. The Holy Spirit is given him for membership in the community and for the *common* priesthood of believers: the latter he exercises in prayer and the reading of Scripture together with his brothers and sisters and in the common celebration of the eucharist. But he is not yet expected to undertake the ministry of an independent 'missionary' of Jesus Christ. It is only after a time of settling into the congregation and of living with the community that prayer is offered for him, for the Spirit of God to reveal in him gifts of testimony and ministry for others.

Here is an important pastoral task to be taken up by the congregational leaders together with the whole group or congregation. It should never be said that someone 'obtains' or 'receives' the Holy Spirit only on the occasion of a laying on of hands in the charismatic prayer group. By the very fact of creation and despite all sin, the Spirit of God is already living in a very general sense in every human being. And he lives for our salvation particularly in everyone who believes; for there is no faith in God except through the operation of the Holy Spirit in us. But even this is not yet the same as being permeated with the Spirit of God, who is revealed in the charisms effecting the salvation and well-being of others in love. Every Christian has the task and the joy of praying for this actualization and renewal of the Spirit and it is not surprising if these first signs of the effective operation of the Holy Spirit are received with special joy and attention and even made the occasion of a celebration in the community.

Confirmation and renewal of the Spirit
We have already said that confirmation in the Protestant Churches has not the importance which it has in the Catholic Church. The reason for this is partly that not all Protestant Churches have had confirmation at all times.

In the course of history confirmation has been understood in a variety of ways. Besides being regarded as a confirmation of baptism, it has also meant: making a personal profession of faith, conclusion of a stage in the catechumenate, award of rights and imposition of duties in the Church (admission to first communion or to the office of godparent). Different aspects have been stressed in the light of different theological interpretations. But the problem of confirmation today lies not so much in differences of emphasis as in the fact that it seems to possess little spiritual significance.

Prayer for the Spirit has of course scarcely ever been lacking in confirmation; at worst it has been thrust into the margin by a more general form of blessing. Also and especially in Protestant confirmation it is a question of the development of this aspect of baptism, which is expressed in the request for the Spirit linked with baptism of water: of *the Holy Spirit becoming effective in the life of a Christian.*

Confirmation has come to be practised widely merely as a custom or a kind of youth-dedication, with instruction closely linked to a particular age group (which to many seems too early). What it amounts to is confirmation as a member of the Church which most people regularly attend. In view of this, the only way to rediscover its meaning is deliberately to meditate on the prayers and words of blessing and to take these in. For those taking part in the course we give some examples in the second part of this initiation ('Prayer and Expectation').

For us, who want to provide an initiation into the basic Christian experience, confirmation is the institutionalization in the Church to which most people belong of this urgently necessary (vitally necessary for the Church) actualizing of baptism and of the Spirit promised and granted at baptism. But it is almost always little more than an outward form, the somewhat timorous first contact with the faith mostly in the part of an isolated individual (who often soon loses his enthusiasm).

This is not to dispute the objective content of confirmation, particularly if it is linked with some such formula as the following:

> Receive the Holy Spirit,
> Protection and defence against all evil,
> Power and aid for all good,
> From the gracious hand of God,
> Of the Father, the Son and the Holy Spirit.

The basic Christian experience of renewal of the Spirit in a living congregation however is then its necessary experiential complement.

(b) The sacrament of confirmation: historical continuation of the Pentecost event (Catholic)

What was said above about infant baptism and conversion is true also for Catholics. We need not go more closely here into differences of emphasis and we have already spoken of the different understanding of confession (third week, fourth section). Neither can it be the point of this 'initiation' to discuss the very difficult historical and theological questions associated with the understanding and administration of the sacrament of confirmation. But it does seem that the charismatic renewal within the Catholic Church has rediscovered this sacrament which has been widely regarded as a secondary matter. The texts of the Church's magisterium and liturgy expressly relate the reception of the sacrament of confirmation to the initial experience of the Church at Pentecost. In 1971 Pope Paul VI adapted the formula of administration of confirmation to that of the Orthodox Church. It now runs: 'Be sealed with the gift of the Holy Spirit'. As we read in the Apostolic Constitution of 1971, authorizing the new rite, this formula is meant to 'recall' more clearly 'the outpouring of the Spirit which took place on the day of Pentecost'. Moreover, the laying on of hands mentioned in Acts 8.15-17 and 19.5f is considered in the Catholic tradition to be 'the beginning of the sacrament of confirmation, *which in a certain way perpetuates the grace of Pentecost in the Church*.'[28]

Of course it must be maintained that the Holy Spirit is promised and given already in baptism; but the grace of God is 'varied' (1 Pet 4.10) and the Catholic view is that the historical separation of baptism from the sacramental authorization to bear witness was not due to purely human considerations. It has in fact a solid biblical foundation:

1. The external sign of baptism, washing or immersion together with the words spoken at this point, indicates and effects the inward washing, the cleansing from sins (1 Cor 6.11). Its effect is rebirth (Tit 3.5; Jn 3.5). Nowhere in the New Testament is it suggested that the exercise of the gifts of the Spirit is the immediate effect of baptism.

2. Nowhere in the Acts of the Apostles does Luke suggest that the Holy Spirit is given already by baptism of water as such (cf. 8.16; 19.6). The exercise of charisms can in fact be granted even chronologically *prior* to baptism of water (10.44-48).

3. The New Testament as a whole therefore distinguishes very clearly between the rebirth effected by one and the same Spirit and the power he gives to exercise the charisms. From this there emerges a *theological* distinction between baptism and confirmation, whatever the historical data may be. If the charisms are scarcely or not at all active any longer, this distinction largely ceases to be important and confirmation becomes in practice an appendix to baptism. The rediscovery of the charisms throws a new light also on confirmation.

4. From the standpoint of my life-history it is clear that, if I am baptized *today*, I cannot immediately testify to my rebirth *tomorrow*. This rebirth must first be tested, so that in any case a testimony solidly based on the new way of living is only possible after a certain time (cf. the seventh day of the seventh week in the second volume of this initiation).

In this light the description of confirmation as 'sacramental baptism of the Spirit' is completely justified and there is no great difference between administering the sacramental sign of confirmation (laying on of hands and/or anointing with the words related to this) to the small child (as in the Orthodox Church) and administering it to the growing boy or girl (as in the Catholic Church).[29] Like all the others, this sacrament is and remains an *offer*, which in any case must be continually freshly accepted. Even the disciples, after the first persecution, renewed with prayer the experience of Pentecost: 'When they had prayed, the place in which they were gathered together was shaken; and they were all filled with the Holy Spirit and spoke the word of God with boldness' (Acts 4.31). Similarly the renewal of the sacrament of confirmation, once received, is part of its inner dynamism. For the Catholic then renewal of the Spirit is always at the same time a *renewal of confirmation*.

How is this to take place? It would not be appropriate to the very personal happening of the renewal of the Spirit for the whole congregation simply to utter a formulary or a prayer on certain occasions. For the renewal of baptism in the Easter Vigil has already become a ritual which does not necessarily grip the individual at a deeper level. It is more appropriate if individual members of the congregation after a personal and intensive preparation (the present 'initiation', for example) come before those present and say an extempore prayer committing themselves to Christ. This can take place about Pentecost or even in small prayer groups. A suitable place for it in the liturgy would be during the eucharistic celebration before the preparation of the gifts. Experience of the Spirit however is possible at any time when Christians pray with one another at home for the fulness of the Spirit; it might well be after the close of this seven weeks 'initiation'. Then, for the laying on of hands, those in particular should come forward who have personally accompanied the one praying for renewal of the Spirit. They lay their hands on his hand and shoulders and say prayers of intercession and thanksgiving.

This procedure is not a new sacrament but an exercise of the *common priesthood* in virtue of which Christians help and strengthen one another in prayer: an expression of the solidarity of all in faith, of social experience of God. For Catholics this laying on of hands is comparable to that of ordination. The latter is not a complement to the episcopal laying on of hands, but an expression of priestly solidarity (it takes place mostly in silence, but it would certainly give new life to fraternal communion if personal prayers were said at the same time).

The symbol of laying on of hands in itself is ambiguous. It can express a blessing, accompany the prayer for healing and so on. The laying on of hands at confirmation and ordination expresses the historical contact with the initial experience of the Church. The person who lays hands on the candidate has himself received laying on of hands from someone on whom in his turn hands had been laid, and so on back to the primitive community (cf. Acts 8.14). In this way it becomes clear that baptism of the Spirit, experience of the Spirit, has something to do with the Church in its whole historical extension and remains linked with the initial experience. The Catholic or Orthodox Christian therefore would never be prepared to found a new Church by appealing to his own experience of the Spirit, however deep or shattering that may have been. He maintains that the Spirit does not come merely from time to time, 'from above' as it were, continually founding new Churches and structures, but in fact by the historical way of tradition in preaching and in the sacraments. He becomes aware of this particularly at the reception of confirmation and consequently this sacrament is dear to him.

Historical experience up to now has shown that certain charisms (as, for example, the gift of prophecy, the gift of healing, the gift of tongues) are simply not active in the major Church or that there is a sectarian split. But for the charismatic renewal it is vital to be led by the Spirit in such a way that the existing traditional Churches are renewed from within. But this again presupposes that the normative *initial experience* of the Church should acquire an historically new shape. From this standpoint the sacrament of confirmation has an important and perhaps indispensable significance for the future of the charismatic renewal. In the 'renewal of the Spirit' the individual lays himself open first of all for *all* gifts of the Spirit which God has promised and granted to him. If someone has already experienced in himself the fact that God has bestowed certain gifts of the Spirit on him, he can also pray at the renewal of the Spirit (or its repetition) particularly for an intensification of these specific gifts of the Spirit. It is a disastrous one-sidedness on the part of the Pentecostal Churches to link 'baptism of the Spirit' only with the gift of tongues.[30] As a rule it is only after the *first* renewal of the Spirit that the individual in a further process rises to the exercise of the diverse gifts of the Spirit.

Sixth week: Gifts of the Spirit

Acceptance of the gifts of the Spirit: The way to the living parish

1. Gifts of the Spirit in the congregation

2. The gift of prophecy

3. The gift of tongues

4. Socio-critical charisms

5. The gift of healing

1. Gifts of the Spirit in the congregation

The exercise of the gifts of the Spirit is part of the Church's nature and has always been active in it. Admittedly, some gifts were absorbed — so to speak — by the Church's ministry as early as the second and third centuries, so that a clear distinction emerged between 'clergy' (concerned with 'spiritual' matters) and 'laity'. After the age of persecution, at the beginning of the fourth century, under the Emperor Constantine, the first Christianization of public life began. The gifts of the Spirit serving the Church's mission receded into the background and the charismatic activity as it had been known in the primitive Church now became increasingly withdrawn into the mysticism of the monasteries.[31] It was from the latter that prophetic impulses continued to emerge (mendicant orders of the middle ages, missions to the people in modern times, and so on). Other charisms too, mentioned in the New Testament, survived in the Church, the charism of teaching, of care for the poor and the sick, of healing (the last especially at places of pilgrimage) and so on. The common priesthood of all believers likewise is an idea that never completely died out. It remained alive in the relationship of parents to their children, of teachers to scholars and so on, but one's *personal relationship to God* became increasingly a private affair, particularly from the period of the 'Enlightenment' in the eighteenth century.

Historians are agreed that the middle of the twentieth century marked an historical turning point of the very greatest importance, the climax of a trend initiated by the rise of industrial civilization in the eighteenth century. People see more clearly than formerly that they are dependent on one another in a life which is continually becoming more complicated. In this step from the 'I' to the 'we', in this socialization and solidarization, a new epoch is being heralded. We can now see more clearly the social experience of God attested in the New Testament — of which we spoke in the third week — and thus at the same time we can look for an experience of Church and community *to which everyone contributes something*. One concern of the Reformers of the sixteenth century now acquires a new importance. The common synod of the dioceses of the Federal Republic of Germany also says in its document on pastoral ministries in the parish: 'One of the most important aims of Church reform is the establishment of living parishes in which a variety of gifts of the Spirit work together' (I.1.i). We must however again insist that the exercise of the gifts of the Spirit cannot be 'introduced' as we 'introduce' liturgical reforms or the setting up of parish councils or similar bodies. For the former a very personal receptivity is necessary on the part of each and every individual Christian, with the act of faith, of baptismal renewal and renewal of the Spirit, preparing the way for the acceptance of the gifts of the Spirit.

In this respect an important pastoral starting point would be for the active members of the parish to rouse the interest of young people in confirmation, so that they want to receive the sacrament. To prepare for their ministry the former might first of all combine to form a prayer group in the parish, helping one another to take the personal step of renewal of the Spirit and to accept the gifts of the Spirit. Such a group would be at the same time a model to prayer-groups of any kind. They are not a circle of friends, not a charismatic circle, not a group of people merely seeking individual personal experience; they want to help in building up and giving new life to the *parish*. If a prayer group does not produce stimulating incentives for parish life, it does not merely remain fruitless, but frequently displays a tendency to withdraw and split off from the parish. This would not be a renewal, but a decline of the Church.

Of course supraparochial groups can and may be formed in the initial phase, but if the members of these groups are not also active in their own parishes, help to sustain them and — when opportunity offers — also help to form prayer-groups there, then the charismatic renewal cannot develop its dynamism for a renewal of the Church.

In what follows we can describe only a few charisms and we are therefore restricting ourselves to those which belong to normal congregational life in the New Testament, but which have largely been forgotten in the course of history. At the same time we shall discuss the prevailing attitude to faith as a private affair with its disastrous consequences for belief in God, for the parish and for society.

2. The gift of prophecy[32]

After the ministry of the apostles, Paul regards that of the prophets as the most important in the Church (1 Cor 12.28) and therefore exhorts everyone to lay themselves open for this gift (1 Cor 14.1), even though it is not given to everyone (1 Cor 12.29). The gift of prophecy is a good example of what a charism is, for it is the primordial form of the charismatic reality as such: 'He who prophesies speaks to men for their upbuilding and encouragement and consolation' (1 Cor 14.3). A fine example of a prophetic speech is recorded for us in 2 Corinthians 5.20: 'So we are ambassadors for Christ, *God making his appeal through us. We* beseech you on *behalf of Christ, be reconciled to God'.* If then someone addresses to the prayer group the appeal, 'Be reconciled to God', those present will perceive in the way the person speaks to them he is not making claims for himself, not coming to make his own demands on them, but that God is at work here: 'No prophecy ever came by the impulse of man, but men moved by the Holy Spirit *spoke from God'* (1 Pet 1.21).

This is a prodigious occurrence and everyone feels immediately: I simply cannot take it on myself to speak for Christ to others. I cannot organize and decide things so that God would deliver a message through me to others. If I am to speak from God, I must first make myself completely dependent on him, surrender myself to him, listen to him. For God does not use me as a talking machine, but uses my feelings, my will, my mind, my mouth, in order to speak to those present. The prophets of the Old Testament have often shown that nothing is more strenuous or more disturbing than this concentrated listening to God and speaking for God. That is why one can rise to this gift only after a deep and personal surrender to God.

A first step is to address words from the Bible to the assembly. The prophetic character of this ministry is then shown by the fact that the words are suited to the situation:

that is, they edify, exhort, console, within the context of the service of prayer. So — for example — someone has prayed at the meeting for the grace of conversion and another has answered him with the quotation from the Book of Revelation: 'So be zealous and repent. Behold, I stand at the door and knock; if anyone hears my voice and opens the door, I will come in to him and eat with him and he with me (3.19f). The possible effects of such words are unbelievable. If Jesus were corporeally present here, he could make this statement and he does in fact make it through the mouth of one of those present.

If someone is granted the gift of prophecy, he listens inwardly to the appeals and instructions of the living, risen Lord and asks himself: What would Jesus say here and now if he were still with us as the man of Nazareth? What does the living Jesus now want to say to those present? That is why prophecies are frequently delivered in the first person, *as if* Jesus were speaking here and now.

A further step is taken when God leads the individual so far that the latter places his ideas, words, images at God's disposal and God speaks through him to others. At the same time a prophecy must not necessarily be expressed in the first person. It is often better if someone stands up and says: 'I think God would now tell us this . . . .' The following prophecy was uttered at the international congress of the Catholic Charismatic Renewal, on Whit Monday 1975 during the eucharistic celebration at which Cardinal Suenens presided, with 750 priests concelebrating and ten thousand people present. It was probably the first time in the history of St Peter's that such an extempore prophecy had been uttered during Mass:

'I have strengthened you with my power. I will renew my Church. I will lead my people to a new unity. I invite you: Turn away from useless pleasures, have time for me. I want to change your life profoundly. Look to me. I am always present in my Church. A new call is going out to you. I am creating for myself anew an army of witnesses and bringing my people together. My power rests upon it. They will follow my chosen pastors. Do not turn away from me. Allow yourself to be permeated by me. Experience my life, my spirit, my power. I will liberate the world. I have begun to renew my Church. I will lead the world to freedom'.

Paul's rule is that those present are to judge whether a prophecy comes from God (1 Cor 14.29), and it may well be necessary for the assembly not to agree. But the prophecy quoted above, spoken by a layman, was confirmed in St Peter's by long sustained applause also by the bishops present, who would be expected particularly to have the gift of discernment (more of this in the seventh week). There are also 'false prophets' (Mk 13.6. 22; Mt 7.15; 1 Jn 4.1; 2 Pet 2.1, etc.). Suppose that in the prophecy above-quoted the words had also occurred: 'Leave your Church, abolish the sacraments. It is my Spirit which produces life and all the rest is the work of men'. It is obvious that such an invitation to schism would not have been inspired by the Holy Spirit, the Spirit of unity.

It is not always possible to make a clear distinction between what comes from God, what from men or even from anti-divine powers. There remains a certain *insecurity* which is rooted in human freedom and the possibility of lapses. God is always *wholly* at work and man is always *wholly* committed. The prophet utters words which come from himself. They express ideas and images which are connected with his own life-history and his experience of life. But at the same time God wants to speak through them to others, to awaken others to believe. It is impossible however to draw an *exact* dividing line and therefore Paul says that those present should 'judge' (1 Cor 14.29, 32). The Catholic view is that a final judgment on the authenticity of gifts of the Spirit rests with the totality of all the bishops as the representatives of the whole Church. For some Christians this function is exercised by the particular local congregation associated with other local congregations (cf. the Protestant contribution at the end of the seventh week).

Anyone who exercises the gift of prophecy then abandons his privacy in regard to God and to the congregation. If it is God himself who *admonishes through you*, then the assumption must be that you have wholly and entirely laid open and placed at God's disposal your feelings, your will, your intellect, yourself. The word 'private' means 'separated'.

If someone speaks in place of Christ, he is not separated from God in this happening, but is one with him by grace. But the prophet gives up his privacy also in regard to the community. He speaks, not as a private individual, but as a member of the congregation and submits himself to the judgment of the other prophets.

3. The gift of tongues

For many the first step to the abandonment of privacy in regard to God is the gift of tongues: 'One who speaks in a tongue speaks not to men but to God; for no one understands him, but he utters mysteries in the Spirit' (1 Cor 14.2). God is not only unknowable, he is *inexpressible*. This is the explicit teaching and dogma of the Church. We can neither comprehend nor express the mystery of God in ordinary human speech. But prayer in tongues is the *utterance of that which remains unutterable for all eternity*. We must therefore allow God himself to penetrate into the depths of our power of speech, to utter his mystery in us. In the prayer of tongues we surrender ourselves to God to the very depth of our humanity. For the power of speech is the most profound expression of being human (no animal will ever acquire a human language). In the word 'I' I am myself wholly and entirely present with body and soul, mind, will and feeling. No one can say 'I' in my place, no one 'you' in my place. Prayer in tongues emerges from the depths of the person as a way of saying 'you' to God, without the person praying being able to understand the 'meaning' (cf. 1 Cor 14.11).

Since this expression of the inexpressible has become almost unknown, we cannot have the remotest idea of it if we have never heard it or never experienced it in ourselves. Consequently this prayer is exposed to many misunderstandings. It is not — as many translations of the Bible suggest — a 'rapturous' or 'ecstatic' talking, but wholly normal speaking in a normal tone. Paul assumes that the person praying in this way can begin or stop whenever he wants (cf. 1 Cor 14.27: 'each in turn'). Prayer in tongues normally sounds like a news broadcast in a language completely unknown to the hearer. It is a question of a sequence of vowels and consonants with a certain speech melody and rhythm, the only difference being that this speaking is 'meaningless' for the understanding and moreover very personal, since it emerges from an attitude of profound adoration.

In our traditional prayer we find what could certainly be regarded as preliminary stages to this speaking in tongues. In Gregorian Chant there are long drawn out melodies in which only the vowel 'a' is sung (for instance, at the end of the Alleluia). The vowel 'a' has no 'meaning' in itself, it contains no communication, no information. In such singing out before God it is solely the linguistic bridge to God and emerges from the deepest levels of my person, which cannot be fathomed solely by reason. We find a similar occurrence in the Eastern Church, particularly in the Jesus-prayer. The person praying often continues for hours repeating the invocation: 'Lord Jesus Christ, have mercy on me'. We need only hear this sentence once and we know its content: in this form of prayer however, what is of primary importance is not the *content*, but the *occurrence*, the fact of expressing myself wholly and entirely to Jesus, to God, and thus experiencing his presence in me. For the mind such a continuous repetition is 'pointless'. Something similar happens in the rosary. During this prayer we do not take in mentally the content of every single word or of the spoken sentences. There is no 'point' in saying the same prayer fifty times. Prayer in tongues differs from all this only in one respect: the spoken vowels and consonants belong to a language which I do not understand, which no one has hitherto spoken in this form; in it I utter myself before God, I gave myself wholly and entirely — even my speech — back to him.

Self-surrender to God in the prayer of tongues can express gratitude (1 Cor 14.16f), intercession (Rom 8.27; Eph 6.18). proclamation of God's great deeds (Acts 2.11; 10.46). But it reaches its deepest level in the *adoration of God for his own sake*. When we praise and glorify God for his creation, we can enumerate the many things he has created. But if we praise and glorify him because he is the unfathomable, incomprehensible, inexpressible mystery (cf. 1 Cor 14.2), words fail us. We can only cry out: 'We praise you, we glorify you, we adore you' and we ought then really to continue repeating these invocations or begin to enumerate God's 'attributes' ('You alone are the Holy One, you alone are the Lord, you alone are the Most High', etc.). If it is a question of God himself, *because he is God*, we do not really know what and how we should pray. We can only be guided by the presence of the Spirit of God in us. He himself then intercedes for us 'with *sighs too deep for words*' (Rom 8.26). The Greek word translated here by 'sighs' is a technical term in the New Testament for prayer which is produced, not by the intellect, but by the Spirit. The same word is found also in Mark 7.34 and 8.12. Mark then probably thought that Jesus too prayed in this way.

When we call God the inexpressible mystery, we mean that the resources of our mind are quite inadequate to grasp or express him. This is true of the words 'God', 'Father', 'Holy' and so on. We associate with them certain ideas and meanings drawn from our human experience. But if God himself, the 'Father', is beyond our experience, as the Bible says from the first book to the last, this mystery can be expressed only in terms other than those drawn from our human experience. Moreover, with our mother-tongue and the many mental concepts we have acquired, we can easily shield ourselves against God, talk *about* him. In the prayer of tongues on the other hand we speak *to* God (1 Cor 14.2). In it therefore we do not even communicate anything to other human beings, but we edify ourselves and present ourselves to God (1 Cor 14.4).

For this reason Paul gives a warning against making the prayer of tongues predominant in congregational worship. If there is no one to 'interpret' it, then no one should speak in this way before the congregation. In this situation one should 'speak to himself and to God' (1 Cor 14.28). This form of prayer then remains private in the sense that it is primarily an enrichment of 'private' prayer. But the occurrence itself is a way of completely *shedding our privacy* in regard to God, for in it I no longer pray as 'separated' from God to a 'supreme being' before and above creation, but *God the Holy Spirit prays in me through Christ in God, the*

Father beyond our knowing and experience.

Communal 'singing in the Spirit' (cf. Eph 5.19f; Col 3.16f) is rather different. Someone strikes a note, all gather round him, each singing his own melody, 'as the Spirit inspires it', and praying at the same time in tongues. Anyone to whom this gift is not given can also link prayers in his own language with these melodies (Alleluia, Jesus is Lord, etc.). This 'singing in the Spirit' often gives an unexpected depth of adoration to the service of prayer. It is not accidental that the call to proclaim 'the mystery of faith', which comes after the words of institution in the eucharistic celebration, is frequently followed by this form of singing.

According to Paul (1 Cor 12.10) the *interpretation* of an individual prayer in tongues is a special gift of the Spirit. Someone who interprets such a prayer tries to reconstruct it and, under the influence of the Spirit, empathetically to give it a content. It is obvious that there can be no question here of a 'translation', for the person praying does not himself attach any content to his speaking. The gift of interpretation and explanation is given mainly so that others too may profit by the prayer of tongues (1 Cor 14.17), so that the social dimension of the experience of God is maintained and the mind too gains something (1 Cor 14.14). Interpretation therefore is more a complement than a translation.

Does God expect you also to pray for this gift? Paul tells the Corinthians, 'I want you all to speak in tongues' (1 Cor 14.5), and expressly thanks God that he himself prays in tongues (v. 18). He therefore exhorts them not to forbid speaking in tongues (v. 39), but also insists that not all are given this gift 'appointed' by God (1 Cor 12.28, 30). It is granted mostly to people who are prepared *to give even their speech back to God.*

Our modern rational outlook admittedly makes us afraid to ask for the gift of tongues. We have been educated constantly to watch ourselves, not to commit ourselves prematurely and uncritically to something we do not know. In the prayer of tongues however we must for once jump ship, get away from familiar surroundings, away from all that protects us. We must attempt the impossible and walk on the water, even though we think it is unlikely to sustain us. At the same time the call of Jesus is addressed also to us: 'Take heart, it is I; have no fear' (Mt 14.27).

On the first occasion you may be very upset, for you really have to cross a threshold. You must let yourself go completely, simply pray like mad, without worrying about what noises you are making. Some people are nervous and therefore the first time you speak in tongues it is helpful if those who have already received this gift speak in tongues together with you. There are some who are not upset by this gift, if they surrender themselves in a wholly childlike way and — in a good sense — naively to God. In itself this prayer has nothing to do with ecstasy or emotional outbursts.

This form of prayer is unlikely to make its way into the mainstream of congregational worship in the near future. We read in Mark's gospel, in the ending which first appeared about the middle of the second century: 'And these signs will accompany those who believe: ... they will *speak in new tongues*' (Mk 16.17). That is, a hundred years after the death of Christ, the meaning of prayer in tongues was generally known and the text suggests that this 'sign' of the presence of the Holy Spirit was not only given to the first generation of Christians but is a phenomenon normally accompanying the Christian mission. Today we have reached a new epoch in the history of faith and have not yet found a language to describe this originality of the ever-new God. The Lord of history wants to *purify* our language, to break it up from within and give us new words. If we offer the depths of our power of speech to his mystery, then we shall be able 'boldly to proclaim *the mystery of the gospel*' (Eph 6.19) in a new way in our intelligible mother-tongue.

In conclusion, it should be emphasized that the charism of prayer in tongues — like every other charism — presupposes a natural capacity: that is, the human power of speech as such. Prayer in tongues therefore, like any other gift of the Spirit, must be *tested* for its authenticity. The utterance of un-intelligible sequences of vowels and consonants is a phenomenon well known to doctors in certain types of illness and it occurs also in states of intoxication. In these circum-stances it is not charismatic, but has a *purely psychological* origin.

4. Socio-critical charisms[38]

In the prayer of tongues I give up my private existence to God, I open myself out to him. If then we follow our discussion of that topic immediately with a study of the charism of social-critical involvement, we are not leaping into an entirely different world: this charism is to be 'desired' by everyone (1 Cor 14.1) just as much as the other gifts of the Spirit which flow from love. In his list of charisms Paul mentions also administrative services, the community's charitable works, the distribution of the love-gifts collected at the eucharistic meal. The word in 1 Corinthians 12.28 (antilempseis), translated by 'aids', means literally 'receiving in turn': the task of those engaged in trade who see that agreements are kept with regard to imports and exports. Behind this gift is the natural capacity for administration. The Spirit of God purifies and strengthens this capacity and makes use of it for building up the Church (and society). Thus it becomes a charism.

Within the Christian community this gift is seen, not only as a charism of charity from one human being to another — as a personal ministry of love to the sick and the needy — but as public administration of the love-gifts in the congregation, as charism of distributing aid (Rom 12.8). This does not mean merely book-keeping, but also provision for a just *balance* of material possessions within the local congregation and between the congregations in different places.

Paul himself takes on this service when he invites the Corinthians to make a collection for the poor community in Jerusalem, so that a *balance* emerges between superfluity and need (in fact both on the material and on the spiritual planes: 2 Cor 8.13f). We would call this sort of thing 'development aid': spiritual and material equilibrium between rich and poor nations, without ulterior motives (cf. Rom 12.8). Such an equilibrium of course presupposes criticism of existing conditions, as Paul makes clear from the start in connection with the love-feast before the eucharistic celebration. He sharply rebukes the Corinthians, because the rich remain rich and the poor are still poor (1 Cor 11.20-22). He does not call for a *change* in the existing social conditions, any more than Jesus himself drew up any concrete socio-critical programmes; but in the changed awareness brought about by Jesus it is logically implied that, not only do men change, but also that structures prevailing at a particular time should be critically examined and occasionally changed.

Paul also makes clear for us that criticism of society, social commitment, for Christians does not rest solely on any kind of political ideology. The latter is not concerned mainly with the truth, but with the attainment of political objectives. On the other hand the social involvement of the Christian is charismatic. It is 'grace' (2 Cor 8.1) and the historical continuation of Jesus' own self-surrender. Paul says of the Macedonians that they have not only given something by way of material gifts, but *'first they gave themselves'* to the Lord and to us by the will of God' (2 Cor 8.5). Some translations smooth out the text ('they committed themselves, first for the Lord, but also for us') and it does at first seem exaggerated to describe the surrender of material possessions as surrender to Christ himself. This however is not merely an emotional expression; for Paul the ordinary daily actions and necessities, which we would describe as 'secular', are *charismatic*, rooted in the grace of Christ: 'You know the grace of our Lord Jesus Christ, that though he was rich, yet for your sake he became poor, so that by his poverty you might become rich' (2 Cor 8.9). Jesus did not keep his divine riches for himself, but humbled himself, made himself poor, in order to be poor with us who are poor (cf. Phil 2. 5-8).

We may ask what this means for each one of us. First of all, if the *social experience of God* in worship does not lead also to a strengthening of social and political commitment, if it remains restricted to a selected group of 'charismatics', it amounts to *culpable* one-sidedness. However much you are stirred and however attentively you are praying during worship, if your faith is not followed by deeds, then you are 'deceiving yourselves' (cf. Jas 1.22). You are stirred more by yourself than by Christ, who gave himself up for others. 'If a brother or sister is ill-clad and in lack of daily food, and one of you says to them, "Go in peace, be warmed and filled", without giving them the things needed for the body, what does it profit? So faith by itself, if it has no works, is dead' (Jas 2.15-17).

On the other hand, as a Christian, you are armed against all ideologies which see the salvation of mankind *solely* in the redistribution of possessions and deduce from this a totalitarian claim: 'If I give away all I have, but have not love, I gain nothing' (1 Cor 13.3). You have experienced in yourself the *mystery* of God and thus you have an inner *standard* by which you can measure all totalitarian claims and intramundane 'doctrines of salvation'. This also assumes that you really cope with these things and co-operate as far as your resources allow in the changing of unjust social structures and power-situations.

The Christian can and must occasionally identify himself with those who refuse to be Christians or even describe themselves as atheists. In the great speech on the judgment in Matthew 25.31-46 the 'righteous' ask: ' "Lord, *when* did we see thee hungry and feed thee, or thirsty and give thee drink? And *when* did we see thee a stranger and welcome thee, or naked and clothe thee? And *when* did we see thee sick or in prison and visit thee?" And the king will answer them, "Truly, I say to you, as you did it to one of the least of these my brethren, you did it to *me*" ' (vv. 37-40). Those who had committed themselves to the hungry, the underprivileged, the imprisoned, *evidently had no idea* that they were doing all this for Christ. There are occasions when you can and must identify yourself with all those who are engaged in changing social structures and in producing a just distribution of possessions, without ulterior motives and without wanting to include you or to allow for you in their plans. Christians were not behind the social revolutions of the eighteenth and nineteenth centuries, because theology and piety had withdrawn into a disastrous privacy, because people had forgotten that the Spirit of God wills also to order the social relationships of men with one another: this is an historical *fault* of the Christian Churches. You can and must redeem it, going as far as making protests and adopting other means of bringing about (non-violent) change.

Perhaps you feel that you are a gifted charismatic, you pray in tongues and play a great part in the act of worship; but you are giving way to a horrible self-deception if you think that this is the true and most important way to God.

Sin often begins by exaggerating the good. Baptism of the Spirit takes hold of all your powers, including your emotions; but if such an experience estranges you from society, if you think that you are now really able to lead a purely private bourgeois life, it would be better if you had never come into contact with the charismatic renewal. Either you strip your faith of its private character for the sake of society of you remain even in regard to God in a private, segregated existence and — in what you call 'experience of God' — you are perhaps enjoying only your own feelings. Jesus took the side of the despised, the underprivileged, the sinners and his commitment to them was certainly also an emotional commitment.

5. The gift of healing

Paul takes it completely for granted that the gift of healing is granted to some people in the community (1 Cor 12.9, 28) and at the beginning of the second century it is still attested: 'And these signs will accompany those who believe: they will *lay their hands on the sick, and they will recover* (Mk 16.17f). The gift of healing never died out in the Church. In the lives of men and women especially called by God ('saints') we continually come across cures. They are 'signs' of the presence of the Holy Spirit in these people, but thus at the same time also signs of the dawn of the future reign of God. Cures then have an awakening effect, calling forth readiness for faith. They provoke our reaction, our faith in the healing power of God and consequently we usually shield ourselves against coming into closer contact with such occurrences. There are those who think that the gift of prophecy might well be given to someone in the congregation, but regard it as *extremely unlikely* that cures could take place even today during worship in the congregation. Many people do not exclude the possibility of cures at Lourdes and Fatima, but these anyway are tested by a commission of doctors. But is there anyone who would get the idea that he himself had perhaps been granted the gift of healing? Nobody *expects* this and that is why the gift is not granted. To exercise it means making an act of deep faith and of self-surrender to God. Perhaps you regard 'inward' healing as possible, because in certain circumstances it can be explained psychologically (this is in fact the background of the prayer for inward healing in the third week), but not *physical* healing of people who have been given up by the doctors.

Let us look again into the New Testament:

> 'He went about all Galilee, teaching in their synagogues, preaching the gospel of the kingdom and *healing every disease and every infirmity among the people*' (Mt 4.23).
> 'Go and tell John what you have seen and heard: the blind receive their sight, the lame walk, lepers are cleansed, and the deaf hear, the dead are raised up, the poor have the good news preached to them' (Lk 7.22).

According to the gospel accounts, all those who come into closer contact with Jesus are cured of their illnesses. God's reign has dawned. This is seen also in the mandate given by Jesus before his passion and in the history of the Christian mission after Pentecost:

> 'These twelve Jesus sent out, charging them, "Preach as you go, saying, 'The kingdom of heaven is at hand'. *Heal the sick*, raise the dead, cleanse lepers, cast out demons" ' (Mt 10,5, 8).
> 'The twelve went out and preached that men should repent. And they cast out many demons, and anointed with oil many that were sick and *healed* them' (Mk 6.12f).
> 'Peter came down to the saints that lived at Lydda. There he found a man who had been bedridden for eight years and was paralysed. And Peter said to him, "Aeneas, *Jesus Christ heals you*: rise and make your bed". And immediately he rose. And all the residents of Lydda and Sharon saw him, and they turned to the Lord' (Acts 9.32-35, cf. vv.40f).

In the charismatic renewal such accounts are once more taken seriously, but without overlooking modern medical knowledge. If someone comes forward during the service and asks to be cured, all are deeply affected and feel that their faith is being questioned: if we should and may now ask God for a cure, will he show his power? A person who is involved for the first time in such a situation is at first taken aback, perhaps even put off. For many there is a long process of surrendering to God before that attitude of basic trust is reached which is linked with the prayer for healing and the acceptance of the gift of healing.

Here too of course, as with all the other gifts of the Spirit, the gift of discernment is necessary. Both in the person who is seeking a cure and also in the prayer of those present, natural forces — concealed in creation itself — are at work. There are accounts in medical literature of spontaneous cure of serious organic illnesses, outside any religious context. Nature heals itself. This possibility of spontaneous cures, rooted in creation itself, is the basis of charismatic healing. The latter is not essentially supernatural, but only in the *way* it takes place. In it healing forces lying within creation itself are mobilized, creation is restored to its pristine state and its own possibilities exploited. God created man in his image, as his partner, and even man's body is taken up into the relationship with God. In the New Testament sickness and death are regarded as signs of separation from God, of sin (Rom 6.23). Christ did not abolish sickness and death, but he deprived them of their anti-divine character. If then someone gives himself back to God totally, in a deep, basic trust, this has effects even in his bodily nature.

At the same time it must be observed that many organic diseases are mentally conditioned. Many patients who now crowd into doctors' surgeries are suffering from neuro-dystonia, which is rooted in personal tensions, worry, stress, pressure to produce results, false ambition, emotional instability, etc. Organic diseases frequently result from this state. Consequently there are some organic illnesses which the doctor cannot cure, even with the best medicines, unless a process of emotional healing sets in at the same time. And this again occurs in happy personal relationships with others. The highest personal relationship which man can experience is with God himself and consequently it is this relationship by which he is most affected and permanently marked. It is understandable therefore that total surrender to God, encounter with him, also sets in motion healing processes in the depth of the person. This is another clear example of the fact that we can never say precisely where the dividing line runs between the efficacy of God's grace and the natural forces of creation. Consequently a premature and exaggerated description of certain occurrences as 'supernatural' is to be avoided. It is only when cures are confirmed by doctors and have stood the test of time that they should be described as charismatic effects of God. In any case the prayer for healing is an act of deep faith, of basic trust. If someone seeks a cure as he seeks a business success or a job, it is a certain sign that his prayer does not come from basic trust in God.

The gift of healing however, like every other charism, has also a basis in conditions present from birth in those to whom it is granted. The involvement of such powers is then *charismatic* in so far as they are purified, intensified and used for the building up of the Church by the Spirit of God. It is also important to note that this gift is promised *to the Church as a whole* and the individual exercises it as representing the whole Church. That is why the whole assembly prays for a cure and everyone is invited to lay hands on the person to be healed. The deepest incentive to this action is the love of the living Jesus himself, with which he loves the sick. His peace, his liberating freedom, his joy, is present when Christians pray for healing for one another. It is a question here, not merely of group therapy, but of the expression of social experience of God. Healing is granted *in expectant faith.*

But what happens if God does not fulfil the request for healing? A group or congregation must *grow* into the exercise of this gift of the Spirit and this happens to the extent that faith grows. Not only the faith required for baptism, but that which 'moves mountains' (Mt 17.20; 1 Cor 13.2). This metaphor shows that obstacles must be overcome which are rooted in creation itself as still unredeemed or even under the influence of anti-divine powers. This was the sort of faith that the centurion at Capernaum had (Mt 8.10) and that is why Jesus said to him: 'Be it done for you *as you have believed'* (v.13). The centurion expected everything from Jesus, even healing at a distance: 'Lord, I am not worthy to have you come under my roof; but only say the word, and my servant will be healed' (Mt 8.8). We repeat this expression of trust before receiving the eucharistic gifts and apply it to ourselves ('and I shall be healed'); but are we at all aware that we are thus also praying for *healing* at this point?

This example makes it clear that the sign of healing is closely linked with the sacramental signs. But healing power is found, not only in the eucharistic presence of Jesus, but also in the sacrament of penance (healing opposition to God), of marriage (healing personal relationships). In the prayer after the anointing of the sick we find the words:

> 'Lord Jesus Christ, our Redeemer, by the power of the Holy Spirit, ease the sufferings of our sick brother (sister) and make him (her) well again in mind and body. In your loving kindness forgive his (her) sins and grant him (her) *full health* so that he (she) may be restored to your service'.

Anointing of the sick is by no means mainly a preparation for death, but a request for healing. There is no need to insist on the fact that neither the charism of healing nor the anointing of the sick is a substitute for expert medical treatment.

A fine example of the view that the gift of healing is granted to the whole congregation is found in a letter of Luther, written in the last year of his life (and therefore with a lifetime's experience behind it). He writes to a parish priest that the congregation of Wittenberg — whose pastor he was — had cured a maniac 'through prayer in Christ' and gives him this advice:

> 'When you do your house-visiting take with you an assistant preacher and *two or three good men*. At the same time be quite *firmly confident*, because you are in the Church's public ministry and you are the pastor there. *Lay your hands on the sick person* and say:

"Peace be with you, dear brother, from God our Father and from the Lord Jesus Christ!" Then pray over him the Creed and the Our Father in an audible voice. Conclude with the words: "God, almighty Father, you have told us through your son: Truly I say to you, if you ask anything from the Father in my name, he will give it to you". Again, you have been quite peremptorily ordered to pray: "Pray and you will receive". Likewise in Psalm 50: "Call upon me in the day of trouble; I will deliver you, and you shall glorify me". Because of these words and because of your Son's commandment, we, unworthy sinners, beg your mercy with *all the power of our faith*: "Look on this man, liberate him from all evil and destroy in him the work of Satan, for the glorification of your name, for the growth of faith and the strengthening of the saints, through our Lord Jesus Christ, who lives and reigns with you for ever and ever. Amen". Immediately before leaving *lay your hands on him again* and say: "The signs that follow those who believe are: they will lay their hands on the sick and they will recover". Do all this up to three times a day. In addition, have prayers said from the pulpit, publicly in Church, till God answers. Let us be one unceasingly in our communal intercession and prayer in the Lord *with all the power of our faith*' (W. Br.11, No. 4120, pp. 111f).

But if God leaves us our sicknesses and sufferings, although we have prayed for healing, then this must be his express will. As Paul experienced it in himself: 'Three times I besought the Lord about this, that it (my sickness) should leave me; but he said to me, "My grace is sufficient for you, for my power is made perfect in weakness" ' (2 Cor 12.8f). Paul sees his suffering as an incentive to a deeper understanding of his missionary activity. The missionary comes 'in fear and trembling', so that faith does not rest on human wisdom, but on the power of God (1 Cor 2.3-5). In addition, Paul takes on himself his sufferings as representative of those to whom he has been sent. 'I rejoice in my sufferings *for your sake*, and in my flesh I complete what is lacking in

Christ's afflictions for the sake of his body, that is, the church, of which I became a minister according to *the divine office* which was given to me for you, to make the word of God fully known' (Col 1.24f).

Seventh week: Discernment

Be guided by the Spirit, test the gifts of the Spirit!

1. Satan wants to separate you again from God

2. Experience of self — sin — gifts of the Spirit:

3. Guidance by the Spirit:
   a) The distinction between human prudence and divine inspiration
   b) The relationship between human fellowship and experience of the Spirit

4. Aids to discernment
   a) Universal distinguishing features
   b) Personal distinguishing features

5. The gift of discernment — gift of the whole Church

6. The Protestant view of the gift of discernment
   a) Decision for a group or congregation in an actual situation
   b) Decision on questions of faith for the community of all Christians

1. Satan wants to separate you again from God

The Greek word (*pneuma*) which we translate as 'spirit' designates in the New Testament, not only the divine Spirit, but also our human spirit and the evil spirit opposed to God. Even here it is not always easy to distinguish between the designations. The Spirit of God is present *in* our human spirit, and the evil spirit can produce a deceptive imitation of the Spirit of God. But if through the Holy Spirit we mortify the sinful acts of our ego, we shall live: 'For all who are led by the Spirit of God are sons of God' (Rom 8.14). Our tendency to sin, our 'hostility to God' (Rom 8.7), remains also in those whom God has justified and liberated from the law of sin and death. You will appreciate perhaps more clearly than before what this means if you pray during this seminar or later for a renewal of the Spirit. Jesus himself, immediately after his baptism of the Spirit, was led by Satan into the temptation to misuse his power for purposes which were not part of his mandate: he was to make bread out of stones, seek wordly power, throw himself down from the temple, trusting in God's word (Mt 4.1-11; Lk 4.1-13). Satan does not in any way question Jesus' baptism with the Spirit, but he wants to twist this baptism of the Spirit into its very opposite.

It will be no different with you. If you commit yourself to the Holy Spirit, you will also have to cope with the evil spirit. You will learn that he is a real force, which seeks to separate you again from God. That is why we read in the Ephesians: 'Put on the whole armour of God, that you may be able to stand against the wiles of the devil' (Eph 6.11). The matter is serious, for we are dealing here not with human beings of 'flesh and blood', but with supramundane powers which are active in and behind world-history, and also in and behind your life-history.

Scholars today disagree as to whether Satan is really a personal being, a 'someone', or whether the biblical writers have presented Satan as a person merely to provide a more concrete description of the origin of evil in man. But this is not the way in which the question should be stated. We pointed out already in the second week that even the Holy

Spirit is not 'someone' with whom we are confronted as with a human person. It would not be appropriate to set up a statue of the Holy Spirit in church, for he did not become man and consequently cannot be depicted in the form of a man (on the other hand it is very appropriate to represent Christ as a man, for he was really and truly man, like us in all things except sin). The Holy Spirit is the divine power and strength in us, the dynamism of God himself. It is likewise misleading to imagine the evil spirit, the devil, as someone whom one might sketch on the wall. On the contrary, he is the power and force opposed to God (but dependent on God for his existence) and wants to separate us from God (Eph 6.12). The anti-God character of this power is seen especially in the fact that it can obtain evil results from good and true intentions or actions: *that is, to turn the good into its opposite*. This Satan achieves mostly by the method of *exaggeration*.

You have certainly experienced this in yourself in the course of this seminar. Perhaps in the third week you recognized more clearly than formerly that you are distrustful in regard to God, that you have insured yourself against him. Satan has put it into your head: 'You are right. You must be distrustful of God, for he will deprive you of your freedom, he will repress you, he is a tyrant'. Satan does not deny that God lives: nor does he deny that God has given you freedom to trust him. Satan wants to persuade you to *misuse* your freedom to give way completely to the ever present possibility of distrusting God and to stand on your own feet.

Perhaps however Satan has caught you at another weak point. He has persuaded you: 'If you entrust yourself completely to God, then you must also be really *completely consistent*. You must radically change your life, renounce everything, sell everything, live in utter poverty, never again strive for success. You must leave father and mother, your family, in the lurch. That is what it says in the Bible. So it would be better to keep your fingers out of it and stay as you are'. By exaggerating, Satan tries *to separate you from God by the word of God*. He is — as John says — the 'father of lies' (Jn 8.44), the 'spirit of error' (1. Jn 4.6). Satan never lies directly, but he exaggerates what is true and so turns it into its opposite.

Such an exaggeration of the good occurs when you think that no more is required once you have experienced the presence of the Spirit in baptism of the Spirit; that you do not need to get involved in criticism of society or in politics. Satan wants to entice you to *misuse* the joy of praising and glorifying God, which has been freshly granted you, to take pleasure — so to speak — in God and in your own feelings, to seek an experience for its own sake. He wants to separate you from your tasks in society and for society and thus turns worship of God into its opposite. We said already in the previous week that, if your faith is not followed up by deeds, you are deceiving yourself, Satan has deceived you.

Satan appears on the scene with all his power when you pray for renewal of the Spirit, when God gives you the gift of prophecy, the gift of tongues, the gift of healing. He will always try to persuade you that *you are fooling yourself,* that basically everything can be explained psychologically and that none of this has anything to do with the Spirit of God. When you feel for the first time the impulse to make a prophetic contribution during worship, doubts will creep in on you as to whether the Spirit of God is really involved here. Perhaps Satan will also entice you to become arrogant, to look down on others, since from now on you are a 'prophet'; he will entice you into *misusing* this gift to increase your own prestige. The same sort of thing happens when you pray for the first time in tongues. You feel odd, since you are still watching yourself too much, and Satan will persuade you that this kind of prayer is something only for lunatics. Be confident then that prayer in tongues is a prayer of victory and do not let yourself be misled by any amount of psychological explanations. Every charism presupposes a natural endowment and capacity, but if this truth is so exaggerated as to suggest that there is no place for the Holy Spirit, we are making ourselves judges of what God can do.

2. Experience of self — sin — gifts of the Spirit

It is of the greatest importance to the charismatic congregational renewal for every individual and for the congregation to learn to distinguish between demonic, human and divine impulses. The Bible teaches us that a special gift of the Spirit is needed to distinguish between these different impulses, the gift of discernment of spirits (1 Cor 12.10).[34] We cannot trust all who claim to be filled with the Holy Spirit: 'Test the spirits to see whether they are of God; for many false prophets have gone out into the world' (1 Jn 4.1). Before we can discuss the characteristic features by which the authenticity of gifts of the Spirit can be recognized, some basic reflections are required. If in the history of the Church the gifts of the Spirit were frequently unable to reveal their full power, there were two reasons for it:

1. Individuals or whole groups have not sufficiently considered the fact that the exercise of the gifts of the Spirit is always threatened by misuse and sin. They have frequently confused their own experience of the self, their wishes and impulses, with the experience of the Holy Spirit and his impulses.

2. Those who are responsible for order in the Church have not always seen their ministry as spiritual, charismatic. They have not fostered and awakened the gifts of the Spirit, but frequently suppressed them.

In the community at Corinth Paul already had to struggle against the formation of parties and the tendency to disruption (cf.1 Cor 1.11). The deeper and — in a true sense — the more moving the experience of the Spirit is, so much the greater is the danger that each will appeal to *his* experience of the Spirit (cf. the fourfold 'I' in 1 Cor 1.12). The experience of the gifts of the Spirit contains in itself from the very beginning the *tendency to disruption*. Even soon after the death of Paul, towards the end of the first century, these tendencies had hardened in the community at Corinth. Some people, invoking their experience of the Spirit, had simply dismissed tried and trusted leaders of the community. The Roman community therefore wrote a letter to the community at Corinth (very probably composed by

Clement, Bishop of Rome), exhorting them urgently but in a fraternal spirit to establish discipline and order. The author of the letter refers at the same time to the order of the Old Testament: high priest — levite. By comparison with that, the relationship of bishop — priest — deacon is not something entirely new.[35]

This recourse to the Old Testament marks the beginning of an historical development during which the Church's ministry frequently came into conflict with the gifts of the Spirit, not always without 'fault on the part of human beings on both sides'. The awakening of a charismatic renewal in all the major Christian Churches cannot be explained without an intervention of God in history, for it was not and is not planned and organized by men. If there are not to be culpable *disruptions* (as a result of appealing to the experience of the Holy Spirit) or culpable *suppression* of this revival (by the 'institutional Church'), we must all be prepared to learn from history and to pray to God urgently for the gift of discernment. This gift too is granted only to someone who is receptive towards it, who surrenders himself completely to God and does not act merely according to the rules of human prudence. Anyone who prays for the gift of discernment assumes at the same time that there really is something to discern, that the impulses of the Holy Spirit are not the same as our own impulses. This distinction is all the more important in that the tendency to sin and thus also to the misuse of the gifts of the Spirit is ineradicable. Every human being, despite justification and sanctification by God, remains a sinner and inclined to sin.

The relationship between experience of the self and experience of the Spirit is expressed particularly clearly in two passages of the New Testament:

'All who are led by the Spirit of God are sons of God. For . . . you have received the spirit of sonship. When *we* cry "Abba! Father!" it is the Spirit himself bearing witness with our Spirit that we are children of God' (*Rom 8.14-16*).

'Because you are sons, God has sent the Spirit of his Son into our hearts, *crying*: "Abba! Father!" ' (*Gal 4.6*).

These two texts are important for several reasons. In the first place they recall the Abba-experience of Jesus, as we showed in the fourth week. But we are sons in the same sense as Jesus of Nazareth was 'Son of God' (the 'Son of God' did not become man in each one of us). If we are sons and daughters of God it is only because Jesus by his self-surrender on the cross has merited our rebirth from God. The sign of this rebirth is the presence of the Spirit of Jesus in us. A comparison of the two texts shows that the *Spirit of God* himself prays in us, but that *we* too pray: 'Abba, Father'. The texts do not say *precisely* what the Spirit does and what we do; they do not indicate exactly where the dividing line runs. All that is certain is that our human spirit and the divine Spirit remain *distinct*. The Spirit of God is sent into our hearts, and 'heart' means man's centre, the depth from which our bodily sensations, our feelings, our mind, our will, emerge. The presence of the Holy Spirit in us does not extinguish any of this. On the contrary, all our powers are roused to adoration and to service when the Holy Spirit 'bears witness' with our Spirit that we are children of God. From this we can deduce a first important principle: *The experience of the Holy Spirit occurs in us, but not without us.*

What is meant by this becomes clear in what follows. Observe once again how you breathe, how your chest rises and falls. This is *your* life, *your* vitality, for no one can breathe in your place. If you make a decision, it is likewise your will to act in this way and not in another. *Your* sin too, for which you are personally responsible, is *your* deed. In view of all this it is also true that no one can be baptized in your place, no one can receive the Holy Spirit in your place. Paul said on one occasion: 'It is no longer I who live, but Christ who lives in me' (Gal 2.20). This does not mean that your own life is destroyed or dissolved by grace. Christ lives in you, but not without you. If we exaggerate this statement of course, it becomes absurd. We cannot say, for instance: When I write a letter, it is Christ who writes in me; when I calculate it is Christ who calculates in me.

It is the same with the exercise of the gifts of the Spirit. No one can or may say of himself: he who sees and hears me

also sees and hears *immediately* Christ himself or his Holy
Spirit. Someone who makes a prophetic contribution during
worship can never say of himself: In me and through me the
Holy Spirit himself speaks immediately. Only in Jesus Christ
was God wholly present, immediately and directly. Anyone
who saw him saw God himself (cf. Jn 14.9). Jesus *is* the Son
of God, but I am *not* Christ, not — so to speak — the Holy
Spirit in person. If God wills to effect the salvation of others
through us, he uses at the same time our mind, our will, our
feelings, our whole person with our whole life history and
all our experiences: we are ourselves wholly involved in the
process. From this we can deduce a second important
principle: *God never acts wholly immediately and directly
on us and through us.*

Furthermore, the Son of God made man was without any
sin; from the very beginning he never lived separated from
God, his humanity was in no way an obstacle to God's
missionary salvific will. But we are and remain sinners and
can therefore obstruct the presence of the Holy Spirit in us.
In fact our sin is a continual strain on the divine salvific will
as it seeks to reach others through us. We may trust God to
hold back our tendency to sin and misuse if we wholly
surrender ourselves to him; but we must remain alert. When
God bestows his gifts of the Spirit, the anti-God power is
immediately on the spot. Consequently we must submit to a
test by others. What Paul says of the gift of prophecy is true
also of the other gifts of the Spirit: 'Let the others weigh
what is said' (1 Cor 14.29; cf.v.32). From this we can
deduce a third principle: *No one can know with absolute
certainty, excluding all doubt, whether the Holy Spirit is
active in him.* [36]

Only the Church as a whole can give a *final* judgment on
the authenticity of the gifts of the Spirit. But not all exercise
equally in public in the Church the gift of discernment any
more than the other gifts of the Spirit. This is the meaning
of 1 Thessalonians 5.12: 'We beseech you, brethren, to
respect those who labour among you and are over you in the
Lord and admonish you'. That is why the leaders, surrendering themselves to God, must continually pray for the gift
of discernment. If they neglect this, they are trusting solely

in their human prudence and are no longer receptive to the gifts of the Spirit in the Church.

From all that has been said it follows that the exercise of the gifts of the Spirit is always *necessarily* mingled with the tendency to sin, disruption and misuse. The essential thing therefore is to allow the Holy Spirit to *refine* our natural endowments and abilities, to *purify* our impulses. This is a life-long process. The more we surrender ourselves to the Spirit (more frequent prayer for the renewal of the Spirit and laying on of hands is a great help towards this), so much the more may we hope for this purification. It leads to a state in which our own impulses and the tendency to sin have *less and less* control over us and in which we offer *increasing* scope for the activity of the Holy Spirit. The testing of the gifts of the Spirit therefore will never end with the observation that there is no longer any sin in an individual, that he is completely filled with the Holy Spirit. We can only ask whether the Holy Spirit is *more* active than his own deepest instincts (which of course are by no means extinguished), more than the tendency to sin (which always remains). Certain features — which are still to be elucidated — however provide a degree of certainty of the authenticity of gifts of the Spirit. Charismatic renewal is consequently also a renewal of the gift of discernment. This gift is not merely a burdensome supplement. Its exercise is no less pleasing and liberating than that of the other gifts of the Spirit. If after a critical examination someone recognizes the activity of the Spirit in the Church, he will gratefully acknowledge that God is truly present among us.

3. Guidance by the Spirit

(a)   The distinction between human prudence and divine inspiration [37]

The gift of discernment and testing results in a *judgment*. This is indicated by the Greek terms used in the New Testament (1 Cor 12.10; 14.29; 1 Jn 4.1) in this connection. Every charism presupposes certain human abilities and endowments. Through the gift of discernment the power to discriminate — which is not given to the same extent to everyone — is purified by the Holy Spirit and placed at the disposal of the Church. But the gift of discernment, like every other, must be tested for its authenticity. It must be asked whether the person judges more in the light of human discrimination and prudence or relies mainly on the inspiration and guidance of the Holy Spirit. It is obvious that those to whom the gift of discernment is granted must in turn to be 'tested' by others in the exercise of this gift of the Spirit. Just as there are 'false prophets'. the gift of discernment too may be inadequately exercised. It must of course be assumed that those who are now testing and judging have also made themselves wholly dependent on the Spirit of God: 'The unspiritual man (who relies on his own intellect) does not receive the gifts of the Spirit of God, for they are folly to him, and he is not able to understand them because they are spiritually discerned. The spiritual man judges all things, but is himself to be judged by no one. "For who has known the mind of the Lord so as to instruct him?" But we have the mind of Christ' (1 Cor 2.14-16).

Every Christian is a 'spiritual' person and everyone should — as with the gift of prophecy — also seek the gift of discernment, even though not all can exercise this gift equally in public in the Church. At any rate the person who does not 'have' the Spirit of Christ, who does not lay himself open completely to him, cannot judge what comes from God. Only a spiritual person can judge spiritual things. This holds both for those who judge and also for those who test their judgment. An 'unspiritual' person — that is, one who has not surrendered himself to the Spirit of God — will never understand the 'madness' of some inspirations by which the lives of many people, richly endowed with God's grace, have been determined. We shall see in the final section (5) in what sense the gift of discernment is granted to the whole Church.

First however something must be said on the relationship of the gift of discernment to human prudence and discrimination. Someone who acts and judges prudently asks whether an act or occurrence is good or bad. The prudent person selects the best out of several possibilities; he takes advice from others and considers in advance the consequences of his action. It would — for example — be imprudent to begin building a house without the necessary means to do so (cf. Lk 14.28). The prudent man takes account of the foreseeable results and success. Pastoral strategy often emerges in this way. A priest may consider whether it is better to use his limited time for house-visiting or for work in groups and organizations. The more these reflections are influenced by love, the closer they come to 'inspiration'. The result is an inclination towards one of several possibilities of action which is no longer based on rules of human prudence.

It is however obvious that the history of the Church did not develop along the lines of merely prudent reflections. St Francis did not consider whether it was more prudent to be rich and live in luxury or to be poor. On the contrary, he felt himself inwardly impelled to live in poverty. The impulse to poverty for the sake of God and men comes, not from human instincts, but from the Holy Spirit. Someone who is under divine inspiration is therefore driven to act in a very *definite* way without being able completely to foresee the consequences and judge in advance. Here human counsel and shrewd balancing of one course of action against another are of no avail. The person who is driven by the Spirit of God is faced only with the decision as to whether he is ready to give way to the impulse of the Holy Spirit *or not.*

Luther's famous saying, 'Here I stand. I can do no other', deserves to be mentioned here as well as the decision of Pope John XXIII to convoke a council. Luther could not weigh in advance according to the rules of human prudence the consequences of his commitment to the Reformation, nor could Pope John foresee what consequences the calling of a council would have. Anyone who submits to an impulse of the Holy Spirit must allow his human prudence to take second place and perhaps face persecution and ridicule. Many social impulses of the Christian Churches would not have been possible without the readiness to follow the inspirations of God. There were in fact some people — like Don Bosco — who built or bought houses without having the necessary means at their disposal.

A charismatic inspiration in the proper sense however does

not by any means deprive man of his freedom. It is true that he can no longer choose rationally and prudently between different possibilities, but the supreme form of human freedom is total surrender to God, *freedom of commitment.* Before the sealing of the marriage contract each party is still free to make a different choice. But the stronger the love, the stronger also will be the *commitment.* A person who finally commits himself is not on that account unfree, but free for increasingly greater love.

This is true also of the charisms. A person who exercises the gift of prophecy at the prayer meeting does not 'choose' his words, does not consider whether he will now say this or that, but follows a *particular* impulse. This does not prevent him from wondering whether he should deliver the message now or later or even not at all. According to Paul's basic rules (that everything should take place in an edifying way, that all should proceed in order), the basic power of love will show the individual whether his contribution is *now* edifying or not. *Charismatic impulses are never coercive.* The same is true of the gift of tongues. Someone who permits the Spirit of God to take possession of his power of speech does not choose the vowels and consonants which he utters, but he prays (or sings) as the Spirit prompts him (cf. Eph 5.19; Col 3.16). (With the preliminary forms — for example, the Jesus prayer or the rosary — incidentally it is likewise clear that the choice of words has no meaning, no point, in regard to God.) In addition, each should consider whether his contribution is now edifying or not (1 Cor 14.12, 28). The same is true of all the charisms. The history of the Church's mission is full of examples. Peter's decision to preach the gospel to the Gentiles was not due to pastoral strategy and prudent considerations, but to a vision (Acts 10.9-16), and Paul too had such a visionary inspiration (Acts 16.9f) before he made his decision to cross into Europe.

Anyone who tests in the power of the Spirit (in himself or in others) whether certain actions and inspirations come from the Spirit of God therefore does not ask whether the words or actions were prudent, adequately considered, but *whether certain impulses come from God or not.* The judgment refers, not primarily to the words and actions themselves, but to the *impulse* from which they proceed. In some cases it can be established with certainty that an impulse comes, not from God, but from natural instincts or even from anti-divine powers (cf., for example, Mt 16.23; Acts 5.3). But if certain features, still to be discussed, establish firmly the authenticity of gifts of the Spirit, the question can and must always be whether certain words or actions come *more* from the Holy Spirit than from the person's own deepest instincts, which are always ineradicably accompanied by tendencies to failure and misuse.[38] If — for example — actions or contributions during the service of prayer clearly spring from certain dispositions of character (or even faults of character), then we shall have to say that such utterances are due *more* (or wholly) to these dispositions. If on the other hand a person does or says something which does *not* correspond to his natural disposition or which contradicts this, it would be a sign of the activity of the Holy Spirit (assuming that the other features, still to be discussed, are also present). Once again, God never acts on us wholly immediately and still less forcibly.

(b)   The relationship between human fellowship and experience of the Spirit

What has been said hitherto of the relationship between human freedom and experience of the Spirit is likewise true with reference to the experience of human fellowship. As the Second Vatican Council says, the Church is a 'social structure, serving the Spirit of Christ who vivifies it'.[39] Experience of the Church always has a 'social' character. This becomes particularly clear in charismatic services of prayer where each makes a contribution.

The dynamism of the charismatic renewal is directed towards a charismatically renewed Church (not to a new charismatic Church). This however can grow only out of small groups and therefore something must be said briefly about the relation between prayer groups and group-dynamics. In processes of group-dynamics people also come closer to one another, are aware of being accepted by others, experience a deep solidarity which changes their life. The members of the group open out to one another, share their feelings without inhibitions, overcome the taboo of their privacy, become more open to other people's problems, are able to enter into new relationships and so on. No one will deny that all this takes place also in charismatic prayer-meetings. It must however be stressed that the prayer meetings involve more than group-processes. The latter are not predominant, they are not deliberately sought, not brought about by definite methods. What unites the members of a prayer-group with one another is *primarily* the communal witness to Christ and this goes far beyond happenings in encounter-groups. We find this description of the primitive community: 'The company of those who believed were of one heart and soul, and no one said that any of the things he possessed was his own, but they had everything in common' (Acts 4.32). The Christian Church's history over two thousand years does not rest solely on a group-process and still less is self-discovery its main driving force. Self-discovery is bestowed as an additional gift to the extent that those present surrender themselves to the Spirit of God. A prayer group is not a circle of friends, not a 'charismatic circle', not a self-discovery group, but first and foremost an ecclesial community.[40] Those present do not decide the level of the encounter, but are united with one another in the one Holy Spirit *before* they do anything together. This *presence of the Holy Spirit is not dependent on the way in which those present are affected, but precedes this.*

Charismatic prayer-experience is a we-experience, going far beyond other human we-experiences. A prayer-group is so much more charismatic when it does not attach importance to itself, does not seek fellowship, does not want to remain self-centred. Here too the parable of the grain of seed applies. The more a group sets itself apart from the congregation or the Church, so much the less will it be able to exercise the ministry of witness and contribute to the renewal of the *whole* Church. If anyone seeks exclusively or primarily human fellowship in services of prayer, has no other wish but to be accepted in a human sense, to overcome his loneliness, taking pleasure solely in the outward forms of worship — in the sign of peace, in the open, human atmosphere — he will be disappointed and after a time will stay away.

Of course the individual experiences fellowship, is personally approved, liberated from his loneliness; but here too he may be reminded: 'Seek his kingdom, and these things shall be yours *as well*' (Lk 12.31; Mt 6.33). The less a prayer-group as a whole attaches importance to itself, so much the more receptive it can be to the guidance of the Holy Spirit. It will make important decisions, not according to the rules of human prudence, nor by selecting the best among various possibilities, but always interrupting deliberations by prayer and submitting to the ever new impulses of the Holy Spirit.

4. Aids to discernment

There are various distinguishing features by which anyone can perceive whether and to what extent certain impulses come from the Holy Spirit. As a rule one of these features in itself is not sufficient to provide a basis for spiritual discernment. The more the characteristics are combined, the greater is the certainty. The New Testament mentions *universally valid* distinguishing features which hold always and everywhere — that is, are not dependent on our personal experience and do not arise from it — and features manifested in the *person himself* on any particular occasion ('fruits of the Spirit: love, joy, peace). Anyone can observe in *himself* or in *others* universally valid and personal features of genuine charismatic utterances. But generally each needs the help of others in order to gain adequate certainty. An absolute, unquestionable certainty is not possible in regard to the gifts of the Spirit. Only Jesus could say of himself that he knew what was the will of God. This *uncertainty*, which persists in spite of all personal certainty, provides an occasion for surrendering ourselves even more completely to God.

(a)   Universal distinguishing features
    1. *Agreement with the word of God and the teaching of the Church.* We read in the letter to the Romans: 'Having gifts that differ, ... let us use them: if prophecy, *in*

proportion to our faith' (12.6). The prophet should keep to certain limits and should not give way to fanatical enthusiasm ('Faith' means primarily not basic trust, but the insight of faith). But the prophet must also be in agreement with the faith of the others, of the congregation, of the Church, and consequently the others should judge (1 Cor 14.29, 32). The faith of the Church finds its expression in the Bible and in the Church's teaching, the letter presenting the faith in a form suited to the particular historical situation and bringing it home to men. The testimony to Christ recorded in the Bible is absolutely reliable, the statements of faith are 'inspired' by the Holy Spirit. All charismatic utterances are prompted by the Holy Spirit, but all Churches maintain firmly that *only* biblical statements of faith are *absolutely certain and reliable*. The Holy Spirit does not speak only in *us*, but has always spoken in the word of Scripture, and he does not contradict himself. No one can claim that he has had a certain experience and consequently cannot learn from others, that he has the source of faith in himself. Promptings of the Holy Spirit always come about within the framework of the biblical statements of faith.

The latter of course are not always unambiguous and they can be interpreted in different ways. Hence the necessity of the Church's teaching authority, as the history of the ecumenical councils shows.

Even in New Testament times there were 'false prophets', heretical teachers, who had asserted that we do not really need Christ to gain access to God. There are many other ways to God. In regard to these the author of the first letter of John says: 'By this you know the Spirit of God: every spirit which confesses that Jesus Christ has come in the flesh is of God, and every spirit which does not confess Jesus is not of God. This is the spirit of antichrist' (1 Jn 4.2f). Let us suppose then that someone were to come forward today and say: 'I have prayed for knowledge and understanding. I wept in great perturbation and I tell you now as a prophet from God that you do not need to believe in the incarnation of the Son of God. Jesus was one among many other founders of religions'. Such a person would have to be exposed by all as a false prophet. We must always be very cautious with anyone who asserts that he *must* say or do something quite definite in the name of Jesus and who is not prepared to be taught and corrected by others. As we pointed out above, the prophet does not speak as a private individual, but as a member of the Church. Nor is the interpretation of the Bible primarily a matter for each individual, but for the whole Church. It is the same with all the other gifts of the Spirit — of teaching, healing, and so on. They are not a private affair, but can be exercised only in agreement with the whole Church.

If then someone (despite the most profound personal upheaval) is not prepared to submit his experience of the Spirit to the spiritual judgment of the Church as a whole, this is a certain sign that he is following his own impulses more (or entirely) than those of the Holy Spirit.

2. *Service for the building up of the Church and the world.* Gifts of the Spirit are granted 'for the common good' (1 Cor 12.7). 'Since you are eager for manifestations of the Spirit, strive to excel in building up the church' (1 Cor 14.12). 'Let all things be done for edification' (1 Cor 14.26).

The opposite of building up is disruption. The latter never comes from the Holy Spirit. In view of its importance we must again refer to the following text: 'All of you agree and let there be no dissensions among you: be united in the same mind and the same judgment . . . . What I mean is that each one of you says, "*I* belong to Paul", or "*I* belong to Apollo", or "*I* belong to Cephas", or "*I* belong to Christ". Is Christ divided?' (1 Cor 1.10-13). Disruption results mostly from attaching too much importance to ourselves, from appealing to our own personal experience. By 'Christ' Paul means the community at Corinth. He could also have asked: 'Is the Holy Spirit divided?' For the latter is one and the same in the different gifts of the Spirit and in the bearers of the Spirit (1 Cor 12.11). He is not exclusively "mine" or "yours", but always "our Spirit". The deeper the experience of the Spirit, the more it becomes part of our personal character, the more partial it is, and so much the more does it need completion and correction. Because of human limitations no one can reveal the depth of the experience of the Spirit and its whole breadth in his life (cf. the section 'Schism does not come from the Holy Spirit' in the fifth week). Over-emphasis on certain gifts of the Spirit (for example, the gift of tongues or the gift of providing for discipline and order) comes more from human than from divine impulses.

It is not only disruption which prevents the building up of the Church, but frequently also the style of personal *testimony*. If the latter provokes opposition which is not the result of a call to repentance (and who likes to hear that?), it is a sign that the testimony arises from a human desire for conversions or even from a feeling of superiority rather than from the impulses of the Holy Spirit. If — for example — on the very first evening or during the first week of an introductory seminar someone were to confront the participants with an exercise of gifts of the Spirit which they had not yet begun to understand, he would not be edifying but creating unnecessary opposition. We shall return to this topic when we come to talk about love. The isolation also of charismatic groups from the congregation or their refusal to contribute to the building up of the particular local congregation is due *more* to human self-will than to a divine impulse.

The charismatic renewal however does not only serve the building up of the Church, but also the building up and reconstruction of the world. If — for example — someone neglects the daily duties of his calling or appeals to his experience of the Spirit as a reason for being released from political and social obligations, he is not allowing himself to be led by the dynamism of the Holy Spirit, which seeks to direct all relationships between men.

(b) Personal distinguishing features

Anyone can observe in himself the 'fruit of the Spirit': love, joy, peace, patience, kindness, goodness, faithfulness, gentleness, self-control (Gal 5.22). The power of the spirit opposed to God is clearly recognizable in fornication, impurity, licentiousness, idolatry, enmity, strife, jealousy, anger, selfishness, dissension, envy and similar things (vv.19ff). Here we can discuss more closely only a few of these features.

LOVE. It is not without reason that Paul mentions love first. He explains this in the thirteenth chapter of the first letter to the Corinthians. If I were to activate all the gifts of the Spirit in abundance outwardly and in front of others, but had not love, I would be deceiving myself and falling into the hands of the spirit of deception. Love is patient, kind, not jealous; it does not boast, does not seek its own advantage and does not let itself be provoked; it is not resentful (cf. 1 Cor 13.4f). In a word, love is self-surrender, self-sacrifice (cf. first week, first section). It is a basic force which must sustain and mould every kind of charismatic expression from within. Love is not one charism among other charisms, but the motivating dynamism in them. That is why it is never called a 'charism' in the New Testament. Love as understood here is not merely emotional agitation or merely a superficial feeling of being accepted by others. Prayer-groups are not emotional hothouses or circles of friends. If love does not of itself urge people to *bear witness*, it is more a human need that a fruit of the Spirit.

It is recognizable in the fact that the whole person in all his signs of life radiates the selflessness, self-surrender, self-sacrifice of *Christ*. Hence the importance of the *principle* that if you want to show someone that the charismatic renewal comes from God, you must *serve* him, love him. Testimony must not be aggressive, must not humiliate or embarrass the other person. The latter must really be able to understand and accept it. Your helpful action shows that you have no ulterior motives, that you are not thrusting yourself forward, that you want to be available for him. Love is not puffed up and consequently the testimony must be true, without exaggeration. A further danger for the charismatic renewal is *impatience*, which does not come from love. God does not drive us like a belligerent to renew the Church, but guides us amiably. That is why *relaxed* activity is a sign of love. Going about things in a violent way is the result of following one's own impulses instead of the Holy Spirit.   ·

In virtue of its intrinsic dynamism charismatic renewal is not primarily militant reaction against existing conditions but action in regard to the future. This does not exclude confrontation, if it leads eventually to reconstruction. It is often possible only subsequently to say whether words or actions were born of love, that is, of love for the Church. But *hostile* confrontation, correction of others in *anger* never comes from the Holy Spirit.

JOY. Love finds expression in a variety of forms, in particular *as* joy. This comes from fellowship with God and with other people, but has nothing to do with superficial enthusiasm, intoxication or gratification. It is not primarily rooted in feeling, but grips the whole person including his suffering. Neither is it primarily a form of self-satisfaction: it embraces other people, it is a *social* experience. For that very reason there is a basic mood of joy in religious services where everyone makes a contribution. All experience simultaneously and together the fact that God as Holy Spirit is present among them and in their midst, as *one and the same* Spirit in each.

A retreat-giver once said: 'We must finally take Christian joy seriously'. We cannot simply make or will this joy, for it is 'fruit' and gift. And a gift cannot be extorted. That is why joy is always accompanied by *gratitude and obedience*. This was shown — for example — at the Mass in St Peter's at Pentecost 1975, with ten thousand or so participants in the international congress of the Catholic charismatic renewal, when some — particularly South American — groups expressed their joy in a contemplative dance. It was perhaps the first time that there had been dancing in St Peter's. When however it was announced over the loudspeaker that there were many other pilgrims who wanted to visit the church, the group immediately broke off its dance and went out in silence. This was a joy that came from obedience and cannot be confused with an unrestrained carnival spirit. The event of the charismatic renewal might almost be summed up in the phrase: *proclamation through joy.*

A person can accomplish heroic deeds under the influence of the highest motives. But if there is no hint of joy in all this, if everything is done in a spirit of toughness and grim determination, his 'heroism' perhaps comes *more* from human pride than from the impulses of the Holy Spirit. Thus for Paul too self-control is the 'fruit of the Spirit'

(Gal 5.22) and not mainly the result of our own efforts of will. Asceticism, self-punishment, are not necessarily signs of humility; they can also be the expression of vanity (Col 2.23).

The joy described here goes so deep that it also embraces suffering. Paul once said: 'I *rejoice* in my sufferings for your sake' (Col 1.24). And elsewhere we read: '*Rejoice* in so far as you share Christ's *sufferings*, that you may also rejoice and be glad when his glory is revealed' (1 Pet 4.13). Jesus did not show any feelings of joy on the Mount of Olives or at the time of his crucifixion, but he said to one of his fellow-sufferers: 'Today you will be with me in paradise' (Lk 23.43). Even at the deepest point of his forsakenness Jesus still called to *his* God, did not give up communion with him, but held out in the hope of his promises. The Christian's suffering is never without hope and for that reason never without some joy.

PEACE. If joy comes from fellowship, then peace comes from *order*, from harmony with the will of God and with other human beings. As long as we are torn hither and thither, are restless and confused, we have not wholly surrendered ourselves to the Holy Spirit, we are still concealing from him our pride, our aggression, our feelings of inferiority. A person who permits the Holy Spirit to penetrate to the depths of his personality remains serene, composed, free from excessive worry and fear. Peace then is not solely an emotional stirring, a feeling of harmony, but a sign of devotion to God's will. God has a *plan* with every life. Peace is granted to us to the extent that we are in harmony with the plan. It is not the disturbance of our plans, but the disturbance of God's plans, which creates the greatest problem of our life. Anyone who surrenders himself to God's plans at the renewal of the Spirit frequently finds after weeks or months that he is more balanced, is less frequently irritated, does not beg so excessively for recognition by other people: he is living in freedom with God, he has given up protesting against God, even his protest against his own death and against the suffering of the innocent. Having experienced this power, he can get himself all the more involved for peace in the world, can co-operate in transforming unjust social and political structures. All this is not out of hatred, but because the peace of Christ drives him on and because Christ alone can bring true righteousness.

Peace as understood here is really the 'fruit' of the Spirit, does not come at the beginning of being a Christian, but is the outcome of the struggle with the powers opposed to God. The author of the letter to the Ephesians exhorts his readers to fight for 'the gospel of peace' (Eph 6.15). Peace as fruit of the Spirit is consequently a sign of the *victory of Christ.* It survives even when we are outwardly enduring conflicts and opposition.

Admittedly unrest and internal turmoil are not in every case signs of the influence of the anti-God spirit in us. If the love of God spurs us to conversion, the first reaction is frequently one of fear, for we have to give up something of ourselves: that is, our distrust of God, our fear of him. We fear however to give up our fear, since this is a part of ourselves. Consequently unrest *before* conversion can certainly be a sign of the presence of the Holy Spirit. A person who struggles very violently against conversion, perhaps also against taking the step of renewal of the Spirit, may well be very close to it. It is the one who tries violently to ward off a particular gift of the Spirit (for example, the gift of tongues) who often needs it most.

The event of the charismatic renewal might also be described by the phrase: *proclamation through peace.* This is expressed particularly in the sign of peace: sign of harmony with each other in the Holy Spirit, the expression of a solidarity *previously* experienced. The sign of peace cannot simply be 'introduced' as liturgical changes have been introduced: this has been shown by the failure of such attempts in Italy and Spain. The sign of peace is not merely an opportunity to get into contact at worship, but the expression of a harmony already *experienced* which does not come purely from ourselves, but is the fruit and gift of the Spirit.

5. The gift of discernment — gift of the whole Church

It is beyond the human resources and the spiritual gift of a single individual to reach a decision in very serious cases. Consequently others must collaborate in this process. The gift of discernment is in fact primarily expected of those who are charged with leadership (cf. 1 Thess 5.12, 21), but the one who leads is dependent in his ministry on the gifts of the Spirit possessed by others. Consequently, from the very beginning, Christians have assembled in council when questions had to be faced which affected the whole Church or the future of the Church (cf. Acts 15). This essential structure of the Church, this conciliarity, is seen however not only in the great ecumenical councils but whenever Christians are gathered together.

A small 'council' of this kind can meet in a form suited to the group of persons involved: the small prayer-group, the parish council, the different councils and consultative bodies in the dioceses, regional Churches and so on. A 'charismatic' process of discernment may then be carried out in the following way:

After the leader has briefly stated the problem, in the communal silence which follows each places the problem before God, submitting completely to his will, praying for understanding, knowledge and wisdom. After about fifteen to twenty minutes each in turn states briefly and concisely what he has found in prayer to God to be the right decision. At the same time no one examines what has previously been said, with a view to confirming or correcting it, but each puts forward only what he felt to be right during the communal silence. No discussion takes place, but the leader tries to bring the various opinions into harmony. If differences still remain, another period of silent prayer follows. Each one thinks over and prays over what he has just heard and decides whether he must change or correct his own opinion or express it differently. This process may be repeated more frequently and drawn out perhaps even over weeks. Of course discussions and analyses are not excluded here, but it should never be a question of simply defending a particular standpoint or bringing pressure to bear in favour of certain opinions. The more each one is ready to listen to what has been said to others in prayer, the greater the prospect that, not human intelligence and will-power, but the Spirit of God will provide guidance. For it is a question particularly of *discernment* between what comes from human impulses and what from the impulses of the Holy Spirit.

An atmosphere of deep adoration and devotion often prevails in such a process of communal decision-making. Each knows that everyone is coming face to face with God. What would happen if — for instance — the parish council or other bodies were to interrupt their deliberations with such a prayer? Frequently the series of arguments is changed, there is an increased readiness to listen to one another.

The decision-making process just described is related naturally to questions which affect the group involved. Fundamental questions of faith cannot be decided by just any small prayer-group. The Catholic view is that 'the *body of the faithful as a whole*, anointed as they are by the Holy One (cf. 1 John 2.20, 27), *cannot err in matters of faith.* Thanks to a supernatural sense of the faith which characterizes the People as a whole, it manifests this unerring quality when, "from the bishops down to the last member of the laity," it shows universal agreement in matters of faith and morals' (Second Vatican Council, Constitution on the Church, art. 12.1). The totality of believers is made visible particularly at an ecumenical council.

The Catholic view is that the bishops are ultimately responsible for the charismatic renewal. With reference to charisms in the Church, the same council document says: 'Judgment as to their genuineness and proper use belongs to those who preside in the Church, and to whose special competence it belongs, not indeed to extinguish the Spirit, but to test all things and hold fast to that which is good (cf. Thess 5.12, 19-21)' (Constitution on the Church, art. 12.4). The catholicity of the charismatic renewal can also be seen not least in the fact that the individual or individual groups are prepared to submit their spiritual experiences to the judgment of the whole Church. Fanatical tendencies towards breaking away from the Church or to sectarian divisions have not been detected up to now. Spiritual sensitivity may be taken for granted in the prayer-groups: sensitivity for order, criticism and instruction, and also for the constantly fresh, historically effective originality of God.

6. The Protestant view of the gift of discernment

Protestants can fully approve of all that has been said above about the gift of discernment of spirits: for example, on the distinction between experience of the self and experience of the Spirit, on the relationship between human and divine spirit, on guidance, community and the criteria of judgment. Many too will agree with the statement that only the whole Church can reach a finally valid judgment. But how this is to come about in practice and how in this respect the relationship between Bible, Church and the individual is to be determined, is less clear in Protestantism than it is in the Roman Catholic Church.

Many Protestants find it difficult to speak of 'the Church' as naturally as Catholics do. For the former the term often implies a bureaucratic officialdom and they prefer the term 'community' or 'congregation'. The New Testament uses the term *ecclesia* and means by this both the community of Christians *in one place* and also the totality of all believers in the whole world. It does not matter very much how it is translated, so long as the reality is safeguarded: the community of Christians who assemble for the word of God and the sacraments and respond to these with faith in God and service to their neighbours. Wherever such a community exists there is a 'congregation' or 'Church', but only on the assumption that it is in communion with other 'congregations' or 'Churches'. Any independence of the individual congregation is just as foreign to the New Testament as the domination of one congregation over another.

In order to determine the rôle of the Church in the discernment of spirits, it is advisable to distinguish between two situations:

the decision for a group or congregation in an actual situation; and the decision on a question of faith for a larger community of congregations or even for all.

(a) Decision for a group or congregation in an actual situation

All that has been said above on the gift of discernment and on the appropriate criteria applies here. If — for example — a prophetic directive is issued in a particular situation to a particular congregation or group, those who are addressed must pray for the gift of discernment. Here both the universal and personal distinguishing features on the one hand (see 4. Aids to discernment) and on the other hand the spontaneous emotion of those addressed are helpful. It is not possible to be absolutely certain that this decision is right for all and for ever, but we can be certain that God wants a definite response from *us* in *this* situation. Whether a decision will be right, cannot be theoretically predicted, but it will be proved in practice by its fruits. Where there is time the one group should seek the advice of another. It is not necessarily bound to follow this advice, for what God requires from Christians may well vary in different situations. But the group must take care in any case that its decision does not destroy its fellowship with the other congregations or groups. Paul — for example — was satisfied with the revelation he had received, but he came to an agreement with the apostles in Jerusalem, so that he would not be 'running in vain' (Gal 2.2). To require every Christian to adopt the decision granted to one's own group proves to be destructive to the Christian community as a whole, it has a sectarian effect, and this is a sign that the decision did not come from the Spirit of God. The position adopted by a group in regard to a particular decision cannot be made the criterion of being a Christian and therefore may not lead to the exclusion of someone who opposes it; or a diversity of views and conscientious decisions is always possible, particularly in ethical questions.

(b) Decision on questions of faith for the community of all Christians

There are situations in which there is not only a decision to be made by a single congregation, but where the congregations (or Churches) of a region or of the whole world must decide where they stand in regard to a particular question of faith. Like Roman Catholics and Orthodox, Protestants also trust in the words of the Lord: 'The Spirit will guide you into all the truth' (Jn 16.13). They are sure that the truth of Christ will never perish and that the Holy Spirit therefore will never allow the Church as a whole to err. The Reformers always saw witnesses of Christ even in what they regarded as the 'darkest' times of Church history. Admittedly those who continued to sustain the gospel, despite all misinterpretation, were sometimes minorities. If the Roman Catholic Church wants to make a statement on a question of faith it has the machinery at its disposal to bring about a process of decision-making. In this respect the conviction of the faithful, the community of bishops and the word of the Pope work together. This kind of organized machinery is lacking in the Protestant Churches and congregations. The view of the majority of the Protestant Churches is that there is no authority which could speak with final binding force for the Church in the whole world. Must Protestants on that account refrain all together from decisions on questions of faith? This is not the case.

The Protestant view is that precedence in such a decision belongs, not to authorized persons, but to intrinsic criteria.

The decisive question runs: does a view maintained today agree with God's historical revelation in Jesus Christ? Since Son and Spirit do not contradict one another (cf. Jn (16.13-15), every new statement on faith must come within the scope of the revelation of Christ and be a re-statement of this. There are various aids with which to test this agreement:

1. *Scripture* as the original testimony of the revelation of Christ is God's word and thus the binding norm.

2. The *Creed* is the response of the community of Christians to the word of God and at the same time a guide to the proper understanding of the Bible.

3. The *testimony* of Christians of the past ('Fathers') and of the present ('brothers') must be heard.

4. The *clerical ministry* is commissioned in a special way to transmit the gospel

All these factors are involved when a decision has to be

reached on questions of faith. In this respect Scripture takes precedence, read however not in a vacuum, but in the context of the believing and understanding community. There is a chain of interpretation and understanding here, no link of which may be broken and from which there is no outlet.

Although the Bible permits a variety of interpretations, the Reformers and Protestants today hold that the Bible speaks clearly, intelligibly and unambiguously on questions which concern man's salvation. This clarity on essentials makes it possible to put up with uncertainty on other questions.

Since the ministers have a special responsibility for teaching (cf. 1 Cor 12.28ff; Eph 4.11f; 1 Tim 4.13-16; 2 Tim 1.13f), they will try to reach a decision first of all in the light of the criteria mentioned above. The decision can be reached only in a *conciliar process*: that is, by listening to one another in community and by prayer (cf.5. The gift of discernment). But even when it has been taken in this way, it is not yet automatically binding on the congregations. It must be proved and established as the truth for the community of all Christians. Such a process of reception of a doctrinal decision is possible only when the gift of discernment is sought, granted and practised in the congregations and not merely among their leaders. A decision can be binding on the whole Church only if it proves to be an unfolding of the historical revelation of God in Christ. 'New revelations' — visions, for example — may be helpful to individuals or to certain groups, as long as they correspond to the standards of truth and love, but they are never binding on the whole Church.

Appendix

I. Charismatic renewal and the unity of the Church

1. *Self-discovery.* 'There are varieties of gifts, but the same Spirit' (1 Cor. 12.4). This statement applies as a parable to the Churches at present separated through the fault of human beings. Every Church has a particular spiritual tradition and in none of them are all the gifts of grace fully realized. That is why every Church must ask itself in the light of its historical origin what is its own inalienable vocation.

2. *Openness.* Every Church must ask itself in a spirit of self-criticism whether it has made its own gifts of grace absolute and as a result of this how far it shares the blame for the division of the one Church of Christ. In this way it becomes capable of gratefully recognizing also the gifts of grace of the other Churches and of allowing itself to be enriched by them. Charismatic openness to all the gifts of the Holy Spirit can in this way be made fruitful for the future of the Church.

3. *Takeover.* Every Church must ask itself in the light of its inalienable vocation what it can take over — perhaps in a critical spirit — from the other Churches. This readiness to take over from others ought to be pressed to the limit of what is possible, for all gifts of grace are granted 'for the common good' (1 Cor. 12.7).

We pray to the Lord of the Church that the dialogue between the Churches may lead to convergence and consensus. We know that this cannot be attained by human effort or good will, but only through the intervention of the returning Christ (Mk. 10.27).

These theses were adopted at the third European Charismatic Leaders' Conference 23-28 June 1975 in Schloss Craheim, Lower Franconia, and confirmed in the same place 3 November 1975 by the conference of those responsible for the charismatic renewal in the German-speaking countries.

II. Theological guidelines of the charismatic congregational renewal in the Protestant Churches

The charismatic congregational renewal is a movement of spiritual revival within the Church.

It takes its place at the intersection-point of many lines of theological and spiritual impulses in present-day Christendom and seeks to extend its influence to the Church in all its amplitude. In particular it is interested in the building up of living congregations with a sense of their missionary responsibility.

In the charismatic renewal people experience the present activity of the Holy Spirit. These experiences are thought out and articulated in the light of the Church's teaching and theological reflection.

1. In the mission of the Son, in the cross and resurrection of Jesus Christ, the promise of God's love assumed its unsurpassable visible shape, definitive once and for all and needing no further complement.

2. Out of this mission of the Son grew the community of his disciples which — liberated by the Spirit of God for the ministry of witness — transmits to the world the new reality of salvation. The community is essentially 'body of Christ'. The structural principle of the community is the mission to the world. Through the community the triune God acts today in and on the world. The community then takes on a missionary, charismatic and ecumenical form.

3. To secure this formation God promised and bestowed on his community the power of the Holy Spirit which becomes visible and concrete in the fruits and in the gifts of the Spirit.

4. Every Christian who is reborn by faith and baptism lives in this charismatic reality. The Holy Spirit dwells in him and wills to become visible in him for the edification of the community and for service in the world.

5. The life of any Christian is 'charismatic' if he permits himself to be liberated by the Spirit of God to develop his original, divinely willed endowments and form of life, as rooted in creation, and to place himself at the disposal of the community's mission.

6. Anyone exercising a charism acts as a member of the body of Christ. Among themselves all members are of equal value. The charisms are developed and exercised in dependence on Jesus Christ (1 Cor. 12.3), according to the measure of faith (Rom 12.3) and as realization of love (1 Cor. 13), in

the community of believers (1 Pet 4.10).

7. Any order of precedence among the charisms is inconceivable. So for Paul -- for example -- marriage and celibacy, prophecy and diaconate, gift of tongues and administration of funds, are all equally charisms.

8. All charisms are signs of a renewed creation, not 'supernatural' happenings.

9. The charismatic foundation of the traditional 'ministry' is rediscovered in the charismatic renewal as ministry for the liberation, development and co-ordination of the charisms of the rest of the members of the community.

10. The important thing about the exercise of the charisms is not their external appearance, but their function in building up the kingdom of God.

11. In a charismatic form of worship the individual becomes responsive to what God wills to do on us and through us. The Lord's Supper (eucharist) is at the centre of liturgical life. From such a fellowship with God people become more sensitive to one another. They accept a way of life which is binding on them even outside the liturgical assembly. In this way they become practised in witness and service.

12. Charismatic experiences are granted when people admit before God their helplessness and emptiness and therefore expect everything from God and his actual directives and gifts. It is only this admission in theology and diaconate, in community life and ecumenical association, which can produce the conditions for spiritual revival and for the concrete activity of the Holy Spirit (2 Cor 12.9f).

The charismatic renewal puts in question a Church to which people belong as a matter of custom, which is characterized by the passivity and indifference of most of its members. Nevertheless, the charismatic renewal is at the heart of the Church and within the continuity of its teaching tradition. It looks for dialogue with all theological trends which contribute to the renewal of the Church.

Its goal is the charismatically-renewed Church, which would render a special charismatic movement superfluous.

(This text was adopted in Würzburg on 2 March 1976 by the co-ordinating committee for charismatic congregational renewal in the Protestant Church).

Notes

First Week

1. The references to literature on this subject are intended mainly for those with an interest in theology. But they cannot and are not meant to replace a scholarly commentary on the spiritual suggestions and reflections and are restricted, in view of the lay-out of this book, to essential topics:

John Austin Baker, *The Foolishness of God*, London, 1970.

Karl Barth, *Dogmatics in Outline*, London & New York, 1972.

Peter Berger, *The Sacred Canopy; Elements of a Sociological Theory of Religion*, New York and London, 1967; Peter Berger & Thomas Luckman, *The Social Construction of Reality*, New York & London, 1967.

Martin Buber, *I and Thou*, London & New York, 1971.

Arnold Bittlinger, *Gifts and Graces*, Grand Rapids, Mich., 1967.

E. Cardenal, *Love*, London, 1974; *Love in Practice: The Gospel in Solentiname*, London & New York, 1977.

J. Feiner & L. Vischer, *The Common Catechism: A Book of Christian Faith*, London & New York, 1975.

Erich Fromm, *The Art of Loving*, New York & London, 1956.

Gustavo Gutierrez, *A Theology of Liberation*, New York, 1973.

John C. Haughey, *The Conspiracy of God: The Holy Spirit in Men*, New York, 1973.

Rosemary Haughton, *The Transformation of Man*, New York & London, 1967.

Morton T. Kelsey, *Healing and Christianity*, New York & London, 1973.

Soren Kierkegaard, *Works of Love*, New York & London, 1962.

Hans Küng, *The Church*, London, 1968; *On Being a Christian*, New York & London, 1976-7.

Joseph Lange & Anthony Cushing, *Living Christian Community* (3 vols.), New York, 1975.

Francis MacNutt, *Healing*, Notre Dame, Ind., 1974.

John Macquarrie, *Principles of Christian Theology*, London, 1977.

Jürgen Moltmann, *The Church in the Power of the Spirit*, New York & London, 1977; *The Crucified God*, London & New York, 1974; *Theology of Hope*, London & New York, 1969.

A New Catechism (with Supplement): *The Catholic Faith for Adults*, London & New York, 1970.

Wolfhart Pannenberg, *Faith and Reality*, London & Philadelphia, 1977.

Karl Rahner (ed.), *Encyclopaedia of Theology*, London & New York, 1975; *The Spirit and the Church*, London & New York, 1978.

Agnes Sanford, *The Healing Gifts of the Spirit*, New York, 1966.

Michael Scanlon, *Inner Healing*, New York, 1974.

John V. Taylor, *The Go-Between God*, London, 1975.

2. Love is not described expressly by Paul as 'charismatic'; it is on the contrary the source and corrective of charisms. Without love the charisms are useless and worthless (1 Cor 13). But the opposite is also true: if love does not surrender itself in the charisms, it remains unfruitful (cf. 1 Jn 3.16-18; Jas 2.14-17).

Second Week

3. The text is directed against the 'Semi-Pelagians': 'If anyone says that, like the increase of faith, so also the beginning of faith and the very feeling of readiness for faith, by which we believe in him who justifies the sinner and by which we come to the regeneration of holy baptism, is present in us, not by the gift of grace — that is, not by the inspiration of the Holy Spirit — . . . but by nature, he is evidently an opponent of the apostolic teachings' (DS 375). 'Semi-Pelagianism' asserts that all men are equal in the sight of God. Hence God bestows equal grace on all men. Differences in God's disposal of gifts to men are based on differences in each one's readiness and in the individual's own efforts. This

is true even of imparting the very first gifts of salvation. The trusting emotion of faith appears in the text as *fides qua,* the faith by which we believe. On the other hand, the truths — the content — of faith are *fides quae,* that which we believe. We shall return to this and look at the problem more closely when we describe faith as trust in the third week.

It might well be asked if many of the efforts at reforming the Church could not be described as 'Semi-Pelagian'. We set ourselves goals, draw up strategic plans, introduce reforms, without trusting from the very beginning and all the time *more* in the guidance of the Holy Spirit than in our own efforts. It can be shown that both 'atheism of the heart' and the disastrous turning of the emotion of faith into a private affair — or its suppression — are due to a sentimentality detached from the person as a whole, to the separation of *ratio* and *affectus* which started and increasingly developed in scholasticism.

4. In accordance with the character of this 'initiation' the term 'experience' is used in a pre-scientific sense. Consequently we are not dealing with the question of the difference between transcendental and empirical experience. Since man is an *incarnate* spirit, his experience is never purely 'spiritual', but remains tied to the senses in its origin and continuation. Every experience begins with the senses, even if it does not arise from sense-experience alone. Not only in accordance with ancient tradition, but also with the Bible, experience begins with 'seeing and hearing'. It means 'knowing on the basis of our own sense-perception' (R. Bultmann in *Theologisches Wörterbuch zum Neuen Testament,* Vol. I, pp. 689f).

The structure of *personal experience* must be particularly stressed. It means 'becoming acquainted through personal *contact'* (Bultmann, *ibid.,* p.696).

It is doubtful if the phenomenon of the charismatic renewal can be seen adequately if approached from the standpoint of transcendental philosophy.

Charismatic experience is not solely a radicalization of man's transcendality, nor is it merely 'popular mysticism'. Up to the present time we have had no fully worked out 'we-philosophy'. It can be shown that the transcendental

'we-experience' is personologically prior to the 'I-experience'.
5. As I have said elsewhere: the Holy Spirit is the divine power of self-transcendence in God himself, in the world and in mankind.
6. See J. Kremer, *Pfingstbericht und Pfingstgeschehen*, Stuttgart, 1973, pp. 222f.
7.In the original Greek text the same root *phaino* is used to describe both the presence of the Son in the man Jesus of Nazareth and the presence of the Spirit of Jesus in the gifts of the Spirit. In the man Jesus of Nazareth the eternal Word of life 'appeared' (*ephanerothe:* Jn 1.1f) and similarly the gifts of grace are a 'manifestation of the Spirit' (*phanerosis tou pneumatos:* 1 Cor 12.7).

Third Week

8. On the question of original sin P. Schoonenberg in particular should be consulted. He defines original sin as an existential 'being in situation', brought about by the sins of others, claiming that the classical doctrine of original sin should be complemented by the biblical teaching on the 'sin of the world' (*Man and Sin,* London & Melbourne, 1965, especially pp. 124-92).
9. Original sin is frequently seen as having its source in pride, in a monstrous rebellion against God. More recently pride and rebellion have been seen as the consequences of taking the step from a possible to an actual distrust, which is the true source of evil in man.
10. See: R.S. Lee, *The Principles of Pastoral Counselling,* London, 1968; Kenneth Ross, *Hearing Confessions,* London, 1974; J.D. Crichton, *The Ministry of Reconciliation* (R.C.), London, 1974.

Fourth Week

11. See Edward Schillebeeckx, *Jesus,* New York & London, 1978.
12. See H. Schürmann, *Das Lukasevangelium,* Part 1: *Herders*

Theologischer Kommentar zum Neuen Testament, vol. III, Freiburg im Breisgau, 1969, pp. 159, 172, 179, 183.

13. Cf. H. Schürmann, *op. cit.,* pp. 161-83.

14. The expression 'baptism of the Spirit' is not as such found in the New Testament. But it appears frequently in current exegetical literature.

Towards the end of the *Church Dogmatics* Karl Barth has an illuminating chapter on 'Baptism with the Holy Spirit' (*Church Dogmatics,* T. & T. Clark, Edinburgh, Vol. IV, Part 4, 1969, pp.3-40). He sees it as the 'self-attestation and self-impartation of Jesus Christ' (p.33), the divine *turning* in a man's life, the beginning of Christian existence. This makes possible and demands a corresponding decision and thus baptism of the Spirit calls for baptism of water, but is not identical with the latter. Hence Barth's rejection of infant baptism.

In the present 'imitation' we do not need to enter into the complicated exegetical discussion, but we start off from the situation in which most Christians are baptized as a matter of custom as infants. Baptism of the Spirit then becomes the personal acceptance of what is sacramentally offered and promised by God in baptism (and confirmation). It is therefore *renewal of baptism of the Spirit* or *renewal of the Spirit.*

15. See M. Füglister, *Handbuch Theologischer grundbegriffe,* ed. H. Fries, Munich, 1963, pp. 350ff.

1o. Cf. E. Schillebeeckx, *Jesus,* New York & London 1978.

17. Cf. H. Schürmann, *Das Lukasevangelium,* pp. 190f.

18. Cf. E. Schillebeeckx, *Jesus,* New York & London, 1978, and consult his detailed bibliography on this point.

19. We need not enter here into the details of the theological compromise between the Greek and the Latin view of the procession of the Spirit achieved at the Council of Ferrara-Florence (1438-1442). The text is in DS 1300-1302. English translation Neuner/Dupuis (Ed), *The Christian Faith,* Mercier Press, Dublin & Cork, 1973, nn. 322-324.

20. The Christian view is that other founders of religion were also filled with the Spirit of God if and in so far as they followed their conscience and God's offer of Salvation to give all men the opportunity of finding their way to him.

But the experience of the Spirit offered to all men gains through Jesus Christ its unique and unsurpassable *concreteness:* it becomes clearly evident only on the cross of Jesus (Heb 9.14) and can be achieved only in the intersection of human expectations (all attempts at obtaining salvation through our own efforts must be abandoned).
21. There existed in the early Church a 'Spirit-Christology' which took three forms: 1. Christ is merely a human being who was endowed with the Holy Spirit for a certain time in the course of his life. 2. He was a human being conceived by the Holy Spirit in a supernatural way in the womb of Mary. 3. Christ is himself the incarnation of the Holy Spirit.

For systematic theology the connection between the incarnation and the mission of the Spirit arises from the coherence of the mysteries with each other (DS 3016), in particular between the Trinity and the Incarnation. In the light of the New Testament the incarnation of the Son is presupposed to the mission of the Holy Spirit. Something of the 'order' of the inter-trinitarian processions is seen in this relationship of Christ and the Spirit in the economy of salvation. In our analogical understanding the procession of the Son is the *presupposition* for the procession of the Spirit. The Son is united in his incarnation with a single human 'nature' and the 'anointing' of the man Jesus with the Holy Spirit is accomplished at the very first moment of the incarnation, since in fact the 'Son' is himself the source of the Spirit. The Spirit of Jesus is then united historically with many persons and thus the difference between Incarnation and Church is clearly expressed.
22. Cf. W. Kasper, *Jesus the Christ*, London & New York, 1976, pp. 74f.
23. For a detailed treatment of Jesus' charisms see A. Bittlinger, 'Gnadengaben in der Bibel', in *Die Bedeutung der Gnadengaben für die Gemeinde Jesu Christi*, Marburg, 1971, pp. 24-48.

Fifth Week

24. Cf. H. Mühlen, *Die Erneuerung des christlichen Glaubens*, Munich, 1976, pp. 35-42, 55-60.

25. See Karl Rahner, 'Charism', in *Encyclopaedia of Theology*, London & New York, 1975, pp. 184-6.

26. See A. Bittlinger, *Im Kraftfeld des Heiligen Geistes*, Marburg, 1976, pp. 71-86.

27. See Karl Rahner, *Encyclopaedia of Theology*, London & New York, 1975, pp. 1477-88, 1619-23.

28. For the text of the Apostolic Constitution on the Sacrament of Confirmation see *Confirmation — The Rite*, Catholic Truth Society (CTS/D482, 1976, pp.1-7). Further liturgical texts and statements of the magisterium are found in the second volume of this 'Initiation', fifth week, seventh day.

29. In this respect Calvin's position on the sacrament of confirmation is revealing. He sees very precisely that the apostolic laying on of hands reported in Acts 8.15-17 and 19.5f is linked with the bestowal of charisms, but he restricts this laying on of hands to apostolic times. But 'neither Calvin — who restricted the charismatic manifestations of the Spirit imparted by laying on of hands to apostolic times — nor the Catholic theologians — who rejected the (purely) charismatic understanding of the effects of the Spirit whom the Apostles bestowed by laying on their hands — recognized that the charismatic pneuma is essential to the building up of the Church. But it is only by appreciating this fact that we are justified in drawing the conclusion that what the apostles did in the primitive Church must also be done in the later Church (H. Schutzeichel, 'Calvins Kritik an der Firmung' in H. auf der Maur and B. Kleinheyer (Editors), *Zeichen des Glaubens*, Zürich/Einsiedeln/Cologne, 1972, pp.123-135; quotation p.131). For this reason Max Thurian thinks that Calvin had some responsibility for the rise of sectarian movements seeking charismatic manifestations of the Holy Spirit outside the Church (*La confirmation*, Neuchatel and Paris, 1957, pp.8-14, 69-71, especially p.14). J. Amougou-Atangana completely overlooks this aspect of confirmation in his otherwise important book *Ein Sakrament des Geistempfangs? Zum Verhältnis von Taufe und Firmung*, Freiburg/Br., 1974. The really essential thing is to keep in mind the difference between *sanctificatory* (with its significance primarily related to God) and *consecratory* grace (with

its significance primarily related to service to others).
30. Cf. Karl Rahner, *Encyclopaedia of Theology*, London & New York, 1975, pp. 66-78, 642-50.

Sixth Week

31. Cf. Karl Rahner, *Encyclopaedia of Theology*, London & New York, 1975, pp. 642-50, 1004-1011, 1406-27.
32. Cf. Karl Rahner, 'Prophetism' in *Sacramentum Mundi*, London/New York, 1970, Vol. 5, pp. 110-113.
33. The charismatic renewal is a very complex phenomenon with diverse roots and moved by a variety of impulses. One of its historical impulses is derived from the Pietism of the seventeenth century and for that reason still tends to stress the personal and private aspect of the movement.

Seventh Week

34. See Karl Rahner, *Encyclopaedia of Theology*, London & New York, 1975, pp. 642-50; J. Feiner & L. Vischer, *The Common Catechism*, London & New York, 1975, pp. 221-32.
35. Cf. the second volume of this 'Initiation', fifth week, sixth day, for more details on this topic.
36. This question of 'certainty' was the object of fierce controversy at the time of the Reformation. Meanwhile theologians have largely cleared up the misunderstandings on both sides. But the question has again become relevant for the charismatic renewal, not so much in theory as in practice. Martin Luther's distinction between *Gewissheit*, a certainty based on God's promises and therefore excluding all doubt, and *Sicherheit*, a certainty based on self-confidence rather than on God's grace should be noted: 'No one can be justified except by faith in the sense that it is necessary for him to believe with firm faith that he is justified and to have no doubt that he has received grace. For if he is *doubting* and *uncertain* (*ungewiss*), then he is not justified, but spits out grace' (WA 2.13); and elsewhere: 'But Christians certainly feel the weakness of faith and are tempted to despair

because of their sense of sin. But, *although nothing is more pernicious than security (Sicherheit)*, you must pull yourself together when you feel the weakness of faith' (WA 25,331). The Council of Trent makes a similar distinction between a certainty relying on God's promises, excluding all reasonable doubt, and the certainty of faith which would remove even the salutary fear of one's own weakness: 'No devout Christian must doubt the mercy of God, the merits of Christ or the power and efficacy of the sacraments; but anyone who considers himself, his own weakness and inadequacy can be anxious and fear for his grace, since no one can know with the certainty of faith, excluding all that is false, that he has obtained the grace of God' (DS 1534). (On the possibility of reconciling Catholic teaching and theology with Luther's views — properly understood — on the certainty of justification, Stephanus Pfürtner, *Luther and Aquinas,* Darton, Longman & Todd, London, 1964, may be recommended. Translator.)

37. The *grace* of discernment, of which we are mainly speaking in this 'initiation', must be distinguished from the power of discrimination acquired by *practice.* The distinction was well known to the older theologians and writers on the spiritual life. They placed 'discernment of spirits' among the *gratiae gratis datae* (literally 'unmerited graces', but — since all grace is 'unmerited' — used to describe those graces which are given more for the benefit of the whole Church than for the sanctification of the individual), as a gift granted only to a few. It was however possible for all to acquire by their own efforts a power to discriminate and to judge in the light of rules given by Scripture and the Church, of the experience of the saints and of one's own prudence.

38. Here it becomes particularly clear that the occurrences in the charismatic renewal urgently demand further theological reflection. In this request there is much to be learned from the discussions over the centuries of the 'inspiration' of the Bible and what this implies in practice for the writers. For inspiration is the charism of the biblical writers. As a result of historical-critical studies it is impossible now to speak of 'verbal inspiration' in the sense that the writer would be merely responding more or less automatically to

'dictation'. What happens is that God makes use of the writer's mind, will and feelings so that he writes down what God wills and as he wills it. It is only when we have studied as closely as possible the historical and personal milieu of the writer that we can perceive *what* God wants to tell us. Even when writing down the 'word of God' the writers do not experience a completely *unmediated immediacy* of God's effects (cf. the works of reference on 'Inspiration'). But charismatic statements and occurrences are not even 'inspired' in this sense. They do not contain any new 'revelation' and for that very reason they must be 'tested'.

39. Constitution on the Church, art.8.1.

40. A psychological analysis of occurrences in charismatic prayer groups is of course appropriate and necessary. But there are obvious limits to be observed in regard to methods. The psychologist can no more analyse the workings of the Holy Spirit with the methods at his disposal than the chemist can come across God in his test-tube. In any liturgical assembly there are occurrences involved which are open to psychological analysis, but the Church's existence cannot be attributed to group-dynamics nor be ultimately explained in this light.

Part II
EXPECTANT PRAYER

Translated by Thomas Linton

Introduction

1. Evangelization and the parish mission

In the introduction to the first part of this programme of initiation I have already expounded certain fundamental aspects of both parts of this work — and of course the two parts are closely connected. In this second part it is less a question of transmitting doctrine than of stimulating people to open themselves up in expectant faith for the renewal of their personal encounter with Christ and for ministering to the faith of others. Recently this ministry has increasingly been understood in the Catholic Church, as well as in other Churches, as 'evangelization'. This marks the appropriation of an impulse which may well have been alive in the traditional Catholic parish mission from the seventeenth century on but which achieved far greater significance within the new Churches of the Reformation. It is thus a genuinely ecumenical event when Pope Paul VI, as he did in December 1975, publishes a document on the subject of evangelization.[1] In this the Pope affirmed 'that the task of evangelizing all people constitutes the essential mission of the Church' and added later: 'Evangelizing is in fact the grace and vocation proper to the Church, her deepest identity'(14). The witness of the living out of the Christian life must be supplemented by the proclamation of the good news by one person to another: 'In the long run, is there any other way of handing on the Gospel than by transmitting to another person one's personal experience of faith?' the Pope asked (46).

Evangelization is thus not just something that happens in far-off mission countries. Instead the Pope affirmed 'that she [the Church] has a constant need of being evangelized, if she wishes to retain freshness, vigour and strength in order to proclaim the Gospel'(15).

It should not be overlooked that this impulse did not arise

[1] Apostolic exhortation *Evangelii nuntiandi*, 8 December 1975: English translation, *Evangelization in the Modern World*, London, Catholic Truth Society, n.d.

from classical Catholic theology. Nor did it emerge from the liturgical movement of the present century, a movement which stressed rather the outward form of public worship. This personalization of the faith had its origin rather in the Reformation of the sixteenth century (though I cannot here explain this in detail). This in turn gave rise to early pietism, to the community movement, to the 'tent mission' form of evangelistic campaign, and in Britain and America to the evangelistic campaigns of the Baptists and the Methodists. For their part these movements were not without influence in the USA in the middle of this century on the eruption of the charismatic renewal movement, which there has included the Catholic Church too. Over the past few years this movement has to an astonishing extent spread throughout the entire world. According to the latest figures the movement at the international level includes some 450,000 Catholics in over 63 countries in about 4,000 prayer groups. At least as many Christians belonging to the Churches of the Reformation regularly take part in the life of prayer groups of this kind — and this does not include the thirty million or so members of the independent Pentecostal Churches. Naturally these figures are imprecise, since the charismatic renewal is not a movement in the precise sense of religious sociology, is not an organization with a definite structure. It is a source of unexpected impulses towards person-to-person evangelization. The information leaflet on 'The Renewal of the Church' — the text of which appears in Appendix I — spells it out as follows: 'The charismatic renewal is a form of evangelization in which on the basis of the common priesthood of all believers Christians lead each other by means of their personal witness to the faith to a direct encounter with Christ himself.'

It should of course be noted that personal evangelization, the passing on of one's own experience of the faith, has often led to the formation of new ecclesial communities. While it is important that hundreds of thousands of Christians should open themselves up to receive the gifts of the spirit, the charisms, that serve the proclamation of the gospel, and while it must be recognized that this will happen in an unplanned, unorganized manner that is impossible to anticipate, it is also important that this historically new gift of charismatic graces should serve the building up of the existing united Church and not lead to the formation of élitist prayer-groups that shut themselves off from others. In this way the emphasis among both Catholics and Protestants in German-speaking countries has been on the renewal of the parish community. This also strengthens the links with the traditional parish mission as it has grown up in both the Catholic and the Lutheran Church.

The traditional form of the parish mission with its strongly individualistic impact, calling on people to save their souls, does not however correspond any longer to the understanding of the Church that has come to life in the present century. Thus for example V. Schurr was writing in 1965 that the contemporary form of the parish mission and the missionary hope of the Church was 'the holy spirit in a small group' and a 'missionary liturgy in keeping with 1 Cor. 14:23 ff.'. It was not the missioner coming in from outside to preach and hear confessions but the parish priest who was the missionary of his parish community, and a parish mission had to be conducted in co-operation by the entire community (*Lexikon für Theologie und Kirche*, Freiburg-im-Breisgau, Herder, 1957-67, vol. 10, col. 859). This brought the primitive Church's missionary technique of every Christian being a missionary back to life again. On the basis of the common priesthood of all believers everyone is called to lead others to Christ by his witness to the faith.

A similar development had been taking place in the Protestant Churches right at the start of the present century: '[The parish mission] is conducted *not by the charismatic individual* (sic) but by the Church, by the parish organization, by every Christian who is aware of being one. The aim is to lead all members of the national Church to personal faith and to fellowship with Christ by means of inspiring preaching and Christian education . . . The parish mission remains nothing but a vain attempt to beat the air if it is not conducted by the parish community and if the parish community is not open and ready to admit people who have been awakened to new faith by the parish mission and to incorporate them into itself. On the other side the community's spiritual life perishes if it looks after only its own life . . .' (H. Rondtorff). The

Church must change from the institutional into the missionary Church. On the basis of what has been said in the intro-duction to the first part of this work, there follows a description in greater detail of how the gifts of the spirit can in practice serve the building up of the parish community.

2. Pattern for a parish mission

(a) The small group

The exercise of the gifts of the Spirit cannot simply be 'introduced', for this presupposes a completely personal surrender to God which cannot be brought about simply by life and education. Nor can a whole parish community awaken overnight to a missionary impulse. This is something that normally grows in a small group that forms a nucleus and lets itself be used by God to arouse the entire community over the course of the following months and years. The ideal is for the parish priest first of all to gather round himself a small group of this kind, which would be composed of those working most closely with him, those with some kind of active public rôle in the liturgy, those taking catechism classes and preparing young people for confirmation, etc. At all events the parish priest must in this case have first of all himself experienced the 'renewal of the spirit' of which we shall have more to say later. In a personal act of surrender undertaken in the presence of other people and with their help he must have taken upon and into himself what had been promised to him by God at his baptism, confirmation and ordination.

Traditional pastoral methods in long-established Churches presuppose the existence of the believing community and have hardly developed any missionary techniques on the basis of which the individual is ready and able not only to bear witness to his personal faith through living a Christian life but also to bear witness to it by expounding it in his own words. If a missionary prayer group comes into existence in a parish, this is something that in every case should happen in close co-operation with the parish priest. Getting it off the ground is often a laborious process which comes up against all sorts of hindrance, and links with other prayer groups can be a great help.

If these exercises are to form the basis of a later parish mission, then every member of the core group must have undertaken a personal course of preparation lasting seven weeks. The parish mission then takes the form of concentric circles of groups studying the faith: members of the core group talk to others on a personal basis, visit people's houses, distribute advance information (the text of a suitable leaflet is given in the appendix to this volume), talk about the cassettes and films available, etc. What is important in this preparatory work is above all personal witness (on which see the seventh day of the seventh week later in this volume).

(b) The study group
Today God is awakening many people in many different ways to a living faith and to the exercise of their gifts of the spirit. Taking part in the study group suggested in this programme of initiation can help towards this. It has been shown that outsiders who now and then visit the prayer meetings of a group that is already in existence only achieve the growth necessary for renewal by taking part in a study group. For this what is needed is not only advance information but also a definite decision in advance. Everyone taking part in a study group should know what it is all about and make a firm resolution to attend its talks and meetings regularly. Everyone, too, must give himself or herself time for prayer and meditation every day: it needs to be at least half an hour during which he or she can relax and not be exposed to the pressures of daily life and work — though perhaps essential obligations cannot simply be declined for the weeks that the study group is meeting. In everybody's life there are definite periods of grace during which he or she perceives God's call more clearly. This does not mean that those taking part in the study group must stick rigorously to the texts that are being used. Above all no one should have the feeling that he or she is being forced into something. It is all a question of the inward guidance of the Holy Spirit, for it is only the living Lord of the Church who is *the* way to God.

Members of the original group become assistants in the

second, enlarged study group. It has been found helpful for a register to be kept of those taking part. The person leading the study group can then organize the formation of small groups of between six and eight people before the study group gets under way. These small groups meet under the leadership of the assistant for personal discussion and prayer after the study group has met to hear each particular talk or during the week that follows. In many cases it is best if people who know each other very well — married couples, for example, or people belonging to the same religious community — do not belong to the same small group. This means that the initial difficulties are not then so great. Above all what is important is that a small group of this kind should not see itself as a mutual admiration society but as a missionary association — and this of course applies too to the original core group: the readier everyone is to place himself or herself at God's disposal for his service in the Church and in the world, the less they consider themselves in this, the more unconstrained and freer will the meetings be. It has been shown that the process of personal discovery and even the effects of group dynamics take place as a gift, without any forcing, if each person acts as the other's 'steward of God's varied grace' in the sense of 1 Peter 4:10 and is chiefly concerned to be at the service of the other's faith. Prayer groups in which everyone centres upon his or her own human or spiritual experiences lead to a state of impractical seclusion and deprive the individual of the stimulus to missionary and political commitment. The personal step to seek the renewal of the Spirit (with the laying on of hands) often needs the advice and encouragement of others, such as the leader of the study group or one of the assistants.

The weekly meetings of the study group can start and finish with a prayer. Two patterns are possible for what follows:

(1) During the course of the week those taking part read through the corresponding section of the first part of this work once again, so as to be able to discuss its content at next week's meeting. In these discussions the objective, expert approach should be avoided: separate meetings can be provided for this. Pride of place should be given to each

individual's personal voyage of discovery. In the week that follows those taking part take as their starting point the corresponding sections of this second volume and meet in small groups for prayer and discussion for the first time on the third evening. After this the second talk is given at a meeting of the whole study group and the entire process is repeated. The exercise on this pattern thus needs fourteen weeks.

(2) At the meeting of the study group the talk is followed by a short discussion and then the participants meet in small groups for prayer and to exchange their views on the suggestions contained in this second volume. In this case the study group lasts for seven weeks.

Weekends spent together can make a considerable contribution to the intensification of the study group's work.

(c) The personal character of the study group

When someone is involved in a personal encounter with God all his powers are mobilized in an undreamed of way. This applies also to defects of character and mental illness. To the same extent that these can be healed by a surrender to God — see the prayer of the third week of the present volume — so too does participation in these exercises normally demand a certain measure of mental health and stability.

Those who have not been able to achieve a certain equilibrium or who suffer from serious psychological disorders should be asked affectionately to begin by recognizing the situation they are in and to look for psychotherapy or should be directed towards other possible means of coming to terms with themselves. Such people can have a notably disturbing effect on the progress of a study group of this kind. This does not rule out individuals being admitted to existing prayer groups and becoming accepted as members of them. But these latter are not to the same extent spiritual hothouses.

These exercises are in particular not suited for those who, on account of their personal history or because of emotional disorder, suffer from depression. The tendency of depressives is to take everything upon themselves, and they derive from a course such as this what they are in any case already burdened with. Everything stands in judgment against them, and the biblical preaching of conversion has the effect of increasing their feelings of guilt (which of course do not have any basis in objective reality). Those on the other hand with a tendency towards hysteria strive in an exaggerated fashion to obtain the 'higher' gifts of the Spirit. Not only can they in this way continue to reinforce their existing defects of character, but they can seriously disturb a service of prayer. (There is a more detailed treatment of this on the fourth day of the seventh week in this volume).

Surrendering one's life, renewal of one's baptism, asking for the fulness of the Spirit in front of witnesses in the way suggested in this programme of initiation are very personal acts of faith. In making them everyone needs the personal assistance of another. For this reason the language of this kind of initiatory course must also be personal. This implies that relationships within the study group will fairly soon be based on Christian name terms.

(d) The renewal of the Spirit
When the study group has come to the end of its course, or later, everyone is given the opportunity of praying for the fulness of the Holy Spirit in a rite marked by the laying on of hands — possibly at a joint celebration of the Eucharist at which all members of the study group take part. This is not a step that should be put off for too long, but should be taken when the inward guidance of the Holy Spirit compels one to do so, with the encouragement of other people's advice. It is something that has so many different layers to it that it cannot simply be summed up in a few words. It is discussed in more detail in the third section of the fifth week of the first part of these exercises.

As history shows us, spiritual advances tend to bring about an overemphasis on certain aspects. But exaggeration does not make what is true any more true. Instead it leads to division and schism. The expression 'baptism of the Spirit' is open to misunderstanding. It would perhaps be better to speak of the renewal of the Spirit, though without wanting to insist on this concept. It is capable of expressing the various aspects of growing up into being fully and completely a Christian, aspects which have been touched on in this work: conversion as a renewal of our human spirit (the first week); a renewed acceptance of what had been done to us by God at baptism (the third week); a renewed readiness to bear witness and to accept the gifts of the Spirit (the sixth week); openness to the guidance of the Holy Spirit and to God's continually surprising newness; as well as a renewed understanding of the sacraments and of the Church's ministry. This kind of renewal of the Spirit is a life-long process. But it is helpful if from time to time we perform some explicit and personal action so that we can receive this renewal of the Spirit anew from the Spirit of God. The aim of this work is to lead up to such a step. What it involves is thus not only turning again to Christ and deciding for him, not only the renewal of our baptismal promises, not only acceptance of the gifts of the Spirit, not only an openness to the guidance of the Holy Spirit that is released by the Church, its ministry and its sacraments, not only a new spiritual approach to the sacraments, but all this combined in one single indivisible event.

3.   What are the views of Church leaders?

Renewal always poses a question for long-established Churches and their traditions. Often movements of revival have led to the formation of élitist prayer-groups that shut themselves off from other people and have thus led to schisms, due of course to faults on both sides.[2] This is all the more ominous in that the Church, as Vatican II recognized, stands in need of continual reform. In Germany however schismatic tendencies do not stand out at the start. Cardinal Julius Döpfner,

[2]   Cf. the report of the pastoral commission of the US bishops' conference, Spring 1975: Statement on Catholic Charismatic Renewal (US Catholic Conference, 1312 Massachusetts Avenue NW, Washington DC 20005). The Canadian bishops published a message in April 1975: Le Renouveau Charismatique — Message des évêques canadiens (obtainable from Pneumathèque, 7 bis, rue de la Rosière, 75015 Paris). The report *The charismatic movement in the Lutheran Church in America* was published by the Muhlenberg Press, Philadelphia, in 1974.

president of the German bishops' conference, said in his report on the plenary session of the German bishops' conference held at Fulda from 22 to 25 September 1975: 'On the first evening of our conference we experienced a charismatic paraliturgy. After a short introduction on the life and development of the Catholic charismatic renewal throughout the world, there was a reading from the New Testament. Out of the silence that followed the bishops present offered spontaneous, personal prayers that expressed their faith. The executive committee will at its next meeting deal fully with the charismatic renewal' (KNA, Documentation 37, 27 September 1975, p.4).

Bishop Tenhumberg of Münster, president of the pastoral commission of the German bishops' conference, published the following in his diocesan journal in March 1976: 'The German bishops' conference has concerned itself with the theological and pastoral basis of the Catholic charismatic renewal. Developments so far in the Federal Republic give rise to the hope that this movement can contribute to the renewal of the Church and provides a means of creating "living parishes in which the many diverse gifts of the Spirit are at work together" (Joint Synod of the Dioceses of the German Federal Republic, Pastoral Service in the Parish, 1, 1.1)' (Kirchliche Amtsblatt Münster 1976, no. 7, p.63).

Pope Paul VI said on Whit Monday 1975 when he addressed some 10,000 participants in the third international congress of the Catholic charismatic renewal and a further 20,000 pilgrims in St Peter's: 'A world that is more and more secularized has no greater need than that of the witness of this "spiritual renewal" which, as we see, the Holy Spirit is bringing about everywhere today and in the most varied surroundings.' He went on to describe the charismatic renewal as an 'opportunity for the Church' and as 'authentic renewal, Catholic renewal, renewal in the Holy Spirit' (L'Osservatore Romano, 19/20 May 1975). So far there has been no official statements by the Evangelical Church in the Federal Republic of Germany.

4. Suggestions for further reading

For background reading to accompany the work of the study group the following works may be suggested:

Cardinal Leo Joseph Suenens, *A New Pentecost?*, London 1975.

Edward D. O'Connor, C.S.C., *The Pentecostal Movement in the Catholic Church*, Notre Dame, Indiana, 1971.

Kilian McDonnell, *Charismatic Renewal and the Churches*, New York, NY, 1976.

Simon Tugwell, O.P., *Did you receive the Spirit?*, London 1972.

Kevin and Dorothy Ranaghan, *Catholic Pentecostals*, Paramus, NJ, 1969.

(edited by) Kevin and Dorothy Ranaghan, *As the Spirit leads us*, Paramus, NJ, 1971.

Donald L. Gelpi, S.J., *Pentecostalism: A Theological Viewpoint*, Paramus, NJ, 1971.

(edited by) Joseph Lange and Anthony J. Cushing, *The Living Christian Community Series* (3 vols.), Pecos, New Mexico & New York, 1975.

The author must conclude by thanking once again Arnold Bittlinger, Erhard Griese and Manfred Kiessig for their co-operation, Erhard Griese in particular for help with the passage about the Evangelical rite of confirmation and the testimony of faith in the second appendix. But his thanks must above all go to those who have taken part with him in study groups. It is from their services of prayer that these suggestions for meditation have emerged, and it is these prayer services that have given him new hope and strengthened his faith with their manifold gifts of the Spirit.

Paderborn, Easter 1976 *Heribert Mühlen*

First week: Meaning

First day: Listening to God and answering him

At the start of my encounter with God in prayer I remind myself that I was not willed and planned by myself but that I came out of the love of God. I ask him to open my eyes and ears, and I am grateful for the fact that I am now able to make this request, since it is already the effect of the Holy Spirit at work in me. God's Spirit, the Spirit of self-sacrifice and love, is already present in us before we are able to open ourselves up for God. It is not we who have to make the first move. It is instead God who approaches us, who asks us, who makes us welcome. All we have to do is to accept his offer.

Allow the 'words of life' to speak to you personally and to awaken you. God's word is fruitful in itself and powerfully effective (Is. 55:10-11):

> Thus says the Lord: 'For as the rain and the snow come down from heaven,
> and return not thither but water the earth,
> making it bring forth and sprout,
> giving seed to the sower and bread to the eater,
> so shall my word be that goes forth from my mouth;
> it shall not return to me empty,
> but it shall accomplish that which I purpose,
> and prosper in the thing for which I sent it.'

The rain falls on to the earth, but before it is partially evaporated by the sun's heat it waters the ground and makes it fertile: it does not return to the atmosphere without having had some effect. God's word has a similar effect: it falls like rain on to the parched soil and fertilizes our inner aridity. It falls on our uneasy feeling that perhaps everything could after all turn out to be meaningless, it heals our life and saves it from destruction (Ps. 107:20). This word with which God in certain circumstances surprises us quite suddenly like an unexpected shower or thunderstorm returns

to God as our personal answer: it has the effect that we turn
back to him, that we speak to him, that we pray.

The words of life and healing that we take into ourselves
each day are meant to make our answer and return to God
possible and to bring them about. This points to something
extremely important: faith comes from listening to the word
of God, and this above all because we listen very carefully.
What is God trying to say to me in this particular passage,
what effect does he want this passage to have on me, what
must I do or refrain from doing in order to understand it?
If we see someone we are fond of again, perhaps after a
lengthy period of separation, we don't have to force ourselves
to pay attention. Those who are in love do not need any
special technique in order to respond to each other in
conversation; because of their personal presence they are
aware of each other. It is the same with us when we have to
do with God himself in his word. Of course it can be that
certain techniques of meditation can be helpful in order to
collect oneself and be present for God, but for the Christian
such practices are not a procedure in which one sinks into
oneself in the hope of finding there the ground of one's life
and being. Christian meditation is in no way an annihilation
of the ego, nor is it in the first place becoming linked with
everything that exists. It is rather a watchful presence for
God.

It is very helpful if one reads the passage of scripture
allotted for each day out loud. Perhaps it is the first time
that you have listened to yourself reading the Bible. This
reading out loud helps us to be collected and to listen carefully.
By speaking out loud listening to God's word becomes
physical, actual. Hence it is an even greater help to read the
passage jointly with other people and then to ask what God
is trying to say to each one of us through this particular
passage. It is not very useful to have a wide-ranging discussion
on the passage. Rather, the passage should be allowed to
address and challenge each individual personally. Hence it is
important for everyone to keep silent so that out of the
silence people's reactions to the passage can be exchanged.
This is already a trial run for that form of service of prayer
deriving from the primitive Church of which we shall have

more to say later.

Try then — perhaps on your own at first — to respond to God in a freely formulated personal prayer. Be convinced from the start that God is present for you, especially in this half-hour that you have set aside for your daily reading of the Bible and for prayer. He will gladly listen to you. Pray out loud, provided this form of praying is not too awkward for you. In the weeks to come we shall often be returning to the difficulties connected with this.

Second day: Chance and terror

The fact that we are alive is either a terrifying or wonderful piece of luck, or there is really a God who loved us even before he created us and who wants to be present for us. Anyone who derives his existence from pure chance must necessarily be godless, and whether consciously or unconsciously you have already made a decision for or against pure chance, for or against God (Wisdom 2:1-11):

> For they [the ungodly] reasoned unsoundly, saying to
> themselves:
> 'Short and sorrowful is our life,
> and there is no remedy when a man comes to his end,
> and no one has been known to return from Hades.
> Because we were born by mere chance,
> and hereafter we shall be as though we had never been;
> because the breath in our nostrils is smoke,
> and reason is a spark kindled by the beating of our hearts.
> When it is extinguished, the body will turn to ashes,
> and the spirit will dissolve like empty air.
> Our name will be forgotten in time.
> and no one will remember our works;
> our life will pass away like the traces of a cloud,
> and be scattered like mist
> that is chased by the rays of the sun
> and overcome by its heat.
> For our allocated time is the passing of a shadow,

and there is no return from our death,
because it is sealed up and no one turns back.
Come, therefore, let us enjoy the good things that exist,
and make use of the creation to the full as in youth.
Let us take our fill of costly wine and perfumes,
and let no flower of spring pass by us.
Let us crown ourselves with rosebuds before they wither.
Let none of us fail to share in our revelry,
everywhere let us leave signs of enjoyment,
because this is our portion, and this our lot.
Let us oppress the righteous poor man;
let us not spare the widow
nor regard the grey hairs of the aged.
But let our might be our law of right,
for what is weak proves itself to be useless.'

This passage makes clear that if it is only through chance that we have come into being, then life lacks purpose and principle, then utility is made the real and final purpose of life — and that with recourse to force and violence. The result is a reign of terror by those best able to succeed. What is weak is regarded as without use or value. Consider whether you too do not in your heart of hearts regard only what is of use to you as significant. Do not you too try to exercise power, to do better than others in order to lord it over them, to subordinate them to your plans and aims, even if you do not always let this be seen? Who does not tend towards the relentless pursuit of success in the struggle for prestige and power in a competitive society geared to achievement? Who renounces his own advantage for the sake of someone weaker?

Third day: Who or what is your God

It can be shown that every human being worships some power superior to himself and that in this worship he is seeking confirmation and justification for his existence — the meaning of life, in other words. Those who lived in a primitive agricultural society worshipped the stars and other powers of nature as gods. They sought security and protection in their relationship with them. Basically they were seeking God himself. In modern industrial societies there are other gods and higher powers: technical and medical, social and political progress, film stars, Olympic athletes, political leaders. When you read the following passages (Wisdom 13:1-6); Wisdom 14:27 and Galatians 4:8-9) ask yourself who or what in your life is your 'god':

> For all men who were ignorant of God were foolish by nature;
> and they were unable from the good things that are seen to know him who exists,
> nor did they recognize the craftsman while paying heed to his works;
> but they supposed that either fire or wind or swift air,
> or the circle of the stars, or turbulent water,
> or the luminaries of heaven were the gods that rule the world.
> If through delight in the beauty of these things men assumed them to be gods,
> let them know how much better than these is their Lord,
> for the author of beauty created them.
> And if men were amazed at their power and working,
> let them perceive from them
> how much more powerful is he who formed them.
> For from the greatness and beauty of created things
> comes a corresponding perception of their Creator.
> Yet these men are little to be blamed,
> for perhaps they go astray
> while seeking God and desiring to find him.

> For the worship of idols not to be named
> is the beginning and cause and end of every evil.

Paul writes: 'Formerly, when you did not know God, you were in bondage to beings that by nature are no gods; but now that you have come to know God, or rather to be known by God, how can you turn back again to the weak and beggarly elemental spirits, whose slaves you want to be once more?'

Today it is not so much the powers of nature that people worship as the powers and authorities in economic and political life, in the entertainments industry and in television. So it is a great help if you write down for your own purposes what the major thing is in your life, who or what attracts you so much that you can no longer break free, who or what exercises a dominion in your life. It will be very important for your future progress for you to be honest with yourself about this:

(1) What am I fascinated by, attracted by, enthusiastic about?

. . . .

(2) What plans and aims have I got for the weeks and months ahead?

. . . .

(3) What do I want to possess? What do I dream about?

. . . .

The exercises presented here are only possible if you answer these questions completely honestly and at the same time ask yourself how much effort you invest in pursuing these plans and aims of yours, what the genuine and ultimate point of your life is. It is of the most decisive importance for you to recognize the extent to which you squeeze God out of your heart.

There is something you should take careful note of. It is right and proper and in fact necessary that in your working life you should aim at securing your livelihood. But if it is only in earning money that you see the point of your life and if you do not have any other goals beyond this, then money is your God. Again, everybody needs to be appreciated to some extent, but if all our aims and efforts are concerned only and exclusively with being appreciated then the other people from whom we beg for appreciation are our Gods. Again, you must of course provide for your children, but they too can become your gods who rule your entire life (cf. Wisdom 14:12-15). If we worship people or things to an excessive degree or make an inordinate effort to achieve something, then we no longer have the strength to go beyond what we worship or strive after, and what we worship or strive after takes the place of God for us and thus becomes an idol.

Evil often starts with the exaggeration of what is good. To avoid this exaggeration it can be necessary for us to give certain connections, aims, favourite ideas up completely: 'If your right eye causes you to sin, pluck it out and throw it away . . . And if your right hand causes you to sin, cut it off and throw it away' (Matt. 5:29-30). It is worth while being so thoroughgoingly tough with oneself because it is only in this way that we get to dealing with God himself. Perhaps you do not need to cut your hand off but only to switch your television set off and at last give yourself time: for the Bible, for your family, for prayer, for contributing to the community.

Fourth day: The personal, living God

The God we are dealing with in the weeks to come is the God of the Bible, not the God of philosophers. God is not simply a first or highest principle, unchangeable, immutable, remaining unmoved by what goes on in the world and not reacting to human history. The Old Testament presented God with human characteristics. The Old Testament God is jealous, shows mercy, has passions, although at the same time he is infinitely other than a human being: 'I am God and not man, the Holy One in your midst' (Hosea 11:9).

What is and remains important is that he is a living person, lord over the history of mankind, lord also over the personal history of your life. If you genuinely seek him, he can at any time intervene in your life just as in his own person he led the people of Israel out of bondage and slavery (Deut. 4: 24, 29, 31, 34-35, 37, 39; Isaiah 43: 10-12):

> For the Lord your God is a devouring fire, a jealous God. . . . you will find him, if you search after him with all your heart and with all your soul. . . . For the Lord your God is a merciful God; he will not fail you or destroy you or forget the covenant with your fathers which he swore to them . . . Or has any god ever

attempted to go and take a nation for himself from the
midst of another nation, by trials, by signs, by wonders,
and by war, by a mighty hand and an outstretched
arm . . . ? To you it was shown, that you might know that
the Lord is God; there is no other besides him . . . Because
he loved your fathers and chose their descendants after
them, and brought you out of Egypt with his own
presence, by his great power, . . . know therefore this
day, and lay it to your heart, that the Lord is God in
heaven above and on the earth beneath; there is no other.

'You are my witnesses,' says the Lord,
'and my servant whom I have chosen,
that you may know and believe me
and understand that I am He.
Before me no god was formed,
nor shall there be any after me.
I, I am the Lord,
and besides me there is no saviour.'

God reveals himself as 'I', a personal God who has always
intervened in the history of his people. He will break into
your personal history too if you ask him to. He will show
himself to you.

Fifth day: He loves you and is with you

This personal God has created all men and women, including
you, out of love, and he wishes to enter into a completely
personal relationship with all men and women, including
you (Wisdom 11:24-25; Isaiah 45:10-12; Isaiah 43:1-3, 5):

For thou lovest all things that exist,
and hast loathing for none of the things which thou
hast made,
for thou wouldst not have made anything if thou hadst
hated it.
How would anything have endured if thou hadst not
willed it?

Or how would anything not called forth by thee have
been preserved?

'Woe to him who says to a father, "What are you
begetting?'
or to a woman, "With what are you in travail?"
Thus says the Lord, the Holy One of Israel, and his Maker:
'Will you question me about my children,
or command me concerning the work of my hands?
I made the earth, and created man upon it.'

'Fear not, for I have redeemed you;
I have called you by name, you are mine.
When you pass through the waters I will be with you;
and through the rivers, they shall not overwhelm you;
when you walk through fire you shall not be burned,
and the flame shall not consume you.
For I am the Lord your God, the Holy One of Israel,
your Saviour . . .
Fear not, for I am with you.'

The last passage applies to the whole people, but you can
perfectly well apply it to yourself personally, for in a number
of places in the Old Testament God says to individual men and
women: 'I am with you.' You did not will and plan yourself,
whether you like it or not you must accept your life from
outside yourself. But is it not a message of liberation when
the Bible tells us that it is not blind chance, not human
society, not other people that are the cause of your being,
but a loving God who does not reject anything of what he
has made? A God who accepts and endorses you at the
deepest level, more than any human being can accept and
endorse you? Of course there are days and moments —
perhaps they are close at hand — when we want to cry out
with Job: 'Let the day perish wherein I was born . . . Why did
I not die at birth, come forth from the womb and expire?'
(Job 3:3, 11). If we had been able to plan and determine our
lives, our characters, our capabilities ourselves, no doubt we
would have done many things differently. Have you already
reproached God on this account? Trust in his word: he is
with you, he will free you. He accepts and supports you

just as he has created you. He is with you, even in impossible situations.

Sixth day: He has a plan for your life

If God called us into existence out of love, then this was no arbitrary action, but instead there is a plan behind it. The God of the Bible affirms of himself that he has a plan for your life and mine, for human society and its future development in the world (Isaiah 46:9-11; Eph. 1:11-12; Isaiah 55:8-9):

> 'For I am God, and there is no other;
> I am God, and there is none like me,
> declaring the end from the beginning
> and from ancient times things not yet done,
> saying, 'My counsel shall stand,
> and I will accomplish all my purpose,'
> calling a bird of prey from the east,
> the man of my counsel from a far country.
> I have spoken, and I will bring it to pass;
> I have purposes, and I will do it.'

> In him, according to the purpose of him who accomplishes all things according to the counsel of his will, we who first hoped in Christ have been destined and appointed to live for the praise of his glory.

> But:
> 'For my thoughts are not your thoughts,
> neither are your ways my ways, says the Lord.
> For as the heavens are higher than the earth,
> so are my ways higher than your ways
> and my thoughts than your thoughts.'

The major problem of our life is not our unfulfilled wishes, our plans that have come to naught, but God's unfulfilled wishes and his plans that have come to naught.

The Bible states that God has a plan for your life, your family, your nation, and for the world as a whole. The Bible does not say that we shall perceive and understand this plan. On the contrary, the letter to the Ephesians describes God's plan that he has revealed to us in Jesus Christ and in the Church as a 'mystery'. In Jesus Christ God has revealed to us his plan for the world and also his plan involving each individual one of us. But this does not dispel the mystery but rather makes it plain. Even Jesus himself did not know God's plan for him right from the start, and on the Mount of Olives his human nature rebelled against it so that the passage of scripture might be fulfilled in him: 'And he was reckoned with transgressors' (Luke 22:37-46). The evangelists often stress that incomprehensible necessity that makes God's plan for Jesus clear. He entrusted himself to this plan right up to and including the pointlessness of his death. On the cross he experienced God's plan as an incomprehensible mystery in itself. On the cross God realized his eternal purpose (Eph. 3:11).

We too will experience what God plans to do with us and to us, but we shall never comprehend this purpose. God indeed wants to give himself to us, to surrender himself to us, as he revealed it in the cross of his son. Who was willing to comprehend something of this nature? That is why Paul also writes in the letter to the Ephesians: 'In whom [Christ Jesus] we have boldness and confidence of access through our faith in him. So I ask you not to lose heart over what I am now suffering for you, which is your glory' (Eph. 3:12-13). We experience the mystery of God's plan for us to the extent that we entrust ourselves to this mystery. Being a Christian does not mean that all questions are solved at a stroke, but that by following Christ one can learn to live with unsolved questions. Our own plans and wishes are continually being frustrated, but we would never describe such experiences as pointless if we allow God to give back to us that original confidence of which Jesus Christ provides us with the pattern and which he bore witness to in his death.

The Christian co-operates in and contributes with all his might to all useful developments and to the changes that are needed in society, but not because of any secular doctrine or ideology which is concerned not primarily with the truth but with the accomplishment of political ends. Rather he does so because he knows God has a plan for the world and loves all men and women. For this reason he does not despair of unjust structures being reformed even when others have perhaps become resigned to the perpetuation of injustice. His weapons are provided not by hatred but by self-sacrifice. Hence he maintains a critical distance from all doctrines of political salvation that are the work of men. He knows that if the world, if politics, if economics are controlled solely and simply by plans made by men, then this leads to an intolerable domination of men over men, then oppression is inescapable, the oppression exercised by money and by bureaucrats. Someone who by contrast surrenders himself to God's plans can change the world.

Seventh day: He who loves his life loses it

> Now among those who went up to worship at the feast were some Greeks. So these came to Philip . . . and said to him, 'Sir, we wish to see Jesus' (John 12:20-21).

At the end of the first week it is clear to us that we have already in fact decided either for chance or for God, even though we may not have been completely aware of the decision we were making. So we are in the same situation as those Greeks whose interest had been awakened in getting to know this God better. This has brought us up against Jesus, and naturally we would like to be able to see him, as it were. Will he receive us?

> Jesus answered them, 'The hour has come for the Son of man to be glorified. Truly, truly, I say to you, unless a grain of wheat falls into the earth and dies, it remains alone; but if it dies, it bears much fruit. He who loves his life loses it, and he who hates his life in this world will keep it for eternal life. If any one serves me, he must follow me; and where I am, there shall my servant be also; if any one serves me, the Father will honour him' (John 12:23-26).

Jesus is not some performer of miracles who knows everything and can do everything, someone people would like to stare at as at a curiosity. He who wants to get to know Jesus has no choice but to follow him along the path of self-sacrifice. In the simile of the grain of wheat the evangelist John proclaims the celebration of death: the grain of wheat must not want to remain alone, that is, itself. It must die, break through its husk and surrender itself if it wants to bear fruit. A grain of wheat that is concerned only for itself and as it were for its private existence remains pointless and meaningless in itself: it decays. But if it surrenders itself, breaks through its husk and dies, it fulfils the meaning and purpose of its existence and brings forth fruit in plenty.

This shows the extent to which the Christian experience of meaningfulness is the acceptance and anticipation of one's own death. Someone who lives solely for the motive and aim of realizing his own potentialities and obtaining as much as possible in the way of recognition, honour, power and possessions will not attain that God who has given him existence. Fundamentally his life remains meaningless, because he takes himself too seriously. Someone who has too much consideration for himself will never find himself. The discovery of oneself is something that is given as an additional gift if we follow Jesus, if we die with him.

Naturally these are hard sayings, unpleasant demands. No one likes hearing them, and even those who proclaim them to others can seem insincere to themselves. Perhaps God will be willing in the course of the following six weeks to show us a little more who he is and how he is. He himself was at our service in Jesus Christ, and Jesus Christ in his turn challenges us to serve others. We will only learn the meaning of our life when we take up Jesus's commission to continue his work and let ourselves be equipped for this with those ministerial graces, those gifts of the spirit and charisms, that the Spirit of Jesus wishes to bestow on each and every one of us according to his or her capabilities (cf. 1 Cor. 12:4-11). If we open ourselves up for these gifts and serve Jesus in their power, the Father will 'honour' us. That means that we experience God's profoundest approval, recognition, honour when in the power of our gifts of the Spirit we intervene 'charismatically' on behalf of others and serve them. But a renewal of the charismatic gifts in the Church and an openness towards them after they have been almost forgotten for so many centuries is only possible if we ourselves die, if we are concerned to proclaim and propagate not ourselves but Jesus Christ as the Redeemer and as the unique revelation of God. For this reason acceptance of one's own death stands right at the beginning of the charismatic experience, and this like nothing else makes us aware of our own unimportance. We need approval and support for our existence just as we depend on air to live, but we only experience it to the extent that we give this existence of ours and with it ourselves back to God.

During the last four weeks of this course of study we shall look in greater detail at these ministerial graces or charisms. Before we can become open for them and for the intense self-awareness, joy and love that is often given with them, God calls us to conversion. Consider once again the question you noted on the third day of this last week: Who or what is your God? Which 'God' is it that you pray to? Who or what do you look to for the meaning and purpose of your life?

> 'Do you not know that God's kindness is meant to lead you to repentance? (Rom. 2:4).

Second week: God

First day: Praying personally and out loud

Now you have begun to get involved with God, and he promises you a new life, a new start. He wants us genuinely to experience him, he wants to penetrate not just our intellect, not just our will, but the depths of our feelings and emotions: he wants to embrace the entire person that is you. The innermost core of your personality where sense-perception, will and intellect are united and live is called by the Bible the 'heart'. God promises you that it is into this heart that he wants to send the Spirit of his Son (Gal. 4:6), and this Spirit makes you capable of a method and style of praying that perhaps you have not known before.

During the first week, did you ever once try to talk to God personally and out loud? Not in remembered formulas that one recites more or less without thinking but on something like these lines: 'My God, I thank you for having created me. You loved me before you created me, and I would not exist here and now were it not for this love. I trust your promises and ask you to free me from all associations that prevent me from giving my life and my death back to you.' If you try to talk to God out loud in this personal way, you may well find yourself coming to a halt after a few sentences. Perhaps you found yourself being ashamed of yourself — at all events, that is what happened to me the first time. Now why should this be? Not because you are not used to this style of praying, but because you have admitted and expressed something that is not completely covered by your everyday experience. When you pray out loud and personally, you are presupposing that the person you are addressing is present here and now. It doesn't make sense to talk out loud to someone if this someone isn't there and can't therefore hear you. Probably you are not that fully convinced that God is really present and quite near to you and is willing to listen to you. Making this presupposition strikes you as somehow insincere, and you are frightened at the thought of encountering God quite directly and as it were face to face. When for the first time you hear yourself talking to God in this way, your relationship to God becomes as it were tangible, for you can hear yourself talking. It is now something you have to take seriously, and you can no longer retreat, for talking in this way is at the same time an admission or acknowledgment to yourself. And that is why you are ashamed of yourself.

Someone once said: 'The first time I prayed in this way I had the feeling I was doing something indecent.' What did he mean by that? When we repeat to ourselves prayers we have learned by heart we often fail to involve our feelings and emotions. Perhaps we have the will and intention of loving God with all our heart, but in such an act of will our entire heart and all our powers are not really present with God. But if on the contrary we say out loud: 'My God, I love you,' then our feelings and emotions are aroused and we are suddenly made aware that these feelings and emotions have not in any way been made Christian and are not really present with God. As far as our hearts are concerned we are for the most part not present with God but scattered among a multitude of concerns and duties, we are fascinated, affected, attracted by so many things, so many people. So, when we want to pray, we must first collect ourselves and concentrate, we must as it were allow ourselves a run up to the wicket; and very soon we catch ourselves being inattentive. We cannot really say of ourselves that we love God with our whole heart, and so we seem to ourselves to be doing something indecent when we hear ourselves saying: 'My God, I love you.'

Part of the reason for this is that for centuries we have been told from the pulpit that religion is primarily a matter of the intellect and that emotions are untrustworthy and should not be treated as evidence. Joy in believing in God or joy in God's presence was not something you should ever express, especially to other people, for religion was a private affair that belonged to the silence of one's inner life and should not be exposed to public view. This kind of joy had become taboo. But God himself is here to break the taboo by arousing many people throughout the world to a new freedom. A process of liberation begins when we are no longer afraid of surrendering ourselves to God in fundamental confidence and of admitting to ourselves and to others our love for him.

Of course, you cannot overcome your shame and fear unaided. The Second Council of Orange, held in 529, taught that the origin of faith and the very desire of faith whereby we believe in Christ and are led to (repentance and) baptism is not something natural in ourselves but is due to the effect within us of the Holy Spirit who leads our will from unbelief to belief. So when we pray we must not rely on our own resources to prepare ourselves and collect ourselves in tranquillity. Rather it is God's Spirit himself who prays in us: 'Likewise the Spirit helps us in our weakness; for we do not know how to pray as we ought, but the Spirit himself intercedes for us with sighs too deep for words' (Rom. 8:26). It is he who cries out in us and we with him: 'Abba, Father' (Rom. 8:15, Gal. 4:6). God is therefore not only a reality outside ourselves towards which we direct ourselves by an effort of the intellect or will; as the Holy Spirit it is his wish to be present in the depths of our being and in this way to lead us to himself. Prayer is thus something that happens within God himself. God's Spirit prays in us through Christ to the Father, to that God we cannot see and hear. God's own dynamic energy is thus at work in us. It is never only to God, but also in God that we pray.

Are you really convinced of this, or do you, like I myself, have to admit at first that in the depths of your heart you are Godless? Do you have to admit that this kind of unbelievable presence of God in yourself is something you do not regard as at all possible or that the idea is unwelcome because of its consequences and implications? Trust in God's promises: he himself wants to make a new start in you, he will lead you and he will also make you capable of drawing the necessary consequences. Abandon yourself to God's guidance and to his dynamic energy that wants to be set free in you. In the depths of your being there is a spring of living water: it is not true that within yourself you are completely dry and arid like a desert without any water to bring it life. You need only ask God to clear away the rubbish, and the spring will begin to flow. Prayer is then for you no longer just an obligation, a duty. Instead you will understand what Paul meant when he urged us: 'Pray constantly' (1 Thess. 5:17).

If it is possible for you, discuss all this with other people, let them discover the Godlessness of your heart, let yourself be stimulated and enriched by their experiences. Certainly it is a major step when you start praying out loud and personally to God in front of each other and when in this way you confess to each other your faith in God and your love for him. This is indeed foreseen in the New Testament: 'Every one who acknowledges me before men, the Son of man also will acknowledge before the angels of God' (Luke 12:8), but we are simply not used to this kind of thing. Perhaps your experiences will be like that of the unbeliever who entered the community of Corinth at prayer: the hidden resistance of his heart was disclosed thanks to the witness to the faith of those present (1 Cor. 14:24-25). Perhaps then like him you will cry out in astonishment: 'Truly God is among us.' But if this style of praying creates difficulties for you, then wait a little time. We shall have more to say about this kind of 'group' prayer at the start of the fifth week.

But even when you are praying alone you are not alone. Praying with you and for you are hundreds of thousands of Christians throughout the world whom God has similarly aroused to experience his mighty presence. He remains the living and true God who in the second half of the twentieth century gathers his people together anew and leads them into the future he has promised.

Second day: Being awakened by God's Spirit

In the traditionally Christian countries, as far as mainstream Christianity is concerned, fewer and fewer people each year go to church. More and more people turn away from the Churches, even when there is no pressure on them from outside to do so. At the same time God is awakening people in all the Churches to a new joy in believing, to the experience of his mighty presence. The prophet Ezekiel showed the process of God's people being awakened in a vision. In the passage that follows the phrase: 'You shall know that I am the Lord' occurs three times. This promise remains valid for the whole Church today and in a quite personal manner for each individual member of it (Ezek. 37:1-14):

> The hand of the Lord was upon me, and he brought me out by the Spirit of the Lord, and set me down in the midst of the valley; it was full of bones. And he led me round among them; and behold, there were very many upon the valley; and lo, they were very dry. And he said to me, 'Son of man, can these bones live?' And I answered, 'O Lord God, thou knowest.' Again he said to me, 'Prophesy to these bones, and say to them, O dry bones, hear the word of the Lord. Thus says the Lord God to these bones: Behold, I will cause breath to enter you, and you shall live. And I will lay sinews upon you, and will cause flesh to come upon you, and cover you with skin, and put breath in you, and you shall live; and you shall know that I am the Lord.'
>
> So I prophesied as I was commanded; and as I prophesied, there was a noise, and behold, a rattling; and the bones came together, bone to its bone. And as I looked, there were sinews on them, and flesh had come upon them, and skin had covered them; but there was no breath in them. Then he said to me, 'Prophesy to the breath, prophesy, son of man, and say to the breath, Thus says the Lord God: Come from the four winds, O breath, and breathe upon these slain, that they may live.' So I prophesied as he commanded me, and the breath came into them, and they lived, and stood upon their feet, an exceedingly great host.
>
> Then he said to me, 'Son of man, these bones are the whole house of Israel. Behold, they say, 'Our bones are dried up, and our hope is lost; we are clean cut off.' Therefore prophesy, and say to them. Thus says the Lord God: Behold, I will open your graves, and raise you from your graves, O my people; and I will bring you home into the land of Israel. And you shall know that I am the Lord, when I open your graves, and raise you from your graves, O my people. And I will put my Spirit within you, and you shall live, and I will place you in your own land; then you shall know

that I, the Lord, have spoken, and I have done it,
says the Lord.'

Frequently and continually God intervened in the history of
his people, and his intervention often came precisely at the
point when its spiritual life had dried up and all hope had
perished. In the old covenant God intervened through his
mighty deeds. God's greatest intervention in history was the
incarnation of his Son. In the new Covenant God's Spirit is at
the same time the Spirit of Jesus Christ, the Holy Spirit, 'the
Lord, the giver of life,' as we proclaim in the creed. While God
is busy arousing the whole of his people to new life, he also
intervenes in each individual's personal history. The vision
described how the dry bones are raised up. But resurrection,
being raised up, is a very personal matter: 'I will cause my Spirit
to enter you, and you shall live.' We will be made to live as
the same people who formerly were dry and without hope.
No one can be awakened to new life in your place, and so
the vision has a quite direct personal bearing on you. Trust
in God's promise: in the weeks to come he will give new life
to you too, and by means of certain signs you will recognize
that God is also the Lord of the personal history of your life.

**Third day: God's love for us is no less tangible than the love
between man and wife**

In the Bible God's covenant with man is often compared to
the bond of marriage and unbelief similarly to adultery. Two
people who love each other do not merely have the intention
of loving each other: their love is something they experience,
something they know about. They know that they love each
other, and so they can talk about their love with other people.
If you open yourself up completely to the presence of the
Holy Spirit in you, then you will experience God's love in
you with your senses and as it were physically (Hosea 2:16-22):

'And in that day, says the Lord, you will call me,
"My husband," and no longer will you call me,

"My Baal."[1] For I will remove the names of the Baalim from her mouth, and they shall be mentioned by name no more. And I will make for you a covenant on that day . . . And I will betroth you to me for ever; I will betroth you to me in righteousness and in justice, in steadfast love, and in mercy. I will betroth you to me in faithfulness; and you shall know the Lord.'

For the Lord delights in you,
and your land shall be married.
For as a young man marries a virgin,
so shall your sons marry you,
and as the bridegroom rejoices over the bride,
so shall your God rejoice over you (Isaiah 62: 4-5).

'Behold, I stand at the door and knock; if any one hears my voice and opens the door, I will come in to him and eat with him, and he with me' (Rev. 3:20).

It is not by chance that the entire contents of the Bible can be summed up in the one word 'covenant' — the old covenant and the new covenant. A covenant is always a relationship between persons — animals cannot contract a covenant — and it arises from the personal agreement of the partners to the covenant. People who are getting married are explicitly asked if they want to contract a lasting tie with this man or this woman. Marriage finds its profoundest expression in sexual intercourse. For this the original language of the Bible used the term 'know' (Gen. 4:1, 17; 1 Sam. 1:19; Matt. 1:25; Luke 1:34). Here 'to know' does not in any way mean a purely intellectual understanding but experience through the senses. The wedding feast, too, is this kind of experience of community through the senses.

Can you therefore say of yourself that you have experienced God's love for you as a covenant in this sense? When two people love each other steadfastly, faithfully, intensely and fervently, when they have got married, their life changes. At

---

[1]   Baalim are heathen nature gods considered as dwelling in trees, in springs, on mountain tops, in rocks, etc. Jews were strictly forbidden to worship them.

baptism God had already entered your life, but is the covenant formed at baptism as concrete and momentous as the marriage tie for a married couple? Married love is thoroughly emotional. Has God touched you in the depths of your feelings and emotions? He stands at the door and knocks and wants to eat with you. Open the door to him, now. Pray to him in the power of his Holy Spirit.

When we make a covenant, we bind ourselves to remain faithful. God is always faithful, and this faithfulness of his does not change. He always keeps his offer open, even when we have turned away from him. How is it with your faithfulness? Have you really cleared all the false gods out of your life? Faithfulness also entails perseverance. Make up your mind to persevere throughout these seven weeks, and give yourself time for God — at least half an hour a day. If you really let the word of life enter into you, it will accompany you throughout the entire day.

Fourth day: I will seek your face

The Bible states that in everything we do and try to do we are basically seeking God himself. In you too lives the longing to experience God, to see him and hear him, even and in fact precisely when you have turned away from him and worshipped other powers. But God is always asking you, and asking you at this moment too, to seek him with the entire love of your heart (Psalm 27: 8-9):

> Thou hast said, 'Seek ye my face.'
> My heart says to thee,
> 'Thy face, Lord, do I seek.'
> Hide not thy face from me.
> Turn not thy servant away in anger.

When the people of Israel were wandering through the desert and enduring heat and lack of water, Moses wanted to be certain once again whether God himself had intervened in the history of his people, he wanted to see and experience him himself (Exodus 33: 18-20, 23):

Moses said, 'I pray thee, show me thy glory.' And he said, 'I will make all my goodness pass before you, and will proclaim before you my name "The Lord"; and I will be gracious to whom I will be gracious, and will show mercy on whom I will show mercy. But,' he said, 'you cannot see my face; for man shall not see me and live . . . But my face shall not be seen.'

You too will be led by the Lord. True, you will not see him and hear him himself, for he remains the blessed mystery of your life, but you will see and hear something of this mystery if you open yourself up to him in the coming weeks, and your longing for God will grow.

Fifth day: He who has seen me has seen the Father

The new covenant far surpasses the old. In it God outdoes himself, since he has given up for us the person closest to him, his Son (Rom. 8:32). The man Jesus of Nazareth is for us the image and face of God, and in the power of his Spirit we shall come to the knowledge of the glory of God in the face of Christ (2 Cor. 4:6). Jesus knew and experienced God as no one else has done before or since. He lets us share in this experience of his, in what he himself has seen and heard (John 3:31-36):

He who comes from above is above all; he who is of the earth belongs to the earth, and of the earth he speaks; he who comes from heaven is above all. He bears witness to what he has seen and heard, yet no one receives his testimony; he who receives his testimony sets his seal to this, that God is true. For he whom God has sent utters the words of God, for it is not by measure that he gives the Spirit; the Father loves the Son, and has given all things into his hand. He who believes in the Son has eternal life; he who does not obey the Son shall not see life, but the wrath of God rests upon him.

What Jesus said to Philip applies to you too (John 14:6-9):

> 'I am the way, and the truth, and the life; no one comes to the Father, but by me. If you had known me, you would have known my Father also; henceforth you know him and have seen him.'
>
> Philip said to him, 'Lord, show us the Father, and we shall be satisfied.' Jesus said to him, 'Have I been with you so long, and yet you do not know me, Philip? He who has seen me has seen the Father.'

Believe this saying. The God who created you in order to make a covenant with you you will find only in this man Jesus of Nazareth.

Sixth day: He who meets Jesus is beside himself

The passage we read from St John's gospel yesterday takes on form and colour when we read of the way in which people found themselves beside themselves in meeting Jesus. Whatever one may think of the details of the reports of what Jesus said and did — they were formed by the early Church's experience of the Spirit, something which made everyone, including non-Christians, beside themselves, as Luke stresses in Acts 2:12 — one thing that stands out is that someone who actually meets Jesus in the flesh is fascinated by him. We shall read only one of the many accounts (Mark 6:46-52):

> And after he [Jesus] had taken leave of them, he went into the hills to pray. And when evening came, the boat [with the disciples in it] was out on the sea, and he was alone on the land. And he saw that they were distressed in rowing, for the wind was against them. And about the fourth watch of the night he came to them, walking on the sea. He meant to pass by them, but when they saw him walking on the sea they thought it was a ghost, and cried out; for they all saw him, and were terrified. But immediately he spoke to them and said,

'Take heart, it is I; have no fear.' And he got into the boat with them and the wind ceased. And they were utterly astounded, for they did not understand about the loaves, but their hearts were hardened.

Everything that Jesus says and does comes out of the prayer and worship for which he is continually withdrawing. No man experienced God to the same extent as he: we shall come back to this in the fourth week. His contemporaries must have noticed this. They were profoundly disconcerted, fascinated, frightened and at the same time attracted by his appearance, his words, and his miracles. Jesus was an extra-ordinary man who broke all criteria. After a dumb man had been healed the crowds marvelled and said: 'Never was anything like this seen in Israel' (Matt. 9:33). This fascination at Jesus's presence has played a part in shaping the account quoted above.

When we actually meet Jesus, when he passes by us quite unexpectedly, then we are frightened. We are disconcerted at his invitation to self-sacrifice (cf. Mark 10:24), but it is to us that this Jesus says: 'Take heart, it is I; have no fear.' You will be beside yourself when you reach the point of having to do with Jesus himself, when you experience the presence of his Spirit inside you. You will receive the strength to transcend and leave behind you what used to fascinate and stimulate you: you reach the point of having to do with God himself when you encounter Jesus. So do not let him pass you by.

Seventh day: Jesus is the Lord

Among the Christian community at Corinth the question arose how one distinguished genuine experiences of the presence of the Holy Spirit from those that were not. Paul's answer was (1 Cor. 12:1-3):

Now concerning spiritual gifts, brethren, I do not want you to be uninformed. You know that when you were heathen, you were led astray to dumb idols, however

you may have been moved. Therefore I want you to
understand that no one speaking by the Spirit of God
ever says, 'Jesus be cursed!' and no one can say, 'Jesus
is Lord' except by the Holy Spirit.

The Christian community at Corinth was surrounded by a
paganism marked by a high degree of religious excitement
and fervour, and this did not remain without effect on its
worship. So there were plainly nominal Christians who were
really pagans, who denied that the crucified man Jesus Christ
was God's revelation of himself to the world. That was why
they cursed him. Paul derives this cursing from a state of
emotional excitation that is not caused by the Holy Spirit.
He reminds the Corinthians of their former way of life when
they were overpowered, fascinated and attracted by dumb
idols. It is not this experience in itself that Paul is concerned
to criticize but rather what it is aimed at, its content. Go
back now and read once again what you wrote down on the
third day of the first week in answer to the question: 'What
am I fascinated by, attracted by, enthusiastic about?' If it is
some man or woman, technology, athletic heroes, pop singers,
political leaders, or some hobby of yours that fascinates and
attracts you, then this is not wrong in itself and need not
separate you from God. But if you remain stuck at this level,
if your enthusiasm does not transcend these people or things
and reach out to God, then as far as you are concerned they
have become dumb idols. They are dumb because they
cannot tell us who God is and what kind of existence is his,
since for us they replace God, the supreme being, the supreme
power. It is part of human nature to be fascinated by,
enthusiastic about, and attracted by some person or thing, but
the Christian is able to maintain a critical distance from all
purely worldly powers. This he can do because it is Jesus
Christ, whom in a completely personal way he has abandoned
himself to, who fascinates him and arouses his enthusiasm
above all other people and things. The force that brings this
about the New Testament also calls the Holy Spirit, since it is
the divine energy that leads us through Christ to the Father
who is beyond our experience. For the Christian who is filled
with the Spirit Jesus is higher, mightier, greater than every-

thing that he is otherwise still fascinated by: 'Jesus is Lord.'

Perhaps during the past week you have already been praying out loud and personally and God's Spirit himself has overcome within you your initial feelings of shame. Let yourself be led yet further along this path, and perhaps you should now say, quite personally and out loud, this oldest profession of faith: 'Jesus is Lord.' Whoever believes this profession of faith with his heart and confesses it with his lips, is justified and saved (Rom. 10:10). Repeat this formula over and over again for several times. You will find that there is power in it. It makes us ready to entrust this Jesus Christ with dominion over our life, to surrender ourselves to him. It is he who will overcome your fear. You will discover that your feelings too are laid claim to, for love and admitting one's belief are matters of emotion. It is with alarm that we acknowledge that our feelings have not been that thoroughly converted to Christianity, that our heart and the strength of our enthusiasm and love are all over the place and not solely with God. Let yourself be led further by the Spirit of God and go on praying: 'Jesus is Lord.' Your prayer may well develop into something more complex: 'You alone are the holy one, you alone are the Lord, you alone are the most high, Jesus Christ, with the Holy Spirit in the glory of God the Father, Amen.'

Third week: Separation

First day: Praying with the body

One of last week's suggestions was that you should pray out loud and that you should make your prayer a personal thing. This method of praying may well have long been your normal practice. But on the other hand last week could well have been the first time you heard yourself talking to God out loud. After you had overcome your initial feeling of shame you will have found that your prayer had become more intense and more concentrated. You stripped yourself before God, surrendered yourself to him in the spoken word and not just in your thoughts. This involves our physical body and our senses in talking to God and thus affects us to the depths of our emotions. We are not pure spirits who by some unlucky chance happen to be imprisoned in a body. Our body is just as much a part of us as our soul and our mind. It can be shown that everything a human being does, including the most spiritual actions imaginable, are at the same time physical and that without his body man cannot accomplish any actions at all. Hence prayer is fundamentally physical. We do not pray just with our mind and our intellect, but also with our body. Talking out loud already provides a physical process of this kind, and it is strengthened and intensified still more by means of gestures. Gestures associated with prayer are to be found in all religions: speech, after all, began as gesture. Before man reached the point of addressing his God in words, he had already expressed his innermost feelings through gestures. Here we strike the primeval rock of our relationship with God, and it is not without significance for the renewal of the traditional Churches that long forgotten gestures associated with prayer should be revived. They are not merely an expression of inward feelings, but have an independent effect on one's internal attitudes. Gestures are also a form of avowal of and witness to one's faith — faith at the service of others.

In nearly every religion the gesture of prostration is to be found. It expressed total surrender to God, the greatest possible degree of submission to his will. Man buries the most important part of his body, his face, in the dust. Already in the Old Testament this attitude of prayer is to be found in use: 'Then Abram fell on his face; and God said to him, "Behold, my covenant is with you, and you shall be the father of a multitude of nations" ' (Gen. 17:3-4, cf. 24:26). When disaster struck Job he fell upon the ground and worshipped God (Job 1:20). 'O come, let us worship and bow down," says the Psalmist, 'let us kneel before the Lord, our Maker!' (Ps. 95:6; cf. Sirach 50:17, 21, 1 Macc. 4:55 etc.). Jesus too used this attitude of prayer, and is indeed recorded as doing so at the time of his profoundest submission to his Father's will: 'Then he said to them, "My soul is very sorrowful, even to death; remain here, and watch with me." And going a little farther he fell on his face and prayed, "My Father, if it be possible, let this cup pass from me; nevertheless, not as I will, but as thou wilt" ' (Matt. 26:38-39, cf. Mark 14:35). Tertullian records this attitude of prayer as still in general use as an expression of private devotion around the year 200 AD (adv. Marc. 31:8). In the public worship of the Catholic Church it is only normally used today in the Good Friday liturgy and at ordination.

Does the fact that Jesus himself is recorded as having prayed in this posture encourage you to imitate him in this respect too? If you have already been brought to the point of being ready to bring your life and your death, your lack of trust in God and all your sins once again before God in an act of the profoundest self-surrender, then do not shy away from expressing your abandonment of yourself to him in this way. In baptism God concluded a covenant with you just as he did with Abram. And Abram when he accepted this covenant fell on his face on the ground. It was in this attitude of prayer that Jesus accepted and approved his own death. No doubt at first you will think it odd when you start adopting this posture in your private prayer, but it will have an effect in turn on your inner feelings.

Another gesture to be found in many religions is that of stretching the hands out upwards. Like every gesture it is ambiguous. When the palms of the hands are turned upwards it expresses the openness of someone who accepts God's gifts. But this gesture can also express submission: the person who is praying comes to meet God unarmed and with empty hands. It is often recorded in the Old Testament: 'I stretch out my hands to thee; my soul thirsts for thee like a parched land' (Ps. 143:6); 'O God, thou art my God, I seek thee, my soul thirsts for thee; my flesh faints for thee, as in a dry and weary land where no water is . . . So I will bless thee as long as I live; I will lift up my hands and call on thy name' (Ps. 63:1, 4; cf. Ex. 9:29, 33; 1 Kings 8:22; Job 11:13; Ps. 28:2; Ps. 141:2; Isaiah 1:15, etc.). In many places in the Old Testament to stretch out one's hands is used as a synonym for to pray. And in the New Testament this attitude of prayer is not unknown: 'I desire then that in every place the men should pray, lifting holy hands without anger or quarrelling' (1 Tim. 2:8).

In antiquity it was almost exclusively this attitude that Christians used for prayer, and to begin with they adopted the same posture as the pagans with their arms fully stretched out and their hands raised up high to heaven. Then to make the distinction clear between them and the pagans, in the second and third centuries they brought their arms down level with their shoulders. This was interpreted as imitating the Lord praying with his arms stretched out on the cross. Around the year 200 Tertullian says: 'We do not lift our hands up but stretch them out and, modelling ourselves on the suffering of the Lord, we confess Christ in our prayer' (de Orat. 14). This attitude remained usual well into the middle ages, but became progressively reserved for the priest. St Thomas Aquinas retains the interpretation we have mentioned: 'The priest stretching his arms out after the consecration signifies Christ's stretching out of his arms on the cross' (S. Th. III:83, 5 ad 5). Today this form of praying is still usual at places of pilgrimage and in some religious orders.

Everything new is strange at first, but you can grow into this attitude of prayer by understanding it as an expression of your readiness to accept your own death in the power of the cross of Christ. But at the same time it expresses our joy that we have already risen with Christ and conquered death. In the Roman rite the congregation are asked before

the great thanksgiving of the preface: 'Lift up your hearts.'
Why should one not give physical expression to this inward
lifting up by stretching out one's hands? It is not only in our
thoughts that we rejoice but with our entire person, which
includes our body. This gesture is in no way reserved for
private prayer. In the Christian community it is a living
profession of faith in Jesus's death and resurrection and
hence in our own resurrection that will conquer death.

What we think of today as the normal position of the hands
in prayer — with the fingers extended and the palms pressed
together, as in Dürer's famous picture — was for the most
part unknown to the Christians of the early centuries of the
Church's history. It is not recorded among the Fathers of the
Church and first came into general use with the conversion
of the Germanic tribes. Originally it expressed the submission
of the vassal to his feudal superior. As a gesture of prayer
this attitude of obedience presupposes that the ability to obey
is something that is given, and thus presupposes also having
received God's grace as this is expressed by stretching out the
arms.

Recently the gesture has been adopted among prayer
groups of stretching the arms out in front of the body with
the palms of the hands turned upwards while keeping the
elbows in to the sides. This too shows that we receive
everything from God.

Second day: God, you know me and have searched me

The suggestions for prayer in this third week are meant to
lead to a renewal of your baptismal promises, to an answer
to the question: 'Do you renounce Satan?' or, to put it
another way: 'Do you renounce your lack of trust in God?'
So in this week try to look into yourself and to recognize
the roots of your lack of trust in God and your suspicion
of him. God, who created you, is the Lord of the personal
history of your life. He knows your antecedents, he knows
the situations and circumstances that separate you from him
without any personal guilt on your part. It might be an
idea to take a little more than each day this week end

to pray Psalm 139 daily:

> O Lord, thou hast searched me and known me!
> Thou knowest when I sit down and when I rise up;
> thou discernest my thoughts from afar.
> Thou searchest out my path and my lying down,
> and art acquainted with all my ways.
> Even before a word is on my tongue,
> lo, O Lord, thou knowest it altogether.
> Thou dost beset me behind and before,
> and layest thy hand upon me . . .
> For thou didst form my inward parts,
> thou didst knit me together in my mother's womb.
> I praise thee, for thou art fearful and wonderful.
> Wonderful are thy works!
> Thou knowest me right well;
> my frame was not hidden from thee,
> when I was being made in secret,
> intricately wrought in the depths of the earth.
> Thy eyes beheld my unformed substance;
> in thy book were written, every one of them,
> the days that were formed for me,
> when as yet there was none of them . . .
> Search me, O God, and know my heart!
> Try me and know my thoughts! . . .

What could be a great help is if you were to write down all the negative experiences you remember: with your parents and your brothers and sisters, at school, at work, in your marriage or in whatever state of life you are in. Do you remember being disappointed, your confidence being abused, being slighted, being treated unjustly? Maybe you have had negative experiences with the Church too. Maybe you are indignant that it should range itself with the wealthy and the powerful. Maybe you would like to establish a new relationship with God as long as this did not involve the institutional Church, with which you do not want ever to have anything to do again. Write down all your painful memories and disappointments in the order in which they occur to you.

1 . . . .   2 . . . .
3 . . . .   4 . . . .

We ask God to give us strength and the confidence to bring these negative experiences before him at the end of this week.

Third day: You live in enmity with God

There are awkward and unpleasant reasons for living apart from God. There are the positive allurements we spoke of during the second week, the many aspects of our modern civilization that can exert a fascination upon us, being in thrall to other people, etc. But most of those who live apart from God are separated from him because of negative experiences which they have had, which they themselves are not responsible for but which they cannot reverse or alter. As far as their will is concerned they would like to love God. because basically they are convinced that everything did not come into being by chance and that there must therefore be a God, but the negative experiences of their life have taken root in the depths of their being and impel them towards enmity with God. When Paul uses the word 'flesh' he often means the whole human being insofar as he or she has turned away from God: 'For the mind that is set on the flesh is hostile to God . . . But you are not in the flesh, you are in the Spirit, if the Spirit of God really dwells in you. Any one who does not have the Spirit of Christ does not belong to him' (Rom. 8:7-9). It is only the Spirit of God himself, the Holy Spirit, the Spirit of Christ, who can liberate us from the enmity towards God that lives in the depths of our unconscious.

Paul, who had been brought up in a very strict rabbinical tradition, saw the main origin of his enmity towards God in the manifold commandments that were continually provoking him to transgress them. In our present-day civilization it is less religious laws and commandments that separate us from God than rather the entire situation of our life, the 'sin of the world' of which John speaks, the fact that a whole civilization has inwardly turned away from God; and this is something that has affected all Christians. The following passage expresses very clearly the way in which enmity towards God has its roots not only in my own will but in attitudes or situations and circumstances that have their origins outside me and that I am influenced by (Rom. 7: 15-25):

> I do not understand my own actions. For I do not do what I want, but I do the very thing I hate. Now if I do what I do not want, I agree that the law is good. So then it is no longer I that do it, but sin which dwells within me. For I know that nothing good dwells within me, that is, in my flesh. I can will what is right, but I cannot do it. For I do not do the good I want, but the evil I do not want is what I do. Now if I do what I do not want, it is no longer I that do it, but sin which dwells within me.
>
> So I find it to be a law that when I want to do right, evil lies close at hand. For I delight in the law of God, in my inmost self, but I see in my members another law at war with the law of my mind and making me captive to the law of sin which dwells in my members. Wretched man that I am! Who will deliver me from this body of death? Thanks be to God through Jesus Christ our Lord!

The negative experiences you wrote down yesterday lead you astray into adopting attitudes and doing things that basically you do not want to adopt or do and that silently and almost imperceptibly separate you from God. Let yourself be reconciled to God (cf. 2 Cor. 5:20).

Fourth day: God wants to heal us through the power of the Spirit of Jesus Christ

In the New Testament there are certain key passages that in a particularly penetrating way introduce us to the basic

Christian experience. Among them is the story of the healing of the deaf man with a speech impediment (Mark 7:31-37). This passage has since time immemorial found its place in the rite of baptism, when before (or after) being baptized the neophyte is addressed with the words: 'Ephphatha, be opened!' If we read the following passage as God's personal message to us and accept it as such, then it is at the same time a renewal of what happens at baptism. Then what was offered you was the opening of your ears and your mouth, of your entire person. The deaf-mute about whom we read is thus not just some unfortunate who was living in Palestine nearly two thousand years ago. The deaf-mute is we ourselves. Because of our inward hostility and the pattern of our life up till now we have become deaf to God's call and have lost the speech wherewith to praise and extol him with our whole heart. What Jesus did then to the deaf-mute he wishes to do to each one of us each time we read this passage. He takes you on one side, apart from the crowd, he singles you out and wants to liberate you for a new life. It is now, at this precise moment, that he wants to make a new start. He approaches you personally and it is to you that he speaks the word of salvation: 'Be opened!' (Mark 7:32-37):

> And they brought to him a man who was deaf and had an impediment in his speech; and they besought him to lay his hand upon him. And taking him aside from the multitude privately, he put his fingers into his ears, and he spat and touched his tongue; and looking up to heaven, he sighed, and said to him, 'Ephphatha,' that is, 'Be opened.' And his ears were opened, his tongue was released, and he spoke plainly. And he charged them to tell no one; but the more he charged them, the more zealously they proclaimed it. And they were astonished beyond measure, saying, 'He has done all things well; he makes even the deaf hear and the dumb speak.'

Notice first of all that it is other people who bring the deaf-mute to Jesus. We too cannot from our own resources ask Jesus for something; it is others who must lead us to him. Others share responsibility for the fact that we live in an environment in which we cannot really open ourselves up to God. Sin and enmity towards God have a social character: they are not only something rooted in our own will, though they are of course that too. Similarly the experience of God's healing and saving presence is also something mediated by others. The experience of God too has a social character, and it is already a great grace when we find other people who lead us to God. Nobody believes in isolation, and it is only within the community of believers that originally one becomes a Christian. So seek out the company of those who have become aware of God's call to them to let themselves be awakened to a new life. We are so speechless and inarticulate that we cannot even articulate our desire for salvation ourselves. We have neither the confidence nor the courage to regard our salvation as possible; at the deepest level we are inhibited and enslaved by our negative experiences — or by our positive ones too. Other people will lead you to Jesus. God has entrusted the whole Church with the ministry of reconciliation, and it is others who will say to you 'on behalf of Christ': 'Be reconciled to God' (2 Cor. 5:20). This is not something you can say to yourself. It is not simply by sinking into yourself by means of techniques of meditation that you will find God. Salvation and healing come instead through the message of revelation, and this again is something that must be brought to you by others.

In that episode Jesus was asked to lay his hands on the deaf-mute. The laying on of hands is in the Bible an ambiguous gesture. It can signify taking possession, blessing, handing over an office, and also healing. We men and women are bodily beings and so give bodily form to inward events. Similarly it is always in bodily form that God deals with us, through outward and visible signs that others do to us, Christianity is never purely inward and spiritual but is accomplished in outward and visible signs. This becomes even clearer when we remark that Jesus put his fingers in the deaf-mute's ears and put spittle on his tongue. Why did he not heal him by means of a purely internal act of the will? Why did he approach him in such a physical and bodily way, going so far as to touch him and to make physical contact? Not in order to transmit some magic power, not even perhaps on account of some medicinal property of spittle, but because he wanted to demonstrate his personal closeness to him and to express his solidarity with him. If you understand this passage as God's word to you, Jesus approaches you personally, in the power of his Spirit whom he has bequeathed to us. Do not be afraid of statements like this. He has promised us his presence throughout the ages, and this is something quite real and concrete if we are ready to open ourselves to it. But are we ready to do so? Clearly the deaf-mute was not, since Jesus had to tell him: 'Be opened.' This summons applied not just to his organs, to his ears or his tongue, but to his whole person. Clearly, though he could not yet hear, the deaf-mute understood and accepted this summons.

This healing is not something that Jesus accomplishes purely from his own resources. He turns to his Father and prays. The word 'sigh' always means in the New Testament a prayer coming from the depths of one's being. Perhaps at this moment he addresses his Father in the form that has been handed down to us in his Aramaic mother-tongue: 'Abba, Father.' Now too Jesus prays for you and turns to you: 'For God's sake I tell you, Be opened. You need not be thrown to the dogs in your shut-in isolation, in your hostility from which you cannot liberate yourself. I offer you my healing and salvation. I wish to gather a new people for myself, I wish to renew my Church, and I would like to start with you. I want to set the world free, I want to change each individual man and woman, including you. I want to take the Godlessness out of your heart, and you will be astonished at the gifts I have ready for you. Be opened! My holy and healing Spirit is already within you. You need only take the one tiny step towards me that only you can take because you are free, you need only overcome your suspicion of God in the power of this Spirit of mine. Decide now and do not wait any longer. Recognize the anguish you are in and surrender it to me and I will heal it.'

How will you answer? Are you ready really to let yourself go? Or are you afraid of having to surrender a bit of yourself if you surrender your fear of God? Perhaps your fear of God and your suspicion of him, your lack of trust in him, is just an excuse not to have to have anything to do with him, and so you hang on to it. You use your suspicion and lack of trust as a weapon because you are perhaps afraid of the consequences — consequences that would be painful because, if you open the door to God, there are perhaps other doors that you must shut. Remaining completely shut off and isolated is something no one can keep up for long, and every man or woman is open to some external influence, to other people or to a future he or she plans for himself or herself. Just shut all the doors that you have made for yourself to lead out from your isolation, and open that door where Jesus is standing and knocking: 'So be zealous and repent. Behold, I stand at the door and knock; if any one hears my voice and opens the door, I will come in to him and eat with him, and he with me' (Rev. 3:19-20). This is the first of all the consequences if you open the door: he will eat with you and you with him. He will give you food that includes a promise of indestructible life: he will give himself to you.

After the deaf-mute had been healed people were beside themselves with astonishment: 'He has done all things well.' You too will be astonished beyond measure, you will be taken out of yourself by the power of him who has healed you. God himself brings about the reparation that no other man or woman can give you. It is not that he will simply expunge your past and the offences of your past life, but he will transform them, and you will be able to affirm with Paul: 'In everything God works for good with those who love him' (Rom. 8:28).

Fifth day: Repent and break off your false ties

Nobody can live without personal ties and links, and anyone who is suspicious and fearful of God ties himself the more closely to this personality or that or to power, possessions, wealth. The promise of security to be found in these ties prevents thoroughgoing healing and stops the kingdom of God on earth from breaking through. So Jesus calls for repentance, conversion, *metanoia*. But this at the same time is a breaking away from false, exaggerated ties. It is only when we have burned all our bridges, when no escape route still remains open for us, when it is only in the word of Jesus that we trust, that we are healed and saved and thereby made capable of bearing witness to others of the good news. In the passage that in the synoptic gospels follows immediately after the exhortation to have a childlike trust in God (cf. Mark 10:17-27) a wealthy man is challenged to sell all he has and follow Jesus. In reading this well-known passage what is often overlooked is that Jesus looked at him. Mark indeed says: 'And Jesus looking upon him loved him' (Mark 10:21). Christian repentance is not a question just of contempt for the world. It is something that takes place within a personal relationship to Jesus. It is not an act of the will that I make from my own resources that makes me capable of abandoning everything, but love for Jesus in the power of his Spirit. Jesus himself gives the power to follow him to those whom he calls on to do so. But it is not only wealth and riches that make turning to Jesus in repentance difficult but every tie, bond, link that is carried too far, as this passage goes on to make clear (Mark 10:28-30):

> Peter began to say to him, 'Lo, we have left everything and followed you.' Jesus said, 'Truly, I say to you, there is no one who has left house or brothers or sisters or mother or father or children or lands, for my sake and for the gospel, who will not receive a hundredfold now in this time, houses and brothers and sisters and mothers and children and lands, with persecutions, and in the age to come eternal life.'

The passage is clear and does not admit of any compromise. With the innocent and total confidence of a child we must first of all burn all our bridges behind us for the sake of God and the gospel. That does not by any means imply that you are now freed from all obligations that you have towards your parents, your brothers and sisters, your children or to whatever property you may own. On the contrary: it can be that your decision for Christ and your conversion to him demands of you a strengthened commitment and involvement on behalf of your parents, your brothers and sisters, your children, a strengthened social and political commitment and involvement with the liberation of the world as its aim (which would entail your placing your 'houses' and your 'lands' at the service of this liberation). It is not everyone who is called to live as a monk in poverty and chastity. But what you are called on to give up are the excessive ties that bind you, and when you do this these ties are then transformed and healed: you will get back houses, brothers, sisters, mothers, children and lands — that is to say, all your relationships will be radically healed if with deep-rooted trust and confidence you turn to God. God himself is for us father and mother and wealth, he himself gives us his recognition and approval.

A conversion of this kind does not remain unchallenged, both inwardly and outwardly. If we bear witness to our new relationship to God, to the people close to us and to the world in general, then this claim of ours evokes contradiction and disagreement. But inward challenges are not lacking either. Many people are today awakened to a new life in the Spirit but are afraid of the consequences. 'I would have to change my life radically overnight,' they think. But there is a satanic element lurking in this consideration: 'If you turn to Jesus then you must be completely consistent, you must leave your wife and children in the lurch, you must live in real poverty, because otherwise it is all sham and hypocrisy. So keep well away and stay as you are.' The power of evil always knows how to step up the good we are aiming at to such a pitch of exaggeration that it serves to separate us even further from God. In this perspective of excess we cling on to ourselves out of sheer fear that we just cannot live up to the standard demanded of us. For fear of this fear we avoid any decision and any consequences. But leaving everything means in the first place abandoning oneself. When you are no longer tied to yourself in fear you can give up the many other ties that separate you from God.

Sixth and seventh days: Prayer for the healing of memories and hopes (renewal of baptismal promises)

The sacraments are and remain invitations, opportunities.

In baptism God offered us the opportunity of freeing us from our ancestral and social suspicion of him that has its origin in other people's sins and in our own tendency to sin. But God does not free us without effort on our part. In the power of his Holy Spirit we must entrust our suspicion to him in surrendering the whole of our life's history to him: 'My God, I reject my suspicion of you.' Every human being has negative experiences, painful memories, unfulfilled wishes which he has suppressed in the depths of his unconscious life. There they as it were lead an autonomous existence and continually come up to the surface as warnings against God. In addition they often lead to physical malaise, emotional over-excitement, depression, and feelings of isolation. If we offer God the depths of our soul and open them up to him, healing strength will not only lead us back to him but also make us physically healthier and heal our relationships with other people.

The effect on someone of the remarks and prayers that follow can be to make him or her very uneasy. Problems can come to the surface that he himself or she herself is not capable of dealing with. In this case he or she should entrust himself or herself to someone with suitable skills and experience in psychological medicine. What follows is not a substitute for psychotherapy. It will also expound before God on problems and questions that do not effect everyone personally. In bringing these to God bear in mind people known to you, not in a spirit of pride and superiority, but in order to be able to understand and love them better. It is helpful to make this prayer together with others and to help each other mutually to recognize hidden points of opposition or resistance to God. In this way God has often in an astonishing way healed and set in order the fundamental relationships between parents and children, between married couples and brothers and sisters, and not only these primary relationships but also relationships in the world of labour and between friends and neighbours.

It is best if you choose a time when you are relaxed and at ease and a place which you find really peaceful. Your posture should be comfortable, composed, relaxed. Approach your creator in humility and trust. The longer you pray, the more will your inhibitions fall away before God.

'My Lord and my God, my origin and my goal: you are the Lord of history and the lord too of the history of my life. You were present with your creative power when my parents came together and later when I grew in my mother's womb. It is you I have to thank for my existence, and I thank you too for giving my whole existence back to you now in this present moment in the freedom of that trust that you yourself have given to me. For myself my memories cannot reach back to the original beginning of my existence, but 'your eyes beheld my unformed substance' (Psalm 139:16). You know all the circumstances in the life of my parents, of my mother, that still weigh me down today and prevent me from discovering you and discovering myself fully. I did not will myself, I did not develop my character and my talents myself. I do not understand why there should be suffering right from birth, but I have trust in you. With your loving care you have accompanied me and all men and women throughout our lives. Your son took all my, all our disappointment and despair on himself and suffered them through to the bitter end. I thank you for being ready to heal me in the power of his suffering and for beginning now in this present moment.

'I may know nothing more about my birth and also about the first year of my life. But this I do know today that my mother, or whoever took her place, was for me a paradise of trust and security. Perhaps it was then already that suspicion, anxiety, enmity began for me. Perhaps my then as yet unawakened spirit store up disappointment and disillusion in its depths . . .'

Make the effort to remember all you can of your childhood. What was your mother's attitude to you? Did you need more mother-love than you got, so that today you are still driven by a hunger for recognition? Or did you grow up in an atmosphere of excessive care and love so that today you make excessive demands of the people around you? And what was your attitude to your father? Did you perhaps need more fatherly love in the whole of your life as a child to give you stability and self-confidence, a strong love such as can come only from a father? You cannot of course go back and re-write your personal history, but God himself was already and always father and mother to you, and his wish is to be so now anew. You must really leave your father and mother, your brothers and sisters, your children, in order to regain them afresh in God. Go over the following 'words of life' in your mind according to the circumstances you are in. God's spirit will put your answer into your heart (Isaiah 45:9-12; 49:15-16; 66:13; Psalm 103:13; 27:9-10):

> 'Woe to him who strives with his Maker,
> an earthen vessel with the potter!
> Does the clay say to him who fashions it, "What are you making?"
> or "Your work has no handles?"
> Woe to him who says to a father, "What are you begetting?"
> or to a woman, "With what are you in travail?"

> Thus says the Lord, the Holy One of Israel, and his Maker:
> 'Will you question me about my children,
> or command me concerning the work of my hands?
> I made the earth, and created man upon it.'

> 'Can a woman forget her sucking child,
> that she should have no compassion on the son of her womb?
> Even these may forget,
> yet I will not forget you.
> Behold, I have graven you on the palms of my hands.'

> 'As one whom his mother comforts,
> so I will comfort you.'

> As a father pities his children,
> so the Lord pities those who fear him.

> Cast me not off, forsake me not,
> O God of my salvation!
> For my father and my mother have forsaken me,
> but the Lord will take me up.

Give your childhood back to this God who is both father and mother to you. He will heal it: 'My Lord and my God, you alone are perfect, you alone are perfect, selfless love. Let me experience ever more deeply the fact that I am your child, that in my uniqueness I am important to you, that you give me your support and approval. Heal my innermost impulses and efforts of all kind of excess. Let me experience your loving closeness whenever I have been too little loved or praised or recognized. But if as a child I already experienced excessive praise and false appreciation then take away from me all false security, all excessive self-confidence and every kind of anxiety for myself.'

Ask God also to heal all the wounds and injuries that have survived from your relationship to your brothers and sisters. Perhaps your brother or your sister was given preference over you. Perhaps you never really loved your brother or your sister:

'In thinking of them let me be ready at the profoundest level to be reconciled with them, and the next time I meet them may your forgiving selfless love be present among us. Settle everything that stands between us. Already I thank you, God of my life, for the fact that you can put all this in order and will do so.'

For many of us it is when we first went to school that the burdensome experiences and inward wounds began: strange grown-ups to teach us, strange children as our fellow-pupils, the compulsion of having to be there and having to learn, envy, failure. Try to remember what your school-days were like. Some belonged to those who were top of the class, and this aroused excessive expectations in them with regard to the rest of their life. They were successful right from the start, became aware of themselves, enjoyed being powerful and strong. They hardly learned how to understand others, and they trust only their own resources. If your surroundings, your parents and your teachers bred such attitudes in you, bring them before God. For others it was then that life started being a burden. They were unjustly treated by the teaching staff, they were slighted, seldom were they praised.

Perhaps other children mocked you on account of some peculiarity. You began withdrawing into yourself, becoming

anxious. Perhaps the ability to express yourself and communicate yourself to others was never aroused in you. Your
self-confidence was never able to develop, and now, as an
adult, you have your revenge by a lack of consideration for
other people and by oppressing them. Bring all this now in
personal prayer before your God and pray him that a society
may arise in which children grow up without being oppressed
and at the same time without a false lack of ties and
obligations.

Then came adolescence, the first profound enthusiasms and
obsessions, the first personal disappointments. What view of
life was dominant in the world you lived in? Ambition?
Submissiveness? Excessive desire for wealth? What expectations were aroused in you or suppressed in you? Were your
first sexual experiences such as to leave wounds that even
today have not yet been healed? Call it all back into your
memory, peacefully and in a relaxed manner, remembering
all the details and circumstances and with thanks for God's
presence and his ever greater love. He is the Lord of the history
of your life.

'I ask you, my God, to heal all those experiences I had as
an adolescent. For the first time my enthusiasm was really
aroused, I became fascinated by other people, and I grew
into a society in which my heart could never fully awaken
to you. The sinfulness of the world surrounded me and left
its deep imprint on me, an imprint that has persisted until
this moment. Give me the ability to distance myself from all
this, so that I may be able to fulfil my duties in society and
in my job in your power and with you as my starting point.

'I ask you for forgiveness for the disappointments and
injuries I have inflicted on others. Heal the wounds that the
first abuse of my trust and confidence has left in me, the
wounds caused by the first lasting experience of evil that
still continues to make me suspicious of you. Heal too all my
shattered hopes, my expectations that were pitched too high,
that my memory has stored up from this period of my life.
Transform all these experiences and let me recall them without
sorrow, shame and suppressed anger. On the cross your son
did not annul all the destruction and evil in history but
instead transformed it. Your grace is always greater still than

the sins and the sinfulness of the world, however great they may be. Reconcile me with you, with myself and with my fellow-men.'

How have things gone with you in your career? Perhaps you have not progressed as far or as fast as you would have liked. This led to envy, hatred, and fresh feelings of hostility in a pitilessly competitive society where people are measured by what they have done. You looked for security, built up a livelihood, but perhaps to an excessive extent you looked for security in yourself, in your success, in what you own and how well off you are:

'Heal me, Lord, from an excessive need for private security so that I may become more capable not only of working for my private advantage but of seeing my work as a service to others and to society, as a gift of your grace. Heal the wounds that groups within society inflict on each other, heal the remembrance of mutual oppression in the world of labour, and let me contribute to the social changes that are needed being sought not out of hatred but because you are the lord of history.'

Perhaps the ground for your separation from God lies yet further back, not in your own life but in the preceding history of the society in which you must live. If you belong to those whose forebears were exploited during the initial stages of industrial society, or if you live in a country where social justice has hardly yet begun to be implemented, then bring these painful awarenesses too before God. The Church of every age is measured according to Jesus's standard to see whether it has shown its solidarity with the poor and the humble and actually fought for them. Do not let yourself be separated from God by the guilt of the Churches, and be reconciled with your Church — without depriving it of the stimulus of your criticism. It is only in the community of believers that you can find your way to God, and this applies even when that community has become unfaithful to the message of Jesus. Forgive your Church for what it has done to your forebears and you. In that way you will contribute to its rediscovery, in the commemoration of what Jesus said and did, of its liberating power in a society dominated by the wealthy and the powerful.

The liberating power of reconciliation can and must also have its effect in your personal life. If you are married, call to mind now the history of your marriage, all the disappointments, injuries, examples of lack of consideration, wounds that you have inflicted on each other, and ask God to heal it radically, from the roots upwards, from the beginning. Accept your partner in God's sight just as he or she is. You cannot bring about any fundamental changes in his or her character and gifts. Ask God too to heal your expectations. Do not expect of your partner anything he or she cannot give you. God has already healed many marriages, and he can start now, at this moment, to put your marriage too in order.

If you are single, widowed or divorced, then give the history of your life back to God in confidence. Perhaps you had other plans for yourself, did not personally choose this way of life, experience it as harsh necessity, as the oppression of your possibilities of development. God has a plan for you, and he will give you things to do not as a substitute for something you would have liked for yourself but because he needs you in order to remain present in his Church and in his world. He wishes to heal you at the root of your existence, at the point where you have been most hurt.

If you are a member of a religious order or congregation, then perhaps it is precisely as such that you have had experiences that do not lead you to God. Perhaps your expectations of the religious life were disappointed, and now you are resigned and apathetic. Let God infuse you again with the warmth of his love. Go back to the first realization of your vocation and let every doubt be taken away from you by God himself that he had called you to this way of life. God's love is greater than your heart. Today, in this age when a renewal and a re-awakening is taking place, God sends his life-giving Spirit to abbeys and convents and religious houses too. He is calling new communities of prayer into being and bringing to life again the spiritual experiences of the primitive Church. Renew your religious vows and ask God now for the courage publicly to bring your life and death to God. Lord, renew your Church and in renewing it begin with me. I glorify you that you will do it,

I worship you.

If you are among the Church's ministers, you need healing to a particular extent. Perhaps awareness of the apparent futility of your work has turned you into a bureaucratic executive, perhaps you suppress your feelings of disappointment and disillusion by exercising domination and power — an exercise which does not come from God but is instead a compensation for your feelings of worthlessness, an independent act of self-assertion. Your own disillusion leads other people, especially if you are their superior, to ever greater disillusion, and they break away from you and from the Church. You are irritated by the multiplicity of institutions in your Church or you are grieved by the divisions and the hostility to be found within it. You have more confidence in your own efforts and strategies than in the working of the Holy Spirit. A Catholic bishop once bore public witness at a service of penance in these terms: 'Formerly I was king in my diocese. After I had asked others to lay hands on me in what was for me a renewal of the sacrament of ordination, it is only with shame that I can look back at that time.'

Hence I remind you to rekindle the gift of God that is within you through the laying on of my hands; for God did not give us a spirit of timidity but a spirit of power and love and self-control.

Do not be ashamed of testifying to our Lord, nor of me his prisoner, but take your share of suffering for the gospel in the power of God, who saved us and called us with a holy calling, not in virtue of our works but in virtue of his own purpose and the grace which he gave us in Christ Jesus ages ago (2 Tim. 1:6-9).

Give yourself some time and let the Holy Spirit get to work within you. He is alive and at work in the depths of your being, he who alone searches the depths of God (1 Cor. 2:10): he wants to liberate your depths and your dark places:

Heal our wounds; our strength renew;
On our dryness pour Thy dew;
    Wash the stains of guilt away:
Bend the stubborn heart and will;

Melt the frozen, warm the chill;
Guide the steps that go astray.

If you are a Catholic, then bring your personal sins before God in the sacrament of penance, in the celebration of reconciliation. If your Church offers you the opportunity of personal confession and the pronouncing of a formula of absolution, then follow the practice of your Church. Let yourself be reconciled with God as far as your personal sins are concerned (Cf. the fourth section of the third week in the first part of this work, on confession and penance).

Fourth week: Jesus Christ

First day: How did Jesus pray?

Our aim is to begin each week by making some reflections on prayer. In the talk in the study group for this fourth week it has already been shown that Jesus did not only pray to his Father when he was alone and apart from everybody else but that he also prayed publicly and as a form of witness before others. One of these prayers runs (Luke 10:21-22; Matt. 11:25-27):

> I thank thee, Father, Lord of heaven and earth, that thou hast hidden these things from the wise and understanding and revealed them to babes; yea, Father, for such was thy gracious will. All things have been delivered to me by my Father; and no one knows who the Son is except the Father, or who the Father is except the Son and any one to whom the Son chooses to reveal him.

From the Greek original it can be deduced that here Jesus was using that form of address that distinguished his personal relationship to God: Abba. As was shown in the study-group talk for this fourth week, this form of address was a complete novelty for Jesus's contemporaries, since it came from the trustful language of childhood. Jesus therefore did not hesitate to express his most personal relationship to God in front of others. This prayer is to be found in the oldest sources of all and is undoubtedly not the composition of the primitive Christian community. Here in the form of prayer Jesus reveals that he alone really knows God and has experienced him in a way that is completely unique. At the same time he shows us that we can only imitate him in this experience if we open ourselves up to God with the complete and innocent confidence of a child. Growing up and education have made us know much too much about God, and in his presence we are too grown up. Jesus's example induces and encourages us to praise and glorify God before others quite simply and personally in imitation of him and in the power of his Spirit.

Nor does Jesus hesitate to express his fear of death in prayer in front of others. On the Mount of Olives he allows Peter, James and John to share in his profoundest surrender of himself to the will of God and exhorts them to pray with him. We read in Mark (Mark 14:35-36; Matt. 26:39; Luke 22:42):

> And going a little farther, he fell on the ground and prayed that, if it were possible, the hour might pass from him. And he said, 'Abba, Father, all things are possible to thee; remove this cup from me; yet not what I will, but what thou wilt.'

What community would be capable of inventing a situation like this? The evangelists stress that the three disciples witnessed Jesus's fear of death, his trembling before the holy majesty of God — he 'withdrew from them about a stone's throw' (Luke 22:41) — even if he also at this moment encountered the Father in the profoundest personal isolation. But Jesus does not hug this encounter to himself as his own personal secret but instead makes it public in prayer, just as at his baptism (cf. Luke 3:21-22).

It is above all in the seventeenth chapter of his gospel that John makes us appreciate how before his death Jesus prayed in the presence of his disciples. Let us read a few sentences (John 17:17-19):

> 'Sanctify them in the truth; thy word is truth. As thou didst send me into the world, so I have sent them into the world. And for their sake I consecrate myself, that they also may be consecrated in truth.'

The entire seventeenth chapter of John's gospel is a speech of revelation in the presence of the disciples. Here Jesus expresses in verbal witness what is most personal of all, his self-abandonment to the Father, so as to strengthen the disciples' faith. For Jesus his relationship to the Father and his death are not a private affair that does not concern anyone else. Even on the cross, according to the accounts in Matthew and Mark, Jesus prayed 'with a loud voice' (Matt. 27:46; Mark 15:34).

It is now obvious that for the most part we, unlike Jesus, are not used to expressing our personal relationship to God in a personal way in the presence of other people and together with other people. For several hundred years it has been accepted that religion is a private affair. Your beliefs do not concern anyone else. Indeed, it isn't done to show publicly your personal relationship to God. Entire schools of philosophy have taught that you can only know God with your intellect and that your religious feelings are not capable of demonstrating anything in the slightest. So, the argument ran, keep them to yourself and stick to the teaching of the great philosophers who have attempted to know God. You yourself cannot know God nor even experience him: all you can do is fulfil your duty as a citizen. In this way a regular taboo was established, prohibitions were expressed, frontiers were set.

Anyone can easily confirm this if in a group of Christian believers he or she puts the question: 'How do you personally stand with regard to God?' The response will be an awkward silence. Even among priests and ministers it is not taken for granted that one can speak about one's personal relationship to God and about one's doubts, or that people should join together in personal prayer. If on the other hand one were to begin a conversation on sexual questions among the same group of Christian believers one would have started up a lively discussion which included some extremely personal revelations. The last few decades have seen the breaking of a taboo that is likewise very old and goes back to the time of the Fathers of the Church. We Christians are not completely fortunate about the way it has been broken — at an overwhelmingly biological level — but this example certainly shows what a taboo is in general.

It must emphatically be stressed that, if in society, in public life, and even within the community of the Church one has to hide one's personal relationship to God, then something is wrong. The Sermon on the Mount does indeed tell us: 'But when you pray, go into your room and shut the door and pray to your Father who is in secret' (Matt. 6:6). But that was said as against the hypocrites who loved to stand and pray at the street corners 'that they may be seen by men' (Matt. 6:5) and who were fond of 'practising their piety before men' (Matt. 6:1). They wanted to be praised by men for being so good at praying. But this is the death of genuine prayer.

Read through the whole of the seventeenth chapter of John's gospel once again and ask yourself if you would be ready to bear witness before others in a similar personal way. Someone once said that it was like coming across a very hard nut and being afraid of discovering on cracking it that it was hollow. This is a feeling everybody has to begin with. Trust that God himself will crack the nut and fill its hollow kernel with his Holy Spirit, with his power. Perhaps you were ashamed the first time you tried to talk out loud and personally to God. You will undergo a similar experience the first time you pray in this way with others and in front of them or when you talk openly about your doubts and struggles in front of others — which too is a way of bearing witness. The Lord of the Church himself will take all your shame and anxiety away, and to your great surprise you will discover joy in bearing witness to God.

Second day: He who confesses with his lips

Throughout his entire life Jesus bore witness to God through what he said and what he did. What he expects of us is that we should bear witness to him by imitating him. This involves our entire life and everything we do and say, by means of practical help, by means of co-operation in bringing about the changes that are needed in society, by means of involvement in society. All these different forms of witness share the character of proclaiming and announcing God. Hence the original, basic form of witness is the verbal profession of faith. Note that speaking with one's lips is mentioned three times in the passage that follows (Rom. 10:8-10):

The word is near you, on your lips and in your heart
(that is, the word of faith which we preach); because,
if you confess with your lips that Jesus is Lord and
believe in your heart that God raised him from the dead,
you will be saved. For man believes with his heart and
so is justified, and he confesses with his lips and so is
saved.

At services of prayer in the first Christian communities such
confessions of faith were made by individuals (cf. 1 Cor. 12:3).
When for the first time at a prayer meeting we personally in
this kind of way confess our belief in Jesus as the Lord who
has truly risen we realize that this leads to a growth in our
own faith. It becomes concrete, almost tangible. There is in
reality a great difference between thinking silently 'Jesus is
Lord' and saying this out loud in front of others as a confession of faith. And there is a further distinction between
praying such a creed together with others as one voice in a
chorus and expressing this confession of faith in Jesus as a
completely personal avowal in front of others. From every
individual Jesus expects this completely personal witness
in the world of work, in the family, among the people we live
with (Luke 12:8-9):

And I tell you, every one who acknowledges me before
men, the Son of man also will acknowledge before the
angels of God; but he who denies me before men will be
denied before the angels of God.

What a challenge this is to live and to act in a way in keeping
with our witness for Christ!

Third day: The renewal of the Spirit makes us capable of bearing witness

The Holy Spirit was present in the man Jesus of Nazareth
right from the first moment of his life, but this was only in
the full sense manifest after his baptism by the Spirit.

Similarly God's goodness accompanies us right from the first moment of our existence, and when we were baptized as babies God gave us the effective and true promise that he wanted to confer the entire fulness of his Spirit upon us. In nearly every Church the sign of this promise of God's is the laying of hands on the person baptized. But God's offer is only effective in us to the extent that we accept it personally. Hence the person being baptized is asked publicly in church if he or she acknowledges Christ and renounces Satan. This personal acknowledgment of Christ in public in the Church is something that in the course of our life we must let God continually bestow on us afresh. If in this context those present lay their hands on us, then this is not a second baptism but the renewal of what in our original baptism God had already done to us. Even if we should be or have been baptized as adults, the renewal of the baptismal promises belongs to the essence of baptism itself. The following passage applied to someone whose ministry it was to preside over the community, but is similarly applies to all who were baptized as infants (2 Tim. 1:6-9):

> Hence I remind you to rekindle the gift of God that is within you through the laying on of my hands; for God did not give us a spirit of timidity but a spirit of power and love and self-control.
> Do not be ashamed then of testifying to our Lord, nor of me his prisoner, but take your share of suffering for the gospel in the power of God, who saved us and called us with a holy calling, not in virtue of our works but in virtue of his own purpose and the grace which he gave us in Christ Jesus ages ago.

Ask yourself now whether God has, perhaps over the last few weeks, led you to the point where you can be ready to complete or repeat your baptismal promises before others. God has called each one of us with a holy calling and wishes to liberate you too to bear witness to him. If you are ready to take this step, it is not in virtue of your own services, since before you can personally decide for Christ God has always taken the first step. It is his decision and his tongue that make possible your decision and your surrender to him.

Fourth day: Jesus himself baptizes us with his Holy Spirit

When Jesus let himself be baptized by John in the Jordan the visible and public history of the Christian Church began. At Pentecost Jesus for his part poured out on the disciples gathered for prayer his Holy Spirit, and with that began the Church's missionary expansion. In his sermon at Pentecost Peter said (Acts 2:32-33, 36-38):

> 'This Jesus God raised up, and of that we are all witnesses; Being therefore exalted at the right hand of God, and having received from the Father the promise of the Holy Spirit, he has poured out this which you see and hear . . . Let all the house of Israel therefore know assuredly that God has made him both Lord and Christ, this Jesus whom you crucified.'
>
> Now when they heard this they were cut to the heart, and said to Peter and the rest of the apostles, 'Brethren, what shall we do?' And Peter said to them, 'Repent, and be baptized every one of you in the name of Jesus Christ for the forgiveness of your sins; and you shall receive the gift of the Holy Spirit.'

Being liberated to bear witness for Jesus was not for the disciples a once-and-for-all event. After the first persecution a renewal of the experience of Pentecost was bestowed on them (Acts 4:31):

> And when they had prayed, the place in which they were gathered together was shaken; and they were all filled with the Holy Spirit and spoke the word of God with boldness.

Jesus himself baptized his disciples with his Holy Spirit and made them capable of bearing witness. This does not exclude but rather includes the continuation of what happened at

Pentecost being mediated by the apostles' preaching (cf. Acts 10:44-48) and by their laying on of hands (Acts 8:14-18, 19:6). The Catholic view is that this laying on of hands by the apostles marks the beginning of the sacrament of confirmation. The German Protestant rite of confirmation is also normally linked with the laying on of hands and prayer for the descent of the Holy Spirit.

If during this course of study, perhaps after the sixth week, or at some later stage you go before the others and ask for the renewal of the Spirit, then two things happen. First, a renewal of your baptismal promises: 'I renounce Satan, I renounce suspicion of and lack of confidence in God. Lord, I surrender to you my entire life right from its start, together with everything that separates me from you. I surrender to you my intellect, my will, my emotions, my desires and my death. Help me to be able to die daily with you so that I may become your witness. Be the Lord of my life and transform me into the person you want me to be.' Second, an acceptance of the gifts of the Spirit: 'Lord, I am ready to accept all the gifts of the Spirit that you have promised me. Bestow on me the fullness of your Holy Spirit.'

During the sixth week we shall deal in greater detail with individual gifts of the Spirit. Their exercise, however, presupposes the personal step of surrender to the Lord of the Church, and hence it is only after this first stage of the renewal of the Spirit that many grow into the exercise of gifts of the Spirit that have already been bestowed on them. Many then pray specially for these gifts at the second or third renewal of the Spirit, which may take place weeks, months or years later. God's goodness is always impelling us to turn again and be converted, his Spirit is continually leading us ever more profoundly into the understanding and the exercise of the gifts of the Spirit.

So consider how far God's Spirit has led you so far, and discuss this with the other people taking part in the study-course. God's grace is greater than all our suspicion of him and our lack of trust in him. Has it not affected you in your heart already?

Fifth day: You must decide for Christ in the power of his Holy Spirit

Who would not shrink back from dying with Christ when even he was seized by fear and terror on the Mount of Olives (cf. Mark 14:33)? But anyone who wishes to imitate Jesus does not escape this decision (Matt. 12:30-32):

> He who is not with me is against me . . . Therefore I tell you, every sin and blasphemy will be forgiven men, but the blasphemy against the Spirit will not be forgiven . . . Whoever speaks against the Holy Spirit will not be forgiven, either in this age or in the age to come.

Jesus affirms of himself that everything he says and does does not originate in the powers of demons or have a purely psychological explanation and that in his power he casts out all resistance against God and all evil (cf. Matt. 12:28). Jesus has full power to overcome our resistance to God — that suspicion and lack of trust for which perhaps we ourselves are not really responsible and also our personal sins for which we are responsible before God. If you do not believe this, if you do not accept Jesus's offer, then you are sinning against the Holy Spirit. This sin cannot be forgiven because you yourself do not want it to be. God does not compel us. Instead through his Holy Spirit he wishes to awaken us to complete freedom, God has already taken the first step through his word, in the sacraments and through inner guidance. What Paul wrote thus applies to each one of us (Phil. 1:6, 9-10):

> And I am sure that he who began a good work in you will bring it to completion at the day of Jesus Christ . . . And it is my prayer that your love may abound more and more, with knowledge and all discernment, so that you may approve what is excellent.

Do not be afraid of the consequences of your decision. Your life will not change overnight, and in any case it is always a fruit of the Spirit. Love, joy, peace, kindness, self-control —

all these are the work of the Holy Spirit in you more than the result of your own efforts (Gal. 5:22). And of course the Holy Spirit is not at work within you without your involvement (cf. the fifth day of the third week).

Sixth day: And what if God keeps silent?

At his baptism with the Spirit Jesus experienced the presence of God. Following his prayer he 'saw' the Holy Spirit and 'heard' a voice (Luke 3:21-22). Similarly when they experience the renewal of the Spirit many are so profoundly affected by God that they exult with joy, that they experience a mighty power within them that is comparable to love between two people (cf. the third day of the second week). Others however do not feel anything at the moment of the renewal of the Spirit but experience only a vast inner emptiness within themselves. They stay silent and are perhaps even disappointed and disillusioned. At some time or other everyone is thrust into this inward emptiness and wilderness so that he or she does not cling too fiercely to his or her personal religious experiences and does not seek them and enjoy them for their own sake as it were. At his conversion Paul was told: 'I have appeared to you for this purpose, to appoint you to serve and bear witness to the things in which you have seen me and to those in which I will appear to you' (Acts 26:16). The experience of God's presence is something that is bestowed on us for the sake of witness and not for the sake of the experience itself. The baptism of the Spirit is therefore at the same time always also the baptism of death. Jesus used very clear language in preparing his disciples for this (Mark 10:37-40):

> And they [James and John, the sons of Zebedee] said to him, 'Grant us to sit, one at your right hand and one at your left, in your glory.' But Jesus said to them, 'You do not know what you are asking. Are you able to drink the cup that I drink, or to be baptized with the baptism with which I am baptized?' And they said to

him, 'We are able.' And Jesus said to them, 'The cup that I drink you will drink; and with the baptism with which I am baptized, you will be baptized; but to sit at my right hand or at my left is not mine to grant, but it is for those for whom it has been prepared.'

As Jesus's companions and disciples James and John had looked forward to the splendid experience of taking the places of honour at his side when he established his kingdom in the form in which it was always imagined. They looked for honour and power from following Jesus and expected a binding promise to this effect from Jesus himself. But he showed them that the way to glory led through the suffering of the baptism of death. As in the expression 'baptism of the Spirit', the word baptism is used here in a transferred sense. Its root meaning is of being inundated and at the same time cleansed. Hence anyone who follows Jesus will be inundated by suffering and buried in it, and at the same time this immersion has a cleansing power. It cleanses us from false, self-seeking, self-indulgent expectations.

Jesus experienced this baptism of death, this wilderness of inner emptiness, when he prayed on the Mount of Olives. There he did not see anything, did not hear any voice, but experienced only a profound feeling of being isolated and abandoned. Luke notes that in this hour he did not remain without strengthening from God (Luke 22:43), but it was a strengthening of his hope that God remained true to him and accepted his suffering. On the cross this baptism of death that Jesus underwent rose, according to Matthew's and Mark's interpretation, to the pitch of a separation from God that we cannot imagine: 'My God, my God, why hast thou forsaken me?' (Matt. 27:46; Mark 15:34). This cry of Jesus is anything but enthusiastic. God the Son is here crying to God the Father who did not spare his own Son but gave him up for us all (Rom. 8:32). He who is hanging there on the cross and calls to his God receives no answer. He sees nothing and hears no voice. The only thing that keeps him close to God in his hope.

This baptism of death that Jesus underwent is the prerequisite for the baptism of the Spirit that the disciples experienced at Pentecost. Anyone who is not ready to take on himself the baptism of death with which Jesus was baptized will not be ready either to receive the baptism of the Spirit. What it means is that his or her own experience is more important to him or her than witness for God, than love for the Church. God is the Lord of your experiences too, and he himself allots the places at Jesus's right and left hand. However moving our religious expereinces may be, they have no value if they do not bend us to him who was crucified and whom God raised up from the dead. Jesus's warning to watch and remain alert applies too in the context of our own experiences. Proof that our experience of God really does come from God is the fact that it is continually driving and impelling us out of ourselves, makes us defenceless against God and transforms our life. Too great certainty about the genuineness of our experience of God should make us suspicious. Psychologists will analyse such experiences that we are so certain about and quite rightly trace them back to the stimulus of experiences in our everyday life. In the New Testament the word 'enthusiasm' does not occur at all, and so we should not describe the basic charismatic experience as 'enthusiastic'. It starts with acceptance of one's own death (cf. the seventh day of the first week).

Seventh day: You shall follow me afterwards

When for the first time we surrender our life and our death to Christ in front of witnesses, it marks a decisive step, perhaps even a real turning point in our life. We need to be certain that God has accepted us and made us capable of bearing witness to him. We can and must continually call to mind later this first surrender of our life, because in it God has dealt with us, but woe to us if we appeal to it against God. Conversion is a lifelong process, and we have continually to go on learning better how to distinguish between our own impulses and the impulses of the Holy Spirit. Perhaps our situation is like that of Peter (John 13:36-38):

> Simon Peter said to him, 'Lord, where are you going?' Jesus answered, 'Where I am going you cannot follow

me now; but you shall follow afterwards.' Peter said
to him, 'Lord, why cannot I follow you now? I will lay
down my life for you.' Jesus answered, 'Will you lay
down your life for me? Truly, truly, I say to you, the
cock will not crow, till you have denied me three times.'

The first time we surrender our life we are perhaps convinced
of doing something extraordinary. We are ready to lay down
our life for Jesus, to renounce everything, and in this we are
surely following a call of Jesus. We are ready like Peter to get
out of the boat and attempt the impossible of walking on the
water (Matt. 14:29). But the first generous impulse must be
proved and tested. Too soon we shall be overcome by anxiety
at our trust in Jesus: we sink beneath the waves and will
deny him in our everyday life.

If we follow only the talents and gifts of our own character
we shall not learn to allow ourselves to be guided by the
Spirit of God. The Spirit indeed warns us against following
impulses that are as it were an extension of our own character.
We recognize the Spirit at work in the course of our life-
history by finding ourselves capable of doing things that do not
correspond with our inborn talents. That for example includes
being ready to lead a quite ordinary and unremarkable life,
being available for others, without this bringing honour and
increased recognition. Dying every day with Christ, the witness
of our life as we lead it, is more important than the magnificent
once-in-a-while impulse to lay down our life for Jesus. Some
even think that because of their personal experiences with God
they are absolved from their political and social obligations.
They focus on their own experience and deny Jesus.

The Bible's warnings may make us level-headed but it is
not their aim to give us the excuse to put off our decision
for Christ. If we live in expectant trust, then this saying applies
to us: 'Wait for the promise of the Father, which you heard
from me, for John baptized with water, but before many days
you shall be baptized with the Holy Spirit' (Acts 1:4-5).
Follow Jesus now, before many days. He will then lead you
'where you do not wish to go' (John 21:18), to serve him
and to bear witness to him.

Fifth week: The Church

In its origin the Church is the assembly called together by God. It is not primarily formed by a number of individuals living apart from one another but takes shape in their coming together to hear the word of God and to celebrate the sacraments, in other words in public worship. In it each is for each 'steward of God's varied grace' (1 Peter 4:10). A decisive step towards a living parish community in which the many different gifts of the Spirit are at work together is a service of prayer to which each contributes according to the gifts of the Spirit that have been bestowed on him or her (1 Cor. 14:26):

> When you come together, each one has a hymn, a lesson, a revelation, a tongue, or an interpretation. Let all things be done for edification.

This is the briefest possible description of a service of the primitive Church such as the first Christian began by holding 'in their homes' (Acts 2:46). The great hope of the Church today is once again the Holy Spirit in a small group. The social experience of God bestowed on this occasion leads to a form of social prayer, and from that also to a renewed social and political involvement in society at large. A prayer group is thus in no way an exclusive circle of friends but a missionary association. The level on which those present move is not primarily something they themselves have established but is given them in advance in the word of God, in the presence of the Holy Spirit — a presence that is at first independent of subjective experience. What form is taken by a prayer service of this type to which everybody contributes something?

To begin with it is helpful if everyone can sit in a circle — even if they are meeting in a church or chapel or in similar surroundings where the architecture seems to go the other way. The service starts with someone reading a passage from the Bible and giving a short exposition of it. This should make clear what the passage has to say personally to whoever is giving this exposition: God's word always addresses us immediately and challenges us to make a response. (Anyone with a suitable education should previously have subjected the passage to a historical and critical analysis, and for this reason it is best if it is known in advance what the passage is to be. Learned discussion should however take place outside a prayer meeting.) Those present can also take turns to read a verse of the passage selected. After a silence of, say, ten minutes or so each member of the group can then say whether and in what way the verse he or she has read has spoken directly to his or her condition. Already this is a contribution that everyone can make. After another period of silence personal responses are then given to God's word.

This silence is not therefore a sinking into oneself in which one hopes to discover the ground of all being in oneself — as in certain Far Eastern techniques of meditation — but a fundamental listening to the word of God that challenges the whole man or woman and raises his or her activity to a new pitch of intensity. This silence is furthermore already a social occurrence in itself. Everybody knows of everybody else that he or she is letting himself or herself be called into question by God's word. There is a considerable difference between reading the Bible alone just for myself and letting it affect me alone, and being borne along in this opening up to God's word by the silence of others who are present. Many people find it awkward and embarrassing to start with: people wait for something to happen, for someone to say something. The innumerable inhibitions and reservations that we all have become manifest, and many people therefore experience this silence as a demand, even an excessive demand, placed upon them. Many people start working out in advance what to say and at the same time are thinking: 'What will the rest think of me? Am I doing well enough? Will I make an ass of myself?' We have concentrated so much on ourselves in our piety that to begin with we have the embarrassing feeling that we must place ourselves on display. Hence we disguise our inhibitions with all sorts of excuses. 'That isn't for me,' we say. 'Some things in religion are private and personal.'

For the most part growing into this form of prayer that is also witness is a long and in certain circumstances critical process.

The person praying directs himself with his entire person in the Spirit through Christ to the Father. Because the prayers and invocations are said out loud and in front of others they take on the character of proclamation and, if God so ordains, minister to the faith of others. Worship becomes ministry. The presence of others in this case does not stand in the forefront of one's consciousness. If God uses me to say something to someone else through my expression of faith, then that is his work alone.

Listen, however, to what God is saying to you through someone else's contribution. You will gain more than you can ever expect from someone else's witness to his or her faith. There is a great difference between your keeping silent and praying on your own and your doing so together with others. In praying together there is a growth of social awareness and of solidarity that is undreamed of. Your prayer then becomes something that is not only very personal but also at the same time very social. You are liberated from a false privacy in your life of faith and experience afresh what is meant by saying that faith comes from hearing.

Social prayer means furthermore that the various prayers that are contributed are connected with each other. There is here a distinction to be drawn between spontaneous utterings of prayer and social-charismatic ones. Paul had to admonish the Christians of Corinth to speak in turn, 'for God is not a God of confusion but of peace' (1 Cor. 14:33). The resulting order is shown in everyone not simply uttering spontaneously what comes into his or her head without considering the contributions that had been made beforehand. This kind of spontaneous praying can hardly lead to the group becoming aware of its identity as a group but is ego-related, does not serve the building up of the group, and often leads to prayer groups dissolving. In the initial stages it can happen that one person prays after the other: 'Lord, I thank you . . .,' 'Lord, I ask you . . .,' without either listening to what the other had been saying. All each person displays is his or her own inner concerns. The dimension of a social or charismatic prayer service is only attained when each person asks himself or herself when listening to another's prayer: 'What does God want to tell me through this other person?' The prayer that follows then both answers and confirms the one that has preceded it.

Answering another's contribution can of course always make use of traditional formulations. These then take on what can often be surprising depths. If for example someone has expressed some request, those present can take it up with the invocation: 'Lord, have mercy.' In this case this invocation is not made because it stands in the order of service but because it forms a response to someone else's prayer. Phrases from the traditional prayer of praise, such as 'Glory be to God in the highest', are prayed with great inner conviction when they form the response to someone else's prayer praising God. A prophetic exhortation can be answered with the invocation: 'Praise to you, Lord Jesus Christ.' It thus forms the confirmation demanded by prayers of this kind (cf. 1 Cor. 14:29: 'and let the others weigh what is said').

From what has been said there can already be deduced the two ground rules laid down by Paul for a prayer service: first, everything must be done for edification (1 Cor. 14:26); second, everything should be done jointly and in order (1 Cor. 14:33, 40).

The person presiding over the prayer meeting has the task of keeping a keen eye on this social and charismatic dimension. In certain circumstances he or she will have to intervene, perhaps with a prophetic remark, or even, in extreme cases and in a suitable way, ask someone to restrain himself. What is expected of him or her is above all the gift of discernment of spirits, a power of judgement bestowed by God to discern whether utterances spring from primarily human impulses or from the Spirit of God or from powers opposed to God. He or she must also be alert for a suitable time to bring the prayer meeting to an end, with a blessing or a hymn, if it is not followed by a celebration of the eucharist. A service of prayer of this kind lasts as long as the Spirit of God induces those present — half an hour or even three hours and longer.

Often the charismatic dimension that has been described will only be attained after a long initiatory period lasting some weeks or months. To start with prayers of petition will predominate, while later the worship of God for his own sake will come into prominence. The first phase often debouches in an initial crisis. People start with too great an expectation that something will happen. Prayer is sluggish, the atmosphere often oppressive, and many stay away again. One prayer group had the following experience. When after a few months only three participants were left out of an original twenty, the question came up whether it was really God's will that they should pray together in this way, or whether they were primarily impelled by their own intentions and efforts to renew the Church. Some members of the group then spent a whole night praying for insight, understanding and guidance, and afterwards there began an at first painful process of self-surrender. They learned afresh to accept their own death in a quite personal way and to place themselves at God's disposal. Months later they laid hands on each other and prayed to receive the gifts of the Spirit, and this 'baptism of the Spirit' marked a new start. The group grew quickly to number more than two hundred. Many of these are now active in spreading the word in their local parish communities, where the Spirit of God has through them called new prayer groups to life. Social and charismatic prayer leads to the renewal of the community, while stress on the self leads people astray into sectarianism and schism.

Third day: What kind of a house do you want to build for me?

What the Church is is not something that can be said in a few words. It is no less a mystery of the faith than the incarnation. The Bible uses a variety of images to describe it for us, images taken from the life of shepherds and peasants, from building houses or even from family relationships or the relationship between bride and groom. In this week let us consider some of these images.

Often we link the idea of 'the house of God' with the

word 'Church' and in doing so forget that each one of us is the temple of God, that is, the place of his presence. A missionary liturgy however starts from the presupposition that every individual and the congregation as a whole is aware of the grace of being the temple of the Holy Spirit. Only in this way can the individual personal contributions to the prayer service reflect that reverence that is the starting point of love in such services too (1 Cor. 3:16-17; 2 Cor. 6:16; Act 7:47-49):

> Do you not know that you are God's temple and that God's Spirit dwells in you? If any one destroys God's temple, God will destroy him. For God's temple is holy, and that temple you are.

> What agreement has the temple of God with idols? For we are the temple of the living God; as God said,
> 'I will live in them and move among them,
> and I will be their God,
> and they shall be my people.'

> It was Solomon who built a house for him [the God of Jacob]. Yet the Most High does not dwell in houses made with hands; as the prophet says,
> 'Heaven is my throne,
> and earth my footstool.
> What house will you build for me, says the Lord,
> or what is the place of my rest?'

Temple means literally a piece of land cut off and since the earliest times has been applied to that selected place where the divinity of God is present in a special way. For the Jews of Jesus's time this place was the temple of Jerusalem. 'Day after day' Jesus was there teaching (Mark 14:49; Matt. 26:55). Throughout he respected the temple as the 'house of God' (cf. John 2:16), but in his teaching and in his person he himself is 'greater than the temple' (Matt. 12:6). He himself is the temple of God (John 2:19-21):

> Jesus answered them, 'Destroy this temple, and in three days I will raise it up.' The Jews then said: 'It has taken

forty-six years to build this temple, and will you raise
it up in three days?'
But he spoke of the temple of his body.

Jesus himself is that 'place' marked out and set apart where
God is present in a unique way. If we share in his baptism of
the Spirit, in his experience of the Spirit, then we too become
temples of this kind. Every Christian is therefore for everybody else a place of God's presence, and it is just because of
that that this becomes manifest in a special way when people
are gathered for prayer 'all together in one place' (Acts 2:1).
So it is with great reverence for the presence of the Holy
Spirit that each one listens to what the other has to say, lets
himself or herself be addressed and challenged by him or
her. Granted the need to test the gifts of the Spirit, these are
primarily 'manifestations of the Spirit' (1 Cor. 12:7).

Hence the question arises: if someone who did not know
what was going on or an unbeliever came into a prayer
meeting, would he or she fall on his or her face, worship
God and cry out: 'Truly, God is among you' (1 Cor. 14:25)?

Fourth day: Every one is indispensable

The Church comes alive in the congregation to which every
member has something to contribute. But will the service not
tend to be dominated by those who have the natural gift
of expressing themselves? Will not the need for recognition
make itself felt along with ambition? And what happens if it
is not a small prayer group but the entire parish community
of a Sunday that celebrates a prayer service in place of the
traditional liturgy of the word? (It is conceivable for one of
the Sunday services in every parish to be a 'missionary
liturgy' to begin with.)

Paul was very well acquainted with this problem and
reminded the Corinthians that as a community they were
the body of Christ. Anyone who did not discern the difference
between this body, this gathering (and the eucharistic elements
by reason of which the community is the body of Christ)
and an ordinary gathering (and ordinary bread and wine) was
eating and drinking judgement on himself (1 Cor. 11:29).

Paul goes on to expound the relationship of the different charisms to each other with reference to the relationship of the members to our human body (1 Cor. 12:13-22):

> For by one Spirit we were all baptized into one body . . . and all were made to drink of one Spirit. For the body does not consist of one member but of many. If the foot should say, 'Because I am not a hand, I do not belong to the body,' that would not make it any less a part of the body. And if the ear should say, 'Because I am not an eye, I do not belong to the body,' that would not make it any less a part of the body. If the whole body were an eye, where would be the hearing? If the whole body were an ear, where would be the sense of smell? But as it is, God arranged the organs in the body, each one of them, as he chose. If all were a single organ, where would the body be? As it is, there are many parts, yet one body. The eye cannot say to the hand, 'I have no need of you,' nor again the head to the feet, 'I have no need of you.' On the contrary, the parts of the body which seem to be weaker are indispensable.

No one has all the charisms, nor does every one have the same ones, but the Spirit allots each one his or her own charism as he wills (1 Cor. 12:11). Hence everyone has in the prayer service his or her irreplaceable and indispensable function in a way similar to that of each individual limb or organ in our body. The foot is not the hand, the ear is not the eye, and so on. The proper function of every part fits in with that of every other part, and so each is indispensable. It is only through this mutual relationship and co-ordination of different functions that the body can become active as a totality.

So the apostle, the leader of the community, cannot say to the prophets, 'I do not need you,' and the teachers cannot say to the prophets, 'We do not need you.' Where would the Church be as the body of Christ if it consisted only of an apostle, only of a prophet, only of a teacher and were dominated by only one single charism? God has his plan for every individual man and woman, and to each he has allotted a corresponding task for the whole of the Church.

A special danger of the charismatic renewal is that the more spectacular charisms are given undue prominence while the less striking ones meet with scant consideration. The person for example who sees that there is somewhere for the prayer meeting to be held, the person who takes on all the burden of organization or acts as treasurer is performing an indispensable ministry. And with reference to the prayer service itself the advice applies that someone who is naturally used to expressing himself or herself should restrain himself or herself, and that someone who is naturally restrained should have the courage to contribute to the gathering. Above all everyone should respect the mutuality of the prayers that are contributed instead of waiting as it were impatiently until his or her turn comes, and should start by listening. Perhaps God wants to use some quite unpretentious remark to affect you so deeply that the effect lasts all day. If all respect everyone else, then one charism can evoke another. But if everyone is concerned only with himself or herself, then the service will remain without fruit.

Fifth day: God begins only once

However important may be the coming together of the small community formed by the word and the altar, the Church is something more than a small group, more than the individual parish community. Nor is it simply a federation of groups or communities. Instead it began once and for all with the man Jesus of Nazareth, with what happened at the first Pentecost. In Jesus Christ God acted definitively, and through him he founded his Church definitively. God is true to himself, he does not revoke his decisions, and does not continually refound his Church afresh. This fact is of decisive importance for every renewal in the Church. The dynamic of the charismatic renewal is not directed at a new charismatic Church that would transcend all spiritual traditions. Instead it can only be fruitful if all existing Churches let themselves be seized by it. This train of thought may not interest you for the moment, but if the baptism of the Spirit and the renewal of the Spirit have something to do with Jesus's experience of the Spirit then you will be interested in the historical way in which this experience of the Spirit reaches us, since the Church is the continuation of Jesus's experience of the Spirit.

A decisive step for the early Church was the conversion of pagans. Some twelve years after the first Pentecost Peter was preaching in the house of the pagan Cornelius and explicitly stressed the Church's having begun with Jesus's baptism of the Spirit (Acts 10:36-38, 44-46):

> 'You know the word which he sent to Israel, . . . the word which was proclaimed throughout all Judea, beginning from Galilee after the baptism which John preached: how God anointed Jesus of Nazareth with the Holy Spirit and with power . . .' While Peter was still saying this, the Holy Spirit fell on all who heard the word. And the believers from among the circumcised who came with Peter were amazed, because the gift of the Holy Spirit had been poured out even on the Gentiles. For they heard them speaking in tongues and extolling God.

We see clearly that the proclamation of Jesus as the anointed one, as the one baptized with the Holy Soirit, does not only take place in the power of the Holy Spirit, but in it the experience of the Spirit is as it were bequeathed and transmitted. In the spiritual words of Peter's sermon Jesus's experience of the Spirit has itself a history. In this Peter is not in any way the dispenser of the Spirit. That is the exalted Lord alone, but he makes use of human words to prepare men and women to receive the Spirit. The Holy Spirit is not however as it were included in what Peter said, it is not bequeathed like a sum of money. God's word is always a personal offer, and it affects its hearers only to the extent that they accept it and are ready to respond.

Perhaps already you have had the experience of other people coming to believe through your personal witness of faith — and this not because of your personal skill in persuasion, but because God's Spirit has been making use of your intellect, your will, your emotions. We shall never be able to say precisely what God himself does and what we do in this process. Nevertheless there are two notions we must cling to. First, it is not a question of part being God at work and part us. Instead God is always completely involved, and at the same time we are fully needed too. Second, the Holy Spirit does not only as it were come from above and continually create and re-create new communities and Churches which live separated from each other and exist in mutual exclusion. God founded his Church at the start once and for all, and for this reason this beginning remains a standard whereby the Church's subsequent history can be measured. In the witness of faith Jesus's experience of the Spirit is continued, becomes the Church. Peter himself refers to this when he tells the community at Jerusalem of what happened at the house of Cornelius (Acts 11:15-16):

> 'As I began to speak, the Holy Spirit fell on them just as on us at the beginning. And I remembered the word of the Lord, how he said, "John baptized with water, but you shall be baptized with the Holy Spirit." '

Because all men are sinners and remain sinners, because the tendency towards sin and towards the abuse of what is good cannot be extirpated, this initial experience can never be maintained in its purity. The history of the Church is disfigured by developments that turn out to be distortions, by abuse, sin, division, schism. All this however does not of course come from the Holy Spirit itself, and hence the Church stands in need of continual conversion and reform. We pray that all Christian Churches may be brought together again through the power of the Holy Spirit, that the charismatic renewal may at the same time be the start of a shared tradition, and that they may all be one just as at the beginning Jews and pagans and the different local Churches grew together into the one united Church of Jesus Christ.

Sixth day: Charismatic confusion?

In the course of Church history outbreaks of charismatic activity have already frequently led to groups splitting off and to the formation of new Churches, and this through the faults of people on both sides. The existing Churches were not ready to let themselves be called into question by these revolutionary occurrences and to accept their motivation and aims within themselves. And the charismatics for their part were not ready to subordinate themselves. In some Churches that have arisen since the start of the present century on the basis of outbursts of charismatic activity, the same kind of question has come up as arose for the community of Corinth: whose job is it to look after Church order and discipline? Without the strong authority exercised by Paul the divisive and schismatic tendencies present (cf. 1 Cor. 1:10-13, 3:4-23) would have got worse. And Paul lays down definite rules for the celebration of the Lord's supper (1 Cor. 11:17-34) and stresses with regard to the exercise of gifts of the Spirit in public worship that 'God is not a God of confusion but of peace' (1 Cor. 14:33). 'All things should be done decently and in order,' Paul wrote (1 Cor. 14:40). It was with reference to these statements that in the sixteenth century the Reformers stressed the necessity of the Church's ministerial structure.

In the primitive Church this is charismatic ministry to the other charisms, and there are two aspects to it. First, the leader of the community should be concerned in the love of Christ for the mutual order and relationship among themselves of the gifts of the Spirit. Second, he should be concerned about maintaining links with the other Christian communities and keep the totality of the Church in mind. One of the most difficult problems for the future of the charismatic movement as it has occurred in the major mainstream Christian Churches in the middle of the present century is that of Church leadership, discipline and order.

Hence all should learn from the history of the Christian community at Corinth. Not long after Paul's death its fissiparous tendencies came fully to the surface. Some forty years after the writing of the first letter to the Corinthians and some thirty years after Paul's death the 'Church of God sojourning in Rome' wrote a letter to the 'Church of God sojourning in Corinth' — the letter that very probably was drawn up by the Roman bishop Clement and that is known to us as the first letter of Clement. At Corinth some arrogant younger people who did not enjoy a very great reputation had simply deposed established and trustworthy leaders of the congregation. This had not only caused confusion and disorder among the community at Corinth itself but gave unbelievers an excuse to revile the name of Jesus (cf. 1 Clement 47:7). The writer of the letter therefore admonished the Christians of Corinth to maintain order and to subordinate themselves to their leaders. The letter indicates that the apostles foresaw contention breaking out over the office of *episcope* and therefore appointed presbyters who then entrusted other tried and tested men with the task of taking over their ministry after their death (1 Clement 44:3).

> These men were appointed by them [the apostles] or meanwhile by other men of high reputation with the approval of the entire Church. They served the flock of Christ blamelessly, with humility, gently and dis-interestedly, and for many years they have been commended by all. These men we do not think it right to eject from their ministry.

But how should order be restored? The letter was written between 90 and 100 AD, and at that time no firm structure of Church order had been formed. What was more obvious than to go back to the pattern of the Old Testament? The letter said (1 Clement 40:2, 5):

> He [the Lord] ordered offerings to be made and services celebrated, and these not at random or irregularly but at definite times and hours . . . For to the high priest his own services are allotted, their own place is appointed to the priests, and the Levites are charged with their own ministrations; the lay person is bound by the ordinances of the laity.

One continuation of this Old Testament structure is in the sense of this letter the order Christ — the Apostles — bishops (or presbyters or deacons) (1 Clement 42:1-4). We see here how by going back to the Old Testament there arose something like a spiritual order in the Church that was traced back to God's ordinances.

In the sense in which it is used today the word 'lay' or 'layman' does not appear in the New Testament. It occurs for the first time in the passage quoted above from the first letter of Clement. In this study group we do not need to reflect on the difficult problems that are always still connected with the question of the Church's ministry in the course of its history up to and including today. At the moment no full agreement has yet been attained between Protestants and Catholics. Nevertheless the charismatic renewal gives occasion for the hope that the Church's ministry will be understood and lived more strongly as a charism for the other charisms. This of course presupposes that within the mainstream Churches too the exercise of the gifts of the Spirit will really break through. The Church's ministry can only be exercised charismatically if the other charisms have been brought to life. In the contemporary situation it would thus be an important service on the part of the leader of the Christian community to become aware of his own gifts of the Spirit, to accept them, and then as the missionary of his own community to awaken, in the power of the Spirit, the other gifts of the Spirit.

Seventh day: Trust in God's infallible offer

In the talk for the fifth week it is demonstrated that God does not only offer to be close to us through the word of proclamation but also through signs that collectively we describe as sacraments. The celebration of the Eucharist, the repetition of the words that according to the Church's tradition Jesus spoke at the last supper, is Christ's infallible offer to distribute himself to us and thus continually to renew the Church afresh as his body. We must be absolutely certain that in the eucharistic gifts Christ gives himself to us, for through his Spirit he himself has changed these gifts into his body and blood. The sign of baptism, too, when the person administering the sacrament pours water on the person

being baptized and says: 'I baptize you in the name of the
Father and the Son and of the Holy Spirit,' is the same kind
of infallible offer by Christ, for it is he himself who baptizes
through the human administrator of the sacrament. Does
God offer us participation in Jesus's baptism of the Spirit
by means of a sacramental sign? Catholics and Protestants
are not completely agreed on this question, and so this difference must find expression here.

(a) The Catholic sacrament of confirmation

The Catholic understanding is that the laying on of hands in
Samaria by the apostles Peter and John was the beginning
of the sacrament of confirmation. What happened after that?
The 'evangelist' Philip, one of the seven (cf. Acts 21:8),
had proclaimed the gospel in the Samaritan capital of Shechem,
some thirty miles north of Jerusalem and baptized many
people (Acts 8:14-17):

> Now when the apostles at Jerusalem heard that Samaria
> had received the word of God, they sent to them Peter
> and John, who came down and prayed for them that
> they might receive the Holy Spirit; for it had not yet
> fallen on any of them, but they had only been baptized
> in the name of the Lord Jesus. Then they laid their hands
> on them and they received the Holy Spirit.

In the Acts of the Apostles Luke never speaks, as Paul and
John do (cf. Rom. 8:2-16; Gal. 3:2, 5; John 3:5), of the
Holy Spirit being already bestowed at baptism. We do not
need here to enter in detail into the many problems that
arise from this for experts in biblical exegesis and in dogmatic
theology. Luke places great stress on the new communities
that spring up remaining associated with the original community at Jerusalem. So, for example, Peter visits the
believers in Judaea (Acts 9:32) and Barnabas is sent to
Antioch (Acts 11:22). As far as Luke is concerned the Twelve
had from the start a responsibility towards all communities
that came into being. The Holy Spirit is for him primarily the
power to bear witness (Acts 1:8), and in his view it is
bestowed by God not only directly but also by the laying

on of hands by those who are responsible for the Church's missionary effort. The dispenser and source of the Holy Spirit is and remains Christ himself, but he makes use of the act of laying on of hands by the apostles. These are not without their participation in this process, since they pray for the Spirit to come down. But the Spirit itself is not the gift of the apostles but the gift of the risen Lord.

In Ephesus too the Holy Spirit comes down on people after baptism by Paul laying his hands on them. The signs of this continuation of the original experience of Pentecost are praying in tongues and the gift of prophecy (Acts 19:6). Baptism and the laying on of hands in this case take place one after the other without a great interval between them. But in the later development of the Church in the West the two actions became separated from each other, though at baptism a laying on of hands with a prayer for the descent of the Holy Spirit has been kept. In the Orthodox Church of the East even today the smallest infant is baptized, confirmed and given its first holy communion in one integral ceremony.

The sacrament of confirmation is important and precious to the Catholic to the extent that its historical association with the Church's initial experience is indicated. The priest or bishop who lays his hands on the candidate for confirmation has himself received this laying on of hands, and so on back into the Church's first years. What is at issue here is not a chain of layings on of hands but the awareness shown in this that God only makes a start once and founded his Church only once. This stays valid despite all the sin, failing and inadequacy of the human dispensers of the sacrament of confirmation. The sacramental sign of confirmation provides the absolute certainty that God himself is offering the fullness of his Holy Spirit and offering it as strength and power to bear witness.

Thus in the new rite of confirmation the bishop asks the candidates when questioning them about their baptismal profession of faith: 'Do you believe in the Holy Spirit, the Lord, the giver of life, who came upon the apostles at Pentecost, and today is given to you sacramentally in confirmation?' Similarly the Council of Florence declared in 1439 that in confirmation 'the Holy Spirit is given for strength as it was given to the apostles on the day of Pentecost, in order namely that the Christian may courageously confess the name of Christ. Hence the person being confirmed is anointed on the forehead, where shame has its seat, lest he blush to confess the name of Christ' (DS 1319). The laying on of hands thus indicates that the Christian comes as it were into a tangible, physical contact with the experience that marked the beginning of the Church. The anointing of the forehead is at the same time a banishing of the taboo of false anxiety and introversion. The laying on of hands and the anointing of the forehead are accompanied by the words: 'Be sealed with the gift of the Holy Spirit.' Have you already accepted this offer? Have you already given witness of your faith to other people in church or at work? Have you experienced within you the joy of other people having come to the faith through the Holy Spirit living in you, through your witness to the faith?

The separation of baptism and the sacramental enabling of Christians to bear witness to their beliefs does not according to the Catholic understanding of the matter arise from purely human considerations. God's grace is 'varied' (1 Peter 4:10). God's dealings with us are concerned with our relations with himself, and thus our resurrection, our eternal life, begins here and now. But at the same time they are concerned with our relations to others, and through the gifts of the Spirit God makes us capable of ministering to the faith of others (cf. the drawings at the start of the third week and at the end of the second section of the fourth week in the first volume of this work). These two aspects cannot be separated from each other. They express God's single graciousness. But they are not one and the same from every point of view. This difference is expressed in the different signs of baptism and confirmation. The Churches of the Reformation also adhere to historical contact with the Church's initial and original experience, for there has been no period in the history of the Church in which the message of Christ had not been proclaimed and passed on from one generation to the next. From this point of view Catholics and Protestants are agreed that in the proclamation of the message of Christ the whole Church throughout all ages stands in the succession of the apostles.

(b) The Evangelical rite of confirmation

God's offer has been made to you
There are obviously not many members of the Evangelical
Churches who have been able to recall their confirmation
in a way that is alive and defines their being a Christian.
Is it a question of the age at which it is conferred, that
awkward time of transition between being a child and being
grown up that we call puberty? Is it a question of the social
structure that, despite all assurances that confirmation classes
are voluntary, in practice means that usually the entire
age-group is involved? Does it lie with the parents, whether
pious or superficial, who draw a veil over the personal
questions entailed — and the possible answers? Does it lie
in the method of instruction in which the dour business of
learning by rote gives no room for any kind of experience
of faith? Does it lie in the service of confirmation?

Every empathetic pastor knows that despite all superficial
conformism and despite all youthful disgruntledness nearly
all the candidates for confirmation approach what takes place
in instruction and in the service with great expectations.
But it is seldom that these expectations are expressed directly.
Indeed, the young people often hardly have the linguistic
ability to capture in words what they are looking for and
what they are moved by.

Recall your confirmation to mind. Bring back into conscious
remembrance what happened to you then. What hopes did
you entertain? How would you have liked the instruction and
the service to be? Why did you wish to pray? What disappointments did you experience? Why do you look back in
discontent, aversion or anger?

If you think about your confirmation in this way it will
not escape you that despite everything God's offer was there.
If people refused it or if you yourself refused it, do not blame
this offer of God's for that. Do you still know what was said
to you in the service of confirmation? Perhaps you can
remember your confirmation text — or can find it somewhere
and see whether it has something to say to you now.

Perhaps the age of confirmation, despite young people today maturing earlier, and that intellectually as well as physically, is still too early for a real personal renewal of the baptismal promise. Probably it is also too early for a personally responsible decision of faith — and for the acceptance of the fullness of the Holy Spirit. At the least this serves to argue that quite simply a fourteen-year-old will shy away from the whole depth and profundity of what faith is all about: the cross of Jesus, God's unfathomable love for sinners, God's boundless grace and promise, living the spiritual life on the model of Jesus. While a teenager will only in the rarest cases — much more rarely than a grown-up — reject the message of Christ, he is often not in a position to say yes to it because it all appears too large, too foreign, too powerful for him.

Ask yourself how it was with you and where you stand now. When you were asked earlier whether you remembered what was said to you in the confirmation service, this referred to something other than the confirmation text. Hardly anyone knows — and there are not many places to look it up — the wording of the prayer said on behalf of those being confirmed and of the blessing uttered over them. But what stays in the memory is the laying on of hands by the pastor. This gesture goes back to the witness of the New Testament, where it is often mentioned: examples include Acts 8:14-17, Acts 19:6, 2 Tim. 1:6, and Hebrews 6:2 (where the laying on of hands is included among the basic elements of instruction in the faith). The laying on of hands is always connected with a special blessing that is expected from the Spirit of God: for witness to the faith, for a particular service to the community, for healing the sick, or more generally for the reception of the Holy Spirit. Hence the laying on of hands can and should never be a wordless gesture or a silent ceremony. The words that are spoken in connection with it do not only say what it is all about, as it were in order to provide information for those involved or those looking on, but they form the most important part of what is being done and is being expressed in the outward sign. God wants us to pray to him. And because we are sure of this we can express our prayer at one and the same time as blessing, as exhortation, and as communication of the Spirit to other people. This takes place in the prayers and words of blessing that accompany the laying on of hands in the service of confirmation and that form the nucleus of confirmation — which means strengthening.

Hence there are two things to be considered in your preparation. First, that you personally recollect what happened at your confirmation and bring it before God and surrender it to him along with all the purely human elements that in your memory have marked you up till now. Second, that you accept the offer of God that was spoken over you at confirmation.

Since confirmation refers back to baptism, it renews God's real and powerful activity that lay hold of you at your baptism. In a special way confirmation takes up the prayer for the Holy Spirit that had already been uttered at baptism — not only as a sincere prayer to God but also as a certain assurance of the Spirit. Perhaps at the time you ignored it or were not properly aware of it or could not conceive anything definite by it. If by means of having come so far in the present course of initiation into the basic Christian experience you have moved a little further on from that, then a renewed reading of and meditation on the prayers and blessings of the service of confirmation could help you to prepare personally for the consciously sought primal Christian experience of the renewal of the Spirit. In what follows we offer, besides formulae used in confirmation, further prayers for the Holy Spirit whereby our entire personal prayer can receive assistance.

The assurance of the Holy Spirit

At the start of the rite of baptism the pastor says: 'Accept the sign of the cross on your forehead and on your breast, for you have been redeemed by Jesus Christ the crucified.' Immediately after baptism with water ('I baptize you in the name of God, the father, the son and the Holy Spirit') the pastor lays his hands on the person being baptized and says:

> The almighty God and Father of our Lord Jesus Christ,
> by whom you are born again by water and the Holy

Spirit and who forgives you all your sins, strengthen you with his grace to eternal life. Peace be with you.

Alternatively:

May the God of all grace, who has called you to his eternal glory in Christ, prepare, strengthen, fortify, establish, and by faith preserve you for eternal life.

At confirmation the pastor says:

Almighty God, heavenly Father, we pray you for these who are being confirmed: strengthen them in the power of your Holy Spirit that their faith may be true and permit them to remain in the obedience of your word, that they may acknowledge you always as true God, love you from their heart, and praise you before the world in word and deed, through Jesus Christ our Lord.

Alternatively:

Lord Jesus Christ, son of God, we pray you to strengthen these your servants with your Holy Spirit, that they may hearken to your gospel, fight against the Devil and their own weakness, not afflict the Holy Spirit, cause no scandal to your community, but that their life may serve the praise of you and the salvation of their neighbour, you who live and reign with the Father and the Holy Spirit for ever and ever.

There are various formulae for the actual act of confirmation itself:

The blessing of God almighty, the Father, the Son and the Holy Spirit, come upon you and remain with you now and for ever.

May the God of all grace, who has called you to his eternal glory in Christ, prepare, strengthen, fortify, establish, and by faith preserve you for eternal life.

May God, Father, Son and Holy Spirit, grant you his grace: protection and shield against all evil, strength and help for all good, for the sake of the merits of our one redeemer Jesus Christ.

The actual formulations may vary from one provincial or

national Church to another. In German Free Churches the preacher will for the most part make use of extempore prayers at baptism and confirmation. What becomes clear is that the formula used at baptism and confirmation is often the same. The Evangelical rite of confirmation is meant to be an independent acceptance of baptism, but at it the Holy Spirit is invoked in a special way. The clearest and, in our view, the best expression of this is to be found in a confirmation formula that comes from the Evangelical Church of Strasbourg and of Hesse, that was introduced by the Reformer Martin Luther, and that in the nineteenth century was recommended by August Vilmar:

Accept the Holy Spirit:
shield and protection against all evil,
power and help towards all good,
from the gracious hand of God
the Father, the Son and the Holy Spirit.

There are in Protestant Christendom new approaches towards an understanding of confirmation as a renewal of the Spirit that makes one capable of a missionary life. The theologian Max Thurian from the well-known Taizé community has described confirmation as the consecration and (in quotation marks) 'ordination' of the laity. We would like to offer his proposals with regard to confirmation both as a subject for mediation and as an example of how in our view confirmation and the 'baptism of the Spirit' could in practice be combined in a charismatically aroused community (among Christians aged at least sixteen).[1]

---

[1] Max Thurian, *Consecration of the Layman: New Approaches to the Sacrament of Confirmation*, translated by W.J. Kerrigan, with a foreword by Frank B. Norris, S.S. (Baltimore, Md./Dublin, 1963); originally, *La confirmation: consécration des laics* (Neuchâtel/Paris, 1957). His suggested form of service for confirmation is to be found on pp. 105-110 of the English and pp. 109-114 of the French edition. Thurian's basic model can of course also be used when extempore prayers are preferred. But even in this case, as generally happens in charismatic communities, extempore prayers will tend to base themselves on traditional liturgical texts. Another thing that applies to

Thurian proposes asking those being confirmed:

> Do you desire to serve Christ in his Church: to acknow-
> ledge publicly (*témoigner de*) the good news of the
> Gospel, to take your place in the service of praise, and
> to preserve in fraternal love by practising hospitality
> and by visiting your brother men?

Since the confirmation of several people at one service is
envisaged, the prayer to be said over all of them is
correspondingly long while the actual formula of confirmation
to be repeated over each individual is correspondingly short:

> Almighty and everlasting God, who has wished your
> servants to be born from upon high through water and
> the Holy Spirit, and has given them the remission of all
> their sins! Grant to them now the gift of the Holy
> Spirit, to strengthen them, and to confirm them in the
> faith. Send down upon them from the pinnacle of the
> heavens (*du haut du ciel*) your Holy Spirit, our
> Counsellor; by his unction enlighten them in knowledge;
> and grant to them all his gifts: the spirit of wisdom and of
> understanding, the spirit of counsel and of fortitude,
> the spirit of knowledge and of piety, the spirit of fear
> of the Lord (*l'esprit d'obéissance au Seigneur*). Conse-
> crate them in truth: your word is truth. Inspire their
> testimony and their service, for they are of the race
> elect, the royal priesthood, the holy nation, a people
> singled out by purchase to proclaim your magnificent
> works, o Lord, for you have summoned them from the
> darkness into your wonderful light, which is Jesus Christ,
> your Son, our Lord and God, who lives and reigns with
> you, almighty Father, in the unity of the Holy Spirit,
> world without end.

charismatic groups is that it is not only the celebrant or person presiding at the service who lays his hands on the people being confirmed
(cf. the third section of the fifth week in the first part of this work).
Further, Thurian's use of terms such as 'brothers' should be expanded
or rephrased so that Christians who are women do not feel left out.

Those being confirmed go one by one and kneel before the celebrant, who places his hands on each one's head and says:

The gift of the Holy Spirit: fortitude, light, consecration.

Alternatively (not in Thurian's proposed service):

Receive the Holy Spirit of light and truth,
the royal and prophetic priesthood,
the name of the Lord,
the cross of Christ,
the seal of the Spirit,
that you may enter into the kingdom of God,
into eternal life.

A Pentecostal prayer

A meditative prayer that can be suitable for repeated use is based on the promise of Isaiah 11:2 that describes the way in which the future Messiah will be filled with the Spirit. We know that through Jesus's experience of the Spirit this promise applies to all of us:

Oh God, let the fire of your Spirit
come down on the earth;
let its sevenfold fire run through your people
as your sevenfold Spirit rested
on him whom you sent and anointed, your Christ.

May your Spirit fill us:
breath from eternity
that at the world's beginning moved over the waters,
that breathed life into the dead bones,
that became your message in the mouths of the prophets
and a song of praise on the lips of those you have chosen.

Spirit of wisdom, fill us:
warm our hearts with your gently burning flame
that we may learn to be patient and shrewd.

Spirit of understanding, fill us:
with your deep-piercing ray teach us
to distinguish between great and small
that we may be able to choose what is right.

Spirit of counsel, fill us:
let your inextinguishable light make us willing and able
to be friendly to others in our speech and to help them.

Spirit of strength, fill us:
may your bright leaping flame arm us with power from
    above
that we may radiate love and overcome evil.

Spirit of knowledge, fill us:
may your clear radiance unlock for us God's mysteries
that we may proclaim his salvation and praise him.

Spirit of awe, fill us:
may you be a gale in our hearts to teach us to pray and
    to be amazed
that we may become humble and remain God's children.

Sixth week: The gifts of the Spirit

First and second days: Praying ecumenically

The gifts of the Spirit are always imparted for service in and to the entire Church as a whole. Hence because they are still divided the Churches and ecclesial communities see themselves being called into question when they notice that the Holy Spirit distributes his gifts outside as well as inside their boundaries. Thus in its decree on ecumenism (*Unitatis redintegratio*) the Second Vatican Council recognized: 'Moreover some, even very many, of the most significant elements or endowments which together go to build up and give life to the Church herself can exist outside the visible boundaries of the Catholic Church: the written word of God; the life of grace; faith, hope and charity, along with other interior gifts of the Holy Spirit and visible elements' (3). Because of divisions among Christians the Catholic Church 'finds it more difficult to express in actual life her full catholicity in all its aspects (4). Hence 'whatever is wrought by the grace of the Holy Spirit in the hearts of our separated brethren can contribute to our own edification' (4).

Because of the divisions the separated Churches and communities have over-emphasized certain particular gifts of the Spirit, and this has in turn led to a further hardening of the division. The charismatic renewal contains within itself the power to break through this hardening and to make keener our perception of the gifts of the Spirit in other Churches. Hence in a 'spiritual' ecumenism all the Churches will be led to an admission of their former one-sidedness and will become open to an acceptance — in certain circumstances a critical acceptance — of the experiences of the Spirit that are living in other Churches (cf. the ecumenical theses and principles to be found in the appendix to the first volume of this work).

At the moment it is certainly both important and necessary that prayer groups should arise within the existing Churches and within their existing parish or congregational structures. Every Church must bring its own individual experience with it to contribute to the reconciled Christendom that is hoped for. The Spirit of Christ has been at work in history, at work too in our separated spiritual traditions. It would indeed be a 'sin against the Holy Spirit' not to recognize this. Out of respect for the work of the Holy Spirit in history (despite all human sin and guilt) we cannot just simply jump back into the situation of the early Church and start afresh. So the charismatic renewal must become Lutheran, Reformed, Orthodox, Catholic, etc., before it can be really ecumenical.

Acceptance of the experiences of the Spirit from other Churches is nevertheless not possible if these gifts of the Spirit that are not only different but have up to now been separated from each other are not brought into relation with each other in ecumenical prayer services. This of course presupposes that everyone stays firmly rooted in his or her own spiritual tradition. Experience shows that everyone who lets himself or herself be baptized by Christ with the Holy Spirit gains among other things a new relationship to his or her Church. The Holy Spirit unites the divided Churches without denying his own work in them. Hence prayer services among Christians of different denominations often also lead to a profound awareness of the human guilt and responsibility for separation. This may not affect every individual Christian present at such prayer services, but each one of us is marked by the guilt of others. We do not only ask God to heal the wounds that have made each of us personally suspicious and hostile towards God (cf. the prayer for such healing at the end of the third week), but we also ask God to heal the inherited sin of the division of Christendom. An especial profoundness is often bestowed on ecumenical prayer services when those present ask God to heal this inherited sin.

Churches and ecclesial communities are also social structures that involve community-consciousness in its ecclesial form. An emphasis on this group-awareness arising from purely human impulses is thus just as unspiritual as an emphasis on personal awareness arising from personal impulses is in meetings of the prayer group. What Paul has to say about the divisions within the community of Corinth can thus be applied to the divisions of Christendom today (1 Cor. 1:10-13; 1 Cor. 3:3-4):

I appeal to you, brethren, by the name of our Lord Jesus Christ, that all of you agree and that there be no dissensions among you, but that you be united in the same mind and the same judgement. For it has been reported to me by Chloe's people that there is quarrelling among you, my brethren. What I mean is that each one of you says, 'I belong to Paul,' or 'I belong to Apollos,' or 'I belong to Cephas,' or 'I belong to Christ.' Is Christ divided?

For you are still of the flesh. For while there is jealousy and strife among you, are you not of the flesh, and behaving like ordinary men? For when one says, 'I belong to Paul,' and another, 'I belong to Apollos,' are you not merely men?

What does this mean for ecumenical prayer services? Let us first accept that everyone taking part will be marked and formed by the spirituality of the Church he or she belongs to. To such a service the Lutheran will bring the experience of temptation and consolation, the Orthodox the experience of the presence of the Holy Spirit in the liturgy, the Quaker meditation and listening to the inner light that enlightens every man. A Catholic will contribute the experience of the unity that is always greater than the diversity within the Church, however great that may be, and of the continuity, revision and order brought about by the Spirit; the Baptist awareness of Christianity as a challenge to a personal decision; the Pentecostalist speaking in tongues. Of course everyone will be on their guard against becoming stuck in one particular form and expression of the spiritual life, for no Church wants explicitly and consciously to confine itself to realizing only one aspect of the totality of the Christian life. But it would be a service to the reconciliation of the divided Churches if at an ecumenical prayer service of this kind each Christian quite deliberately brought out his or her own spiritual tradition so that the separated gifts of the Spirit can grow together into the harmony of the one body of Christ.

In any case Christians today sit rather loosely to the inherited traditions of their Church and may have partly rejected them. If then at a prayer service they experience a profound spiritual togetherness with Christians from other Churches such as they have not known before, the impression easily arises that all tradition can be left behind. This would however in the long run lead to a 'super-Church' or even to a new 'supraconfessional' Church. The greater part of Christendom would derive no advantage from that (cf. 1 Cor. 14:17), and the gifts of the Spirit would then be put into practice more for their own sake than in the service of the Church.

Hence an ecumenical prayer group that is spiritually alive will find bearable even the pain of not yet being able to celebrate the Eucharist jointly. The charismatic renewal is active chiefly in the approaches to full Eucharistic fellowship and to the unity that all look for. According to the oldest tradition baptism and the reception of the Spirit are the pre-condition for receiving the Eucharist. Eucharistic sharing that has not been preceded by joint renewal of the Spirit cannot therefore lead to complete unity. Enduring present division and hoping in the future in the power of the renewal of the Spirit is thus throughout a profound spiritual proceeding. The experience of fellowship in the one Holy Spirit makes charismatic ecumenical prayer-groups capable of accepting the 'baptism of death'. If it is clearly stated that an invitation to communion cannot be extended, one should, in keeping with general custom, not turn back those who nevertheless would like to receive communion.

Third day: If I have not love

It is not by accident that Paul's hymn of love is placed between the twelfth and fourteenth chapters of his first letter to the Corinthians. Love is not one charism among others but the permanent source of all charisms. Love is deeper than all mere intention, deeper than all emotion, since it is God's love for other people being transmitted through me and at the same time Christ's love for them. In the coda to John's gospel is to be found the well-known passage (John 21:15):

> When they had finished breakfast, Jesus said to Simon Peter, 'Simon, son of John, do you love me more than these?' He said to him, 'Yes, Lord; you know that I love you.' He said to him, 'Feed my lambs.'

Three times Jesus puts this question to Peter, and three times he demands of him to love other people as he, Jesus, loves him, if he, Peter, wishes to love him. This does not apply just to Peter as the 'shepherd' (Romans 15:2-3, 14):

> Let each of us please his neighbour for his good, to edify him. For Christ did not please himself . . . I myself am satisfied about you, my brethren, that you yourselves are full of goodness, filled with all knowledge, and able to instruct one another.

Christ has a completely personal interest in each one of us, and we should identify ourselves with this. If therefore we make a prophetic contribution to the service, what should come out in this is Christ's interest in the other, his self-surrendering love. If we ask for healing, then we should love other people with the same love with which Jesus Christ looked on people and healed them. But if we want to make an impression on the others with our gifts of the Spirit, then what we leave behind is not the impression of Christ but the impression of our own personality. If our witness humbles the other person, shames him, pulverizes him, if it is aggressive, then it springs more from a feeling of spiritual superiority than from the love of Christ, then we abuse the gifts of the Spirit in order in this way to obtain recognition and respect.

The love that is meant here has nothing to do with sentimentality and emotionalism. It is primarily love for the whole Church, for its unity and its order. You will be led by it 'where you do not wish to go' (John 21:18), since it goes through and beyond the baptism of death, it does not seek itself for its own sake. Perhaps at the end of the sixth week God's Spirit has led you to this kind of love.

Fourth day: He who is mighty has done great things for me

The New Testament continually shows us that we cannot organize the gifts of the Spirit, cannot attain them by our own efforts, but can only accept them. From this the figure of Mary obtains a central significance for the charismatic renewal. She is the archetype of the person who in faith lets happen to her what the Lord has promised her (Luke 1:38, 45). The story of the annunciation has the character of the baptism of the Spirit: 'The Holy Spirit will come upon you, and the power of the Most High will overshadow you' (Luke 1:35). So it is no accident that Luke's description of the subsequent meeting between Elizabeth and Mary has echoes of a charismatic service (Luke 1:41-43, 45-47):

> And when Elizabeth heard the greeting of Mary, the babe leaped in her womb; and Elizabeth was filled with the Holy Spirit and she exclaimed with a loud cry, 'Blessed are you among women, and blessed is the fruit of your womb! And why is this granted me, that the mother of my Lord should come to me? . . . And blessed is she who believed that there would be a fulfilment of what was spoken to her from the Lord.'
> And Mary said,
> 'My soul magnifies the Lord,
> and my spirit rejoices in God my saviour.'

The purpose of this story is to indicate that the relationship of John the Baptist to Jesus was from the start pre-ordained by God. At the same time the whole account has charismatic and pentecostal features. Mary's greeting and the leaping of the baby in her womb induced in Elizabeth a profound spiritual convulsion, since she is filled with the Holy Spirit and exclaims with a loud cry: 'Blessed are you among women, and blessed is the fruit of your womb.' This utterance of praise is the first charismatic confession of faith in Christ to be found in Luke. From many points of view it is very personal. Elizabeth in her praise speaks of what is happening to her personally at a physical and intimate level, with the baby leaping in her womb, and she expresses her faith in 'her' Lord who meets her in Mary. The promise recorded by Luke at the start of the Acts of the Apostles — 'You shall be baptized with the Holy Spirit . . . and you shall be my witnesses' (Acts 1:5, 8) — already applies to Elizabeth.

In her joyful witness Elizabeth also appeals at the same time to Mary's faith: 'Blessed is she who believed.' Elizabeth's faith is service to the faith of Mary, who like all other men and women has made the 'pilgrimage of faith' (Vatican II, Constitution on the Church, 58). Mary's faith is shared and supported by Elizabeth's, and the Magnificat is a response of faith to Elizabeth's faith: one charism arouses another, one song of faith and praise another.

Mary now bears witness to her faith to Elizabeth in the form of a song of praise. She does not answer Elizabeth directly, but stands alone before God in the praise she utters. But, because she is uttering it out loud, it takes on the character of proclamation and has the same basic structure as the Pentecostal gift of tongues (Acts 2:4, 11). Mary too expresses her faith in a very personal way: 'He who is mighty has done great things for me.' In this way Elizabeth and Mary are at each other's service as 'good stewards of God's varied grace' (1 Peter 4:10), each with the gift she has received. Here it is made clear in an exemplary fashion what the common priesthood of all the faithful is.

The charismatic renewal however discovers another side to the figure of Mary, one that is hardly ever considered. The basic Christian experience and hence also the common priesthood of all the faithful starts with the acceptance of one's own death. The apostles Jesus selected were clearly not yet capable of doing so at Jesus's death. When he was arrested they fled (Matt. 26:56; Mark 14:50), nor were they present at the cross. All the synoptic gospels mention is some women accompanying Jesus while he was dying (Mark 15:40; Luke 23:49; Matt. 27:55-56). According to John's account Jesus's mother was among them. Whatever the actual historical details may have been, Mary at the cross, following John's account, represents that part of the Jewish people that was receptive to the salvation proclaimed by Christ (this is the commonest interpretation of experts in New Testament exegesis). This however also means that Mary has shared in the accomplishment of her son's death and approves and accepts it as the saving death that redeems all mankind, and this 'baptism of death' of hers includes the acceptance of her own physical death.

We have already said earlier that a turning point of this kind took place in the lives of the apostles between Easter and Pentecost, a turning point in which they accepted their own death in advance. If it should turn out that the twelve were not present at the foot of the cross, then Mary shared in this turning point in the apostles' lives through the acceptance of her own death. This was her charismatic service in and to the infant Church: the common priesthood of all believers sustains the apostolic ministry. With reference to acceptance of one's own death, the Church is also the historical continuation of Mary's experience of the Spirit.

Fifth day: Strive for the gift of prophecy

Right from its origin in Jesus Christ the Church is prophetic. The word 'prophet' means someone who proclaims or is called. In the broadest possible sense all Christians are called to proclaim the mighty works of God (cf. 1 Peter 2:9; Acts 2:11). Mary, too, was granted the charism of prophecy: 'Do whatever he tells you' (John 2:5). The prophet builds up, admonishes, consoles (1 Cor. 14:3). Something has been said about this in the explanations given in the sixth week of the first part of this work, and these need to be supplemented here by some further consideration of the way in which this gift is exercised.

All that Christians say and do in Church and society has a prophetic character. But it is only a comparative few on whom the gift of prophecy is bestowed in a special way, and it is not everyone who can exercise this gift in public worship (1 Cor. 12:29). Everyone however should thankfully accept and test what happens in this domain. A prophetic statement affects and challenges those who hear it no less than those through whom God wishes to act. It can however happen that the entire congregation speaks prophetically to the conscience of a single individual, as is made clear in the following passage (1 Cor. 14:24-25):

> But if all prophesy, and an unbeliever or outsider enters, he is convicted by all, he is called to account by all, the secrets of his heart are disclosed; and so, falling on his face, he will worship God and declare that God is really among you.

Through the gift of prophecy God calls to conversion, through it he reveals resistance to himself, through it he addresses men abd women (1 Cor. 14:3). In this way God is continually gathering his people afresh, their coming together takes place, and the Church as this coming together is made manifest. Open yourself, therefore, to this gift, since it has been appointed by God himself in the community of this gift of grace.

First, when you place yourself at God's disposal for a prophetic statement you are at the same time giving those present the opportunity as a body, as a congregation, to focus themselves on God. All jointly hear and test this summons. All are jointly involved at a very personal level by listening to this message and the question that arises whether God is really present in this statement. After a prophetic contribution that is accepted as such by all present an intense, almost breathless silence grips the assembly. All are gathered and assembled in a very intensive way: God wishes to be among us, indeed, he is present among us.

Second, when you yourself hear a prophetic contribution and are able to accept it as God's word to you, to the congregation, to the Church, then you experience God's presence more intensively than you would in situations in which you are alone or are merely thinking about God. To take an example, the phrase 'I am with you' occurs frequently in the Bible. When you read this and refer it to the situation you are living in at the moment, then God can by this word speak directly to you and call you to conversion. But if someone else at a prayer service addresses you in terms like this, then it is something you actually hear, it becomes a matter of the physical senses, something real and actual. We have already said many times that the experience of God's presence begins with seeing and hearing, in other words with words and events that reach us from outside. If someone else addresses this message to you, then his or her faith resonates with yours, as does his or her conviction that God is really with you, and this strengthens you in your resolve to accept this message. God's call 'I am with you' does not contain any revolutionary novelty for us, but when it is audibly addressed to you or to the assembled congregation then it contains a dynamic energy that does not come only from the person who utters it but from the power of the Holy Spirit who is the dynamic energy of God himself. What the angel said to Mary applies to every one of us: 'The Holy Spirit will come upon you, and the power of the Most High will overshadow you' (Luke 1:35), but this is not a message we can address to ourselves. If we were to address this message out loud to ourselves we would have the impression of trying to impose on ourselves. But if it penetrates us from outside ourselves, then at the same time it overcomes our inner resistance against trusting God. In genuine prophecy that comes from God, God himself is dealing with you.

So, despite all your legitimate misgivings, open yourself to this gift of grace too. Do not say you are too young or too old, do not say you are not capable and worthy of such a ministry. To you too applies what was said to the prophet Jeremiah when he demurred at what was being asked of him: 'To all to whom I send you you shall go, and whatever I command you you shall speak' (Jer. 1:7). To begin with it is useful advice to read the Gospels widely and note the sayings of Jesus that are recorded in them. During the service of prayer the Holy Spirit will recall them to your mind and indicate when in Christ's place you should bring them before the congregation. Everything happens with the aim of building up. You will grow further into the gifts of prophecy if you let yourself be led by God's Spirit.

Sixth day: Let spiritual songs resound among you as the Spirit gives utterance

In the explanatory passages of the sixth week of the first

part of this work we have said something about speaking
in tongues, and here we would like to supplement that with
some remarks about its exercise in practice. Speaking in
tongues is a form of worship in which the mystery of God
himself enters into our very speech. It is an utterance of
what is unutterable, the worship of God for his own sake,
because he is God. How should we worship the mystery of
God if it remains unknowable and inexpressible? We can
praise God on account of his creation and then go on to
enumerate all the creatures and things he has made. The
content of what we are saying can then be understood
by everyone. St Francis of Assisi's Canticle of All Created
Things (*Cantico delle creature*) is one of the finest hymns of
praise of this kind, praising God for the sun, the moon and
the stars, for wind and weather, for water and fire, for mother
earth with its fruits and plants, and for 'our sister the death
of the body'. But when we worship God because he is God,
then all we can utter is: 'We praise you, we glorify you, we
worship you.' Addressing God as you no longer has any
special meaning because we cannot really imagine or conceive
what this you of God is. None of our human words, and that
includes words like God, Father, holy, etc., can grasp and
comprehend the mystery of God. They remain our human
words, filled with our human experiences. The Bible itself
applies such concepts to God by a species of translation,
but who God is and how he exists in himself remains an
unknowable and inexpressible mystery. If in this situation we
begin to recount God's qualities — you alone are holy, you
alone are the Lord, you alone are the most high — then once
again we are importing certain meanings into our addressing
God as you. But in practising speaking in tongues we are
taking God's inexpressibility quite seriously. Hence this form
of prayer provides a substantial enrichment and offers many
a way in to worshipping God for his own sake.

In the first part of this work (sixth week, third section)
we have drawn attention to some of the preparatory stages
that precede this form of prayer. Paul explicitly refers to
God having appointed 'various kinds' of speaking in tongues
(1 Cor. 12:28). One of these forms is surely the invocation:
'Abba, Father' (Rom. 8:15; Gal. 4-6). Its frequent repetition

does not make any sense to the intellect (1 Cor. 14:11, 14): I am not communicating anything to other people but am asserting myself with reference to the inexpressible otherness of God. In this sense speaking in tongues is a stammering.

If God's Spirit has already led you to take your first steps of faith, or to go beyond where you have already reached, or has begun to lead you to do so over the past few weeks, then you can now ask God for this gift, even without the assistance of other people. It is first of all a natural occurrence, for every human being has from his or her birth the primal ability to speak, and in the infant this is shaped into his or her mother-tongue. In speaking in tongues speech comes forth once more unshaped from the depths of our being and in this way becomes at the same time the expression of our faith. Without the very personal component of faith speaking in tongues remains a psychological event like many others. Recall first of all that God has really appointed this gift and has thus promised it to you too (1 Cor. 12:28). Not everyone can or should exercise this gift in public among the community he or she belongs to, but it is bestowed on everyone in the solitude of private prayer if he or she asks God for it. Be convinced that God is offering this gift to you too. You do not have to accept this gift any more than you have to accept the presents that are offered you on your birthday. Perhaps it will be granted you only much later, after the first renewal of the Spirit.

If you are ready to accept this gift, then pray for a time using your own words at first: ask and you shall receive. God wants to let you share in his mystery, his Spirit liberates you so that you can leave behind you all concepts and images of God and simply approach this inexpressible other. Begin in an attitude of profound surrender and adoration with a few vowels that come into your mind and add some consonants to them without being concerned about what you are saying. Many people find the first experience humiliating and are afraid of the sounds they are giving utterance to. Perhaps to begin with they are only scraps of words, and many people have the feeling they are pulling the wool over their own eyes. But one cannot make up the speechless language of worship, since one must let oneself go completely. Otherwise all one produces is a meaningless artificial language.

Many people find that speaking in tongues develops over the course of time. It contains melody and rhythm and flows like a fountain that had been choked with rubbish but has now become a living spring or worship of God and joy in his presence: ' "He who believes in me, as the scripture has said, 'Out of his heart shall flow rivers of living water.' " Now this he said about the Spirit, which those who believed in him were to receive' (John 7:38-39). Speaking in tongues is a process in which the Spirit received in faith flows out of us again.

Paul wants all the Corinthians to speak in tongues, but he gives the very precise instruction that speaking in tongues by individuals should occur only twice or three times during the service. He would sooner speak five words with his mind before the community in order to instruct others than ten thousand words in the form of speaking in tongues (1 Cor. 14:19). But when on the other hand in the experience of the divine mystery tremendous significance is attached to speaking in tongues the reverse applies: in order to speak five words in the congregation with understanding, words that arouse, convict, build up, admonish, words in which the power of the Spirit is alive, I must perhaps have previously prayed ten thousand words in tongues so that I may inwardly be open for the 'mystery of the Gospel' (Eph. 6:19).

It can be a help if others on whom the gift of tongues has already been bestowed pray with us the first time we pray in this manner. This is in no way a process of initiation by means of suggestion or imitation but a stimulation of one's own spontaneity. What is important is not whether on the the first occasion others helped me but whether thereafter I speak in tongues on my own. If I am learning to swim I am grateful for others helping me to overcome my fear of the water. What is important is simply that I should learn to swim by my own efforts and on my own.

In services with a larger congregation from the whole community 'singing in the Spirit' can find an accepted place (Eph. 5:18-20; Col. 3:16-17):

> But be filled with the Spirit, addressing one another in psalms and hymns and spiritual songs, singing and

making melody to the Lord with all your heart, always
and for everything giving thanks in the name of our
Lord Jesus Christ to God the Father.

Let the word of Christ dwell in you richly, as you teach
and admonish one another in all wisdom, and as you
sing psalms and hymns and spiritual songs with thank-
fulness in your hearts to God. And whatever you do, in
word or deed, do everything in the name of the Lord
Jesus, giving thanks to God the Father through him.

What are meant here are without a doubt not songs that have
been written according to the rules of composition but those
that rise up while the service is being conducted from a full
heart, from the fullness of the Spirit. A preparatory stage
would be intensive joint prayer by the choir before the talk is
given. There is a distinction between a hymn being performed
purely 'artistically' and this performing being at the same
time a spiritual service to the faith of the others present that
arises from the fullness of the Spirit.

Such a service is the consonance of many people speaking
in tongues to form the harmony of the one body of Christ.
Following on one of the usual hymns or arising out of the
fullness of the moment someone sings a note and all the
others take it up and then try to find notes above and below
it that together will provide suitable harmony. This is both a
spiritual and a social event. The melodies are not provided in
advance, but everyone fits into the whole so that 'there may
be no discord in the body' (cf. 1 Cor. 12:25). Everyone can
climb up and down this melodic trellis, can sing and play as
the Spirit prompts him or her to do. There can be invocations
in the vernacular — 'Jesus is Lord,' for example, or 'Lord
have mercy' — an alleluia or a simple vowel. It is not a question
of what one is singing or playing, but simply the fact that
one is singing out of one's whole being before God, in deep
adoration at his inexpressible mystery. Everyone can take
part in this singing in the Spirit, even if he or she has not
been granted the gift of speaking in tongues in the stricter
sense. Everyone is promised the experience of prayer as
something taking place in God, within the inexpressible

mystery itself: God, the Holy Spirit, prays in us through the God-man Jesus Christ to God the Father.

Seventh day: The rediscovery of mystery

Whether a community is alive or not is shown by whether the various different gifts of the Spirit co-operate together. However one cannot introduce the exercise of the gifts of the Spirit as if it were a reform of structure or a liturgical reform. Instead, it demands as a prior condition a profound self-surrender of each individual to the mystery of God. It will always remain a mystery how the gifts of the Spirit are the 'manifestation of the Spirit' (1 Cor. 12:7), and hence they arouse in historically new ways the appreciation and awareness of mystery. In our modern, rational and technological civilization the exercise of the gifts of the Spirit comes up against inward resistance, rejection, mockery or distant coolness not least because this rational civilization is thereby in an unexpected fashion once more confronted with the mystery of God. It is more and more evident that the loss of mystery does not only make man spiritually ill but hands him immediately over to modern doctrines of salvation. Where this loss is experienced as such, these new doctrines of salvation are presented as mysterious and sacrosanct in themselves, above all in totalitarian states. Every man or woman venerates, openly or secretly, some power superior to himself or herself. This can be the party's programme, one's personal standard of life, or some other world view. Mystery is not only the boundary of what we can know, but it belongs to the essence of man to venerate some mystery or other, and this not just occasionally at more or less rare intervals. Rather, man's inner striving has as its goal 'what no eyes has seen, nor ear heard' (1 Cor. 2:9 quoting Isaiah 64:4). This applies to space travel no less than to plans and hopes for the future.

Moreover, without the rediscovery of the divine mystery the deterioration of public worship will progress further. On many sides today there prevails a lack of clarity about what really happens or should happen in the liturgy. This is shown not only by the decline in church-going but also and above all by the many different types of 'experiment': liturgy as a framework for discussion or liturgy as the articulation of a ginger group. This lack of clarity is shown by the release of purely natural spontaneity in keeping with the view that you should feel completely at home in church, that you need not sit still but should move, dance, express yourselves, and so on.

In contrast to this it has expressly been indicated that the fundamental dimension of the liturgy, the liturgy of the word just as much as the actual Eucharist and the administration of the sacraments, is the sense of mystery (Eph. 3:1-5; Eph, 6:18-20; 1 Cor. 4:1):

> For this reason I, Paul, a prisoner for Christ Jesus on behalf of you Gentiles — assuming that you have heard of the stewardship of God's grace that was given to me for you, how the mystery was made known to me by revelation, as I have written briefly. When you read this you can perceive my insight into the mystery of Christ, which was not made known to the sons of men in other generations as it has now been revealed to his holy apostles and prophets by the Spirit.

> Pray at all times in the Spirit, with all prayer and supplication. To that end keep alert with all perseverance, making supplication for all the saints and also for me, that utterance may be given me in opening my mouth boldly to proclaim the mystery of the gospel, for which I am an ambassador in chains; that I may declare it boldly, as I ought to speak.

> This is how one should regard us, as servants of Christ and stewards of the mysteries of God.

Paul speaks on the basis of a personal experience of the divine mystery that was made manifest to him at his 'baptism of Spirit' on the road to Damascus (cf. Acts 9:17, 22:15, 26:16). It is no accident that in the second passage quoted above (Eph. 6:18) he refers to unceasing prayer 'in the Spirit', to speaking in tongues. In it he becomes aware that it is the mystery of the gospel that is the authority that has sent him forth: he is the 'ambassador' of the mystery of the gospel. In another passage he explains what is meant by this (1 Cor. 2:7-10):

> But we impart a secret and hidden wisdom of God, which God decreed before the ages for our glorification. None of the rulers of this age understood this; for if they had, they would not have crucified the Lord of glory, But, as it is written,
> 'What no eye has seen, nor ear heard,
> nor the heart of man conceived,
> what God has prepared for those who love him,'
> God has revealed to us through the Spirit. For the Spirit searches everything, even the depths of God.

The 'depths of God' are his primal and individual mystery that only he himself knows and searches out. Eternal life will consist of us penetrating ever more deeply into this mystery of God and it becoming ever more manifest as mystery. Proclamation of the faith, exercising the gifts of the Spirit, is already a participation in God's experience of himself. He reveals it to us so that we may bear witness to it. If we surrender ourselves to this mystery, then we know what we are saying if in the presence of others we utter the words 'God' or 'Jesus' or 'Holy Spirit'.

The rediscovery of mystery in the charismatic renewal has at the same time a considerable critical power with regard to our relations to society. Experience of the divine mystery enables us to take up a critical distance over against all purely secular doctrines of salvation. No political power will be able to crush and oppress us — not the principle of private profit, a principle that lacks all mystery, nor other doctrines that seek to make out of the state or out of a party the final mystery of our life. We have experienced the mystery of God within ourselves and hence on the basis of this we can, with the fullest commitment and with critical detachment, co-operate in changing society.

Seventh week: Discernment

First day: Your decision for Christ is an indelible seal

Of all distinctions the most important is that between God and the powers that are arrayed against God, between the Spirit of Christ and the evil spirit. Perhaps over the past six weeks you have let yourself be led so far by the Spirit of God that you are able to decide for God and Christ, that you have already taken this step or want to take it in the near future. During the fourth week (on the fifth day) we said that we can be forgiven every sin, but if we consciously fail to decide for Christ God cannot forgive us this sin because we have not asked him to do so. But if we decide for Christ then by this decision we remain marked and impressed once and for ever. It is something that in the full sense we can no longer revoke. We can never again act as if we had never heard anything of God and had never accepted his offer. Our experience is similar to that of a married couple who were once profoundly in love. They remain influenced by each other and even after separating later can never again act as if they had never met each other. They carry in themselves the impression of the other person just as if it were the indelible impression of a seal. Love can turn into hatred and rejection. All it does is to turn it into its contrary.

It is in this sense that on several occasions the New Testament says that in the decision of baptism God has impressed his seal upon us (2 Cor. 1:21-22; Eph. 1:13; Eph. 4:30-32):

> But it is God who establishes us with you in Christ, and has commissioned us; he has put his seal upon us and given us his Spirit in our hearts as a guarantee.

> In him, you also, who have heard the word of truth, the gospel of your salvation, and have believed in him, were sealed with the promised Holy Spirit.

> And do not grieve the Holy Spirit of God, in whom you were sealed for the day of redemption. Let all bitterness

and wrath and anger and clamour and slander be put away from you, with all malice, and be kind to one another, tenderhearted, forgiving one another, as God in Christ forgave you.

It is not only that our decision for Christ takes place in the power of the Holy Spirit, but that this Spirit impresses itself on our innermost self in this decision like a signet-ring on sealing wax. Even today important documents are still provided with a seal and thereby attested and irrevocably confirmed. The letter to the Hebrews says (Hebr. 6:4-6):

> For it is impossible to restore again to repentance those who have once been enlightened, who have tasted the heavenly gift, and have become partakers of the Holy Spirit, and have tasted the goodness of the word of God and the powers of the age to come, if they then commit apostasy, since they crucify the Son of God on their own account and hold him up to contempt.

Through baptism we have tasted the heavenly gift, the powers of the world to come, and if this decision reaches down into the profoundest depths of our being we cannot make a conversion of this kind a second time with the same intensity. Conversion is a lifelong process, but the initial decision for Christ makes such an impression that the impression it makes remains indelible. In this manner we become like Christ, for on Christ too 'the Father has set his seal' (John 6:27).

At the start of this seventh week ponder these passages. They will make you joyful. Deciding for Christ is not something gloomy and deadly serious. In it we 'taste' the powers of the world to come and already belong to those who bear God's seal on their foreheads (Rev. 7:3). The gift of discernment is thus a working out of this fact that you are differentiated from everything that is not God.

Second day: The powers of evil will try to turn your decision for Christ into its opposite

If before witnesses and with their help you have surrendered your life to Christ, then more than previously will you become aware of the temptation to misuse and abuse the power that has been bestowed on you (cf. the first section in the talk for the seventh week). Christ too was led into this temptation after his baptism by the Spirit. Satan does not dispute that Christ has been baptized with the Holy Spirit but seeks to turn this happening into its opposite. Jesus is asked to misuse his power (Luke 4:1-13) and thus to fall away from God in a way that just would not have been possible without his experience of the Spirit. Our experience will be no different. Deciding for Christ must involve an ever clearer differentiation from the powers of evil. This is something that does not happen without a struggle (Eph. 6:10-13):

> Finally, be strong in the Lord and in the strength of his might. Put on the whole armour of God, that you may be able to stand against the wiles of the devil. For we are not contending against flesh and blood, but against the principalities, against the powers, against the world rulers of this present darkness, against the spiritual hosts of wickedness in the heavenly places. Therefore take the whole armour of God, that you may be able to withstand in the evil day, and having done all, to stand.

The strength of the Lord's might through which we become strong is the Spirit of the Lord, as Paul shows when in the same letter he asks 'that according to the riches of his glory he [the Father] may grant you to be strengthened with might through his Spirit in the inner man' (Eph. 3:16). This request God fulfils whenever we ask him for the fulness of his Spirit, for it is only possible to make this request in the fullness of the Spirit — with the result that it has already been fulfilled before we express it. Hence someone who has prayed for the fullness of the Spirit needs to be certain that in the depths of his or her being he or she has grown in power and strength through God's Spirit. This growth provokes the powers of evil to put in an appearance. They tried to induce Jesus after his baptism of the Spirit to misuse his gifts of the Spirit. Your experience will be no different, Every one of us must fight for 'the gospel of peace' (Eph. 6:15).

Hence the letter to the Ephesians uses the equipment of contemporary soldiers to describe the struggle the Christian must wage: the breastplate of righteousness, the shield of faith, the sword of the Spirit. It is all summed up in the exhortation: 'Pray at all times in the Spirit, with all prayer and supplication. To that end keep alert with all perseverance, making supplication for all the saints' (Eph. 6:18). Prayer 'in the Spirit' is the strongest weapon of defence we have. Very probably what is meant here is speaking in tongues (cf. the distinction between praying with the spirit and praying with the mind in 1 Cor. 14:14-15). It is a prayer of victory, for the Spirit of God is himself praying within us. It purifies the depths of our being from the suspicion against God that is continually welling up within us. And particularly in situations that do not seem to offer any way out, when our illusions and expectations have been shattered, when we have been traduced and defamed, when anger wells up within us or enmity or disordered sexuality, it is a prayer that purifies our impulses.

The passage we have quoted from the letter to the Ephesians admonishes us to withstand the wiles of the devil. The devil does not just want to lead us astray into misusing the gifts of the Spirit that have been bestowed on us but wants to persuade us to stop being so stupid as to surrender ourself to God on the grounds that we are someone after all. 'Maintain a healthy suspicion with regard to God,' is the line he takes. 'Do not give your freedom back to God, do not even give him back your power of speech. Keep in reserve the readiness to renounce your covenant with God if he does not fulfil what you want.' Satan goes on trying to persuade us on these lines: 'Perhaps it was only a momentary caprice or whim when you prayed for the renewal of the Spirit. Perhaps you only did it because everyone else was doing it. Perhaps it is all a question of group dynamics. So be honest. You have not turned into somebody else. Don't kid yourself. You will see: after a few weeks all this fantastic nonsense will have disappeared, and you won't notice anything supernatural. You will experience crises and periods of dryness. So leave it all well alone and stand on your own two feet.' Satan attacks each of us at his or her weakest point: fear, suspicion, pride, need of approval, independence, depression, etc. (1 Peter 5:8):

> Be sober, be watchful. Your adversary the devil prowls around like a roaring lion, seeking some one to devour.

Third day: Let the seed of God's word grow within you

We have heard the parable of the sower and its interpretation often enough in church. It may be that at the end of this course of initiation this interpretation takes on a new meaning (Matt. 13:18-23):

> 'Hear then the parable of the sower. When any one hears the word of the kingdom and does not understand it, the evil one comes and snatches away what is sown in his heart; this is what was sown along the path. As for what was sown on rocky ground, this is he who hears the word and immediately receives it with joy; yet he has no root in himself, but endures for a while, and when tribulation or persecution arises on account of the word, immediately he falls away. As for what was sown among thorns, this is he who hears the word, but the cares of the world and the delight in riches choke the word, and it proves unfruitful. As for what was sown on good soil, this is he who hears the word and understands it; he indeed bears fruit, and yields, in one case a hundredfold, in another sixty, and in another thirty.'

The field is the heart and the seed is the word of God. Has the word of conversion touched you to the heart like those who heard Peter's sermon at Pentecost (Acts 2:37)? Or have you not understood the word of conversion because your heart has been hardened (cf. Matt. 13:15)? Dark and mysterious is our struggling against accepting the word of God. All of us are not yet fully converted, are not yet healed and made whole. We have often enough prayed Jesus to lay his hands on us, to open our eyes and ears, but continually we have failed really to understand him. Viewed in ourselves we remain God's enemies, despite all his gifts of grace and despite his having accepted us as his children. 'The evil one' has all too often succeeded in taking away again what God has sown in our heart. We have fallen away from him and will continually go on falling away from him.

Or must you count yourself among those who hear the word of God and immediately receive it with joy but have no staying power outside the immediate moment — those who draw back at the first contemptuous remarks from others and relapse into their old habits? Perhaps the immediate impact on you of a prayer service was to appeal to you: you liked the atmosphere, the openness and frankness, the encounter with other people. You enjoyed your enjoyment, but it did not go very deep, it had not struck any roots. In the truest sense of the phrase your enjoyment was a matter of superficial enthusiasm and thus only an episode in your life, no real conversion, no real turning point. To begin with this is how it happens with nearly everybody.

Or do you belong to those in whom God's word and joy and peace and love may have struck roots but has then been choked by excessive cares and concerns, by excessive consumption of this world's goods, by too much television even? Who can say that he or she is not continually fascinated by a high standard of living, by possessions, or by the technological mastery of modern civilization? Go back and read what you wrote down on the third day of the first week.

Or can you say of yourself that the word of conversion and salvation has penetrated deep into your heart and has borne fruit, the 'fruit of the Spirit' (cf. Gal. 5:22)? The parable exhorts us to be contented with the fruits and gifts that the Spirit allots as he wishes (1 Cor. 12:11). Love is not jealous for other people's spiritual gifts, but rejoices in what God has bestowed on someone else. Perhaps in your case the word has borne fruit only thirtyfold and in someone else's case a hundredfold. No one can himself or herself determine which gifts of the Spirit will be bestowed on him or her and how many of them there will be.

Fourth day: Do not think highly of yourself but remain humble

In the talk given in the seventh week of the study group indications are pointed out by which we can recognize the working of the Holy Spirit in ourselves. There are general signs whereby this can be discerned (agreement with God's word and the teaching of the Church, service in building up both Church and world, fulfilment of one's everyday duties) and personal signs (love, joy, peace). Taken by itself any individual one of these indications remains ambiguous. But when several of them or all of them come together, there is no need to have any more doubts about the genuineness of a particular example of the Holy Spirit at work. Nevertheless the question can still arise whether it is more a case of the Holy Spirit being at work or whether it is more our human impulses, including our tendency to sin. Common to all indications is humility, willingness to serve, since all the gifts of the Spirit involve making us capable of being at the service of others. Humility recognizes that in his eternal plan for every individual God has established the measure of grace. Hence Paul says in his letter to the Romans before he comes to enumerate the gifts of the Spirit (Rom. 12:3, 6; Eph. 4:7):

> For by the grace given to me I bid every one among you not to think of himself more highly than he ought to think, but to think with sober judgement, each according to the measure of faith which God has assigned him . . . Having gifts that differ according to the grace given to us, let us use them.

But grace was given to each of us according to the measure of Christ's gift. This applies to every individual and to the charismatic renewal as a whole. Anyone who on the basis of the general and personal indications knows that he or she has legitimately been called to co-operate in the renewal of the Church easily tends towards an insider's over-estimation of the charismatic movement as such. God renews his Church in a variety of ways, and there is no doubt that the Holy

Spirit is not at work only in those who have opened themselves to the charismatic renewal. Often indeed the numbers of those involved in this renewal are exaggerated. Frequently this does not occur because of any desire to inflate the movement's reputation but simply in order to show how mightily God is at work in this present day and age. But an even greater danger is that of having far too high an opinion of oneself personally, something which has its roots in our ineradicable egocentricity. For this reason Paul exhorted his audience to sober judgement and humility with regard to the gifts of the Spirit. Let us quote a few examples.

First, health. The case can arise of someone involving himself or herself in work for the charismatic renewal to such an extent that too great a demand is placed on his or her physical and mental resources and that he or she suffers physical and psychological harm. Of course we are called upon to do our utmost, but if we place too great a strain on ourselves, go with too little sleep, become bad-tempered, irritable and unbalanced, then this is wrong for a start. There are examples from the lives of holy men and women who in the truest sense of the word have worn themselves out in the service of others, but everyone must adduce reasons that prove to himself or herself and to others that this is God's will in his or her particular case. Otherwise the initial presumption is that too great a strain on someone's health derives more from one's own egoistic drives than from the impulses of the Holy Spirit.

Second, mental illnesses. Often people who are mentally unbalanced join prayer-groups in the hope that through membership of the group or through the charismatic renewal they may be relieved of their inner burdens. Many prayer groups have not been able to stay alive and have come to an end because it was predominantly people of this type who came together in them. What is quite fundamental is that the charismatic renewal places a tremendous demand on every individual involved in it, since conversion and self-abandonment are often connected with long inward struggles and demand mental health as a pre-condition. Hence as a rule prayer groups should not presume to accept as members people who are mentally ill unless they have available an experienced psychologist or psychotherapist. Simply to understand people who are mentally ill or unbalanced as a rule exceeds the knowledge and also the resources of members of prayer groups. The request for inward psychological healing demands in every case a knowledge of the mind's internal injuries or of the causes of the particular mental illness (and so too does the attempt made in the third week to recall one's past). But for those who in a medical sense are mentally ill it is precisely recognizing the fact and nature of their illness that is the most difficult thing. Often they are only ready to do so when the pressure of their inner or outer life is correspondingly great, when in some way they really break down. In this case it is only an experienced psychotherapist who can help them towards becoming aware of their illness. It is a great misfortune when one is not ready to see the reality of things as they are in their proper autonomy and when prayer groups try in a dilettante-ish manner to provide free psychotherapy. Mental illnesses are then often hidden or suppressed and their victims are not able properly to become aware of them. The process of mental healings is thus put off or prevented. But after expert advice has been sought prayer-groups can contribute much to the process of healing through the joy, love and freedom that is alive in them. In any event this once again demands humility of those who are mentally ill, so that they do not make themselves the standard whereby the experience of God's grace can be measured. There are two important cases:

First, the depressive. Many people continually suffer from bouts of depression to such an extent that everything is seen in relation to themselves and stands in judgment upon them. From the biblical call to repentance and from instruction in looking into their own souls they derive what had already been burdening them, and this intensifies their depression. Their feelings of guilt, already more than strong enough, rise to the pitch where they become intolerable. In any event they often perceive more keenly than others what real and genuine conversion is and so they can perform an important service, provided they do not in this turn themselves into an absolute standard by which others can be measured. But also they often try to balance their depression by that much more activity, active campaigns or contact with the real world (manic depressive psychosis).

Second, the hysteric. The hysterical person also sees everything in relation ot himself or herself, but in everything he or she sees a possibility of increasing his or her respect and reputation. While the depressive often emphatically blames the influence of Satan for his complaints, the hysterical person continually lives in an unreal way in 'heaven'. What he or she is primarily concerned about is not conversion and repentance. Instead he or she continually strives after the 'higher' gifts of the spirit so as to demonstrate his or her superiority. Because of a deeply rooted feeling of inferiority he or she is continually trying to show that the others are not yet really charismatic. As this always happens somehow or other, the result in this case is to introduce into the prayer groups a restlessness and disturbance that is not the work the Spirit. Often the consequence is dissension and splitting up.

Mentally unbalanced people should never have anything to do with running prayer groups.

Fifth day: We do not give anyone even the slightest offence

The renewal of the Church is not something that can be bestowed overnight. The very personal step of renewal of the Spirit is something that to begin with can only grow in smaller groups.

These however often have the effect of unexpectedly drawing attention to themselves, and hence members of such groups are watched with an especially critical eye, both with regard to the change in their everyday life and with regard to the critical role they adopt over against society. What one preaches must coincide with the life one lives. The following passage applies first of all to every Christian (2 Cor. 6:1, 3-10):

> Working together with him [God], then, we entreat you not to accept the grace of God in vain . . . We put no

obstacle in any one's way, so that no fault may be found with our ministry, but as servants of God we commend ourselves in every way: through great endurance, in afflictions, hardships, calamities, beatings, imprisonments, tumults, labours, watching, hunger; by purity, knowledge, forbearance, kindness, the Holy Spirit, genuine love, truthful speech, and the power of God; with the weapons of righteousness for the right hand and for the left; in honour and dishonour, in ill repute and good repute. We are treated as imposters, and yet are true; as unknown, and yet well known; as dying, and behold, we live; as punished, and yet not killed; as sorrowful, yet always rejoicing; as poor, yet making many rich; as having nothing, and yet possessing everything.

Someone who for the first time comes into contact with the renewal of the Church feels to begin with that he or she personally is being called into question, because once someone becomes involved with this there is much in one's personal life that must and will change. Hence as a rule the first reaction is resistance: this is something everybody has experienced, and this reaction of resistance never quite dies away completely. One looks for all kinds of reasons why one should not have to become involved in this renewal. Perhaps the people that are involved in it do not exhibit that healthy a spirituality, perhaps they are overbearing and presumptuous. Hence the first question to be raised is frequently: 'How do these people behave in their everyday lives? Are they better than us? With what authority do they come before us?' It is absolutely right for outsiders to use as a criterion for judging the worthwhileness of what is going on the effect of the renewal on the actual local Christian community or religious house affected.

Personal witness on behalf of the renewal can be so 'offensive' that a parish can become split between 'charismatics' (a term that should be avoided for this reason alone) and unaroused traditional Christians. If someone's opinion of himself or herself is: 'Because of my renewal of the Spirit I am better than others,' then this is profoundly wrong. It should rather be a case of other people having occasion to remark that he or she is different from what he or she used to be — and better. If someone attends only the prayer meetings but no longer takes part in the life of his or her parish then he or she is not serving the renewal of the Church and has received the grace of God 'in vain'. Harsh things are then — rightly — said about the charismatic renewal. What should happen is that the individual's contribution to the life of his or her parish should be more intensive and more personal than it was formerly. In actual fact many say that they take part in Sunday worship in their parish with greater inward participation than before, since God's presence in the liturgy has become apparent to them in a new way.

The same applies to religious houses and to monastic and para-monastic communities. Where people are living very closely together a 'separate' prayer group can cause considerable disturbance to community life. If it shuts itself away from the rest of the community and individual members of it only rarely or irregularly take part in the normal services and times of prayer, this does not serve the renewal of the religious community concerned but marks instead the emergence of a new order or congregation within the existing one. This can reach the point of some members of the house coming into conflict with the rules of the order or making an internal migration out of it. But the foundation of each religious order was marked by a charismatic experience, and it would be a sin against the Holy Spirit to want to leave this behind one. The charismatic renewal does not only introduce genuinely new elements into the Christian life but contains in itself the power to bring back to life, and in an unexpected way, genuine achievements of the Spirit from past ages.

Sixth day: Criticism of Church and society

The charismatic renewal sharpens one's eye for improper claims to power in Church and society, but criticism of these is not its starting point. Rather, its starting point is the task of criticism with God as its criterion, and it is only from the spiritual gift of discernment that there grows the criticism that is needed in Church and society. In keeping with its inner and most characteristic impulse the charismatic renewal is not primarily a reaction against what exists but rather a campaign of action directed towards the future of the Church and of society. This does not exclude a protest in particular cases. Paul withstood Peter to his face 'before them all' because he had drawn back from the truth of the Gospel (Gal. 2:11-21). Criticism of unjust social and political conditions, too, can and must in certain circumstances go as far as protest, since such conditions can often not be overcome without a struggle. This kind of criticism in Church and world is necessary above all when those in positions of leadership and power abuse their power. Let us therefore at the end of the seventh week read some suitable passages from the New Testament (1 Thess. 2:5-7; 2 Cor. 1:24):

> For we never used either words of flattery, as you know, or a cloak for greed, as God is witness; nor did we seek glory from men, whether from you or from others, though we might have made demands as apostles of Christ. But we were gentle among you, like a nurse taking care of her children.

> Not that we lord it over your faith; we work with you for your joy.

The history of the Church shows that those holding high office within it have continually become subject to greed and have sought their own honour and glory. Paul indeed says: 'We might have made demands as apostles of Christ,' but did not do so in order that his preaching might be accepted as the word not of man but of God (cf. 1 Thess. 2:13; 1 Cor. 2:3-5). For those who are reputed to be something (cf. Gal. 2:6) the temptation is great to ascribe to themselves the power of Christ and the respect that attaches to his person, and to misuse these to increase their own standing. For this reason, too, the Church stands in need of a 'continual reformation', as the Second Vatican Council has pointed out (decree on ecumenism, *Unitatis redintegratio*, 6), and this is the duty of the whole Church and of every individual member of it. Certain basic attitudes on the part of the Church's ministers that were in part the occasion for the protest of the Reformers in the sixteenth century were labelled by that Council as triumphalism, clericalism, juridicism and were rejected. Similar basic attitudes, however, are not unknown in the Churches that arose from the sixteenth century Reformation. Here too the gifts of the Spirit are often lumped in with the competence of the individual minister.

Doing away with these distortions and corruptions is nevertheless not possible if tackled primarily at the sociological level, by setting up councils, committees, synods. Simply changing the Church's internal structures and making it more democratic is not a spiritual process. But what would happen if the parish council, the senate of priests, the bishops' conference interrupted its deliberations for a period of silent prayer for insight and wisdom, if the process of reaching a decision were a 'conciliar' process, as was described in the study group talk for the seventh week?

This kind of spiritual renewal is not however something that can be imposed arbitrarily, above all not with means taken from the context of political struggle. It is something that is bestowed as a gift if those in positions of leadership allow the very personal process of renewal of the Spirit to take place in them. At the international congress of the Catholic charismatic renewal in Rome in 1975 a bishop publicly confessed to the ten thousand participants: 'Formerly I used to be the king in my diocese. After I had prayed for the laying on of hands — and for me this was the renewal of my ordination — I can only look back with shame on that period of my life.' It is thus conceivable that in the future the parish priest would renew his ordination publicly before his parish and ask his parishioners to lay their hands on him.

The leaders of the major Christian Churches will initially shrink back from such a step, since they would fear a diminution of their rôle as it has developed historically, a lessening of the respect in which their office is held. But objectively speaking there is no reason for this anxiety. Many ecclesiastical crises would never arise if the parish priest looked forward every week to taking part in a service of prayer in which he was given human and spiritual support and in which he received more from the faith of the others taking part than he could ever mediate himself. A guardian of the faith would thus in a spiritual way become a servant of joy: 'For the Son of man also came not to be served but to serve, and to give his life as a ranson for many' (Mark 10:45).

Doing away with power in this way, where it is accepted as a gift, cannot simply be transferred without more ado to the plane of secular and political reality. We can hardly expect those who hold political power to be converted to Christ at once and all together. It is only in the eschatological, heavenly city that God alone will rule: 'By its light shall the nations walk; and the kings of the earth shall bring their glory into it . . .; they shall bring into it the glory and the honour of the nations. But nothing unclean shall enter it, nor any one who practises abomination or falsehood' (Rev. 21:24, 26-27). Right up to the end of time what Jesus is recorded by Mark as saying will hold true: 'You know that those who are supposed to rule over the Gentiles lord it over them, and their great men exercise authority over them' (Mark 10:42). The Christian encounters every secular power with a feeling of reservation that comes from his or her faith, and he or she does not let himself or herself be oppressed or abused by it. The taking of active measures in the political struggle can therefore arise from the experience of faith and thus in certain circumstances be necessary and expedient. The principle of private profit in the wealthy industrialized countries of the West is just as un-Christian as the principle of collective profit in the countries of the East. The charismatic renewal is in itself to a very great extent critical of society because it transcends this principle of profitability as an absolute. Praying to God does not entail any 'profit' but for the progress of society it is more important than a society which is geared to productivity and competition and which has lost all sense of mystery. And criticism of society is involved not least in the silent endurance of the suppression of religious freedom.

Seventh day: How do I bear witness?

Through the renewal of the Spirit we become missionaries of
Jesus Christ, witnesses to the new life that God is offering
to all men and women. We experience fellowship with God
at an especially profound level if we are permitted to be
aware of how other people come to believe through our
own witness to the faith. This was indeed the missionary
system of the primitive Church, for every Christian to be a
missionary. The renewal of the Church cannot be propagated
by means of modern propaganda and publicity, but only
by the personal witness to faith on a person-to-person basis —
which does not exclude the use of such modern means as
film, tape cassettes, periodicals, etc. The reason is that modern
publicity tends towards exaggeration and the creation of
bogus values, and frequently is primarily concerned to
address itself to the emotions. Christian witness on the
contrary is concerned with facts.

Hence one should only bear witness after a certain period
of probation. During the first weeks or even months
following the renewal of the Spirit many are very profoundly
filled with joy at having surrendered themselves back to
God and at being able to experience his presence in their
everyday lives. It is a situation totally comparable with that
of a couple at the start of a passionate love affair. Whether
it is true love that will endure is something that only
emerges after a period of probation. During the first phase
after the renewal of the Spirit many are inclined to bear
witness to their emotions in a rather extravagant manner.
But emotions in themselves do not prove anything. What
does is the fact that God has changed us and our life.

But on the other hand bearing witness is not purely a
matter of providing factual information, since we are testifying to what we have experienced. However it is not primarily
our emotions that we bear witness to but what objectively
speaking has changed, and can be recognized by others as
having done so, as a result of our having been affected. The
experience of Pentecost was certainly something that moved
and affected the disciples deeply, since those who witnessed
the miracle of the gift of tongues were beside themselves

with amazement and some even mocked and said: 'They are filled with new wine' (Acts 2:12-13). Peter's sermon that follows, however, is completely sober. In sparse, concise phraseology it describes the signs and wonders Jesus did, signs and wonders that everyone could discern, at least from outside. Peter then pointed to the fact that the disciples had become witnesses of the resurrection. He does not bear witness to his emotions, so as not to obscure the fact as such. The proof of the resurrection is once again provided by certain signs that every one can see and hear, and by these Luke means above all the gift of prophecy and the gift of tongues: 'Being therefore exalted at the right hand of God, and having received from the Father the promise of the Holy Spirit, he has poured out this which you see and hear' (Acts 2:33). The listener is 'cut to the heart' by this fact that is so discernible, the fact that God has made the crucified Jesus both Lord and Christ (Acts 2:37). The recognizable changes in the disciples' lives — having all things in common, selling their possessions and goods, etc. — then provide a further occasion for the growth of the infant community (Acts 2:43-47).

Personal witness is something like a sermon preached by a layman, even in the case of a professional theologian, and a sermon needs careful consideration in advance. The Holy Spirit will suggest to us what we should say in particular situations (cf. Luke 12:12) — at a prayer service, at meetings of the prayer group, at work. The following general fundamental rules apply if an act of witness is to be suitable to each particular situation:

(a) In every case our testimony must be simple, concise and true. Avoid preaching at others. Give your testimony in your natural speaking voice and with your normal intonation as if you were recounting some piece of news. Paul says: 'My speech and my message were not in plausible words of wisdom, but in demonstration of the Spirit and power, that your faith might not rest in the wisdom of men but in the power of God' (1 Cor. 2:4-5).

(b) Do not start your testimony by saying something negative about other people or things, about other Churches or about ministers or prelates: 'He who is mighty has done great

things for me' (Luke 1:49). The renewal of the Church
starts with me, and I can only ask God humbly to impart his
grace on others, perhaps even through my witness. Personal
witness is no place for the protest that in certain circumstances
is needed against things that are wrong.

Although when Paul was in Athens 'his spirit was provoked
within him as he saw that the city was full of idols' (Acts
17:16), he did not start his speech on the Areopagus with a
presumptuous and aggressive protest but instead took
seriously his audience's search for God: 'Men of Athens, I
perceive that in every way you are very religious' (Acts 17:22).
An act of witness that is true to the particular situation in
which is is being given looks for the particular point of
contact in this situation. There is a difference between
bearing witness before Christians who by upbringing and
tradition fulfil their duty and are committed and engaged
in keeping with their abilities and resources, and bearing
witness before people who are completely alienated from
the Church. Do not talk about something the other person
is still lacking, but about God's offer that promises us more
than we can ever accept.

(c) Love is the fundamental attitude, and therefore our
witness must never belittle the other person or put him or
her to shame. It is God's kindness that leads to repentance
(Rom. 2:4), and this kindness and courtesy must be evident
in our witness too. The call to repentance and conversion
that comes from the gospel itself is already in itself too much
for everybody to take and evokes spontaneous resistance in
each of us. There is also the resistance that arises from the
way in which witness is borne, from our tendency to show
something like a feeling of spiritual superiority. Love therefore
does not begin by confronting the other person with gifts
of the Spirit which at the moment are beyond his or her
experience. The other person must be able to see that God
himself is at work from certain definite changes in your
life that he or she can himself or herself verify. Otherwise
he or she would already have to possess the gift of discernment in order to be able to test the genuineness of particular
gifts of the Spirit. But this gift presupposes conversion, and
it is towards that that God's kindness is supposed to be leading

the other person by means of your witness.

For these reasons it is important to devote some time to thinking out the style and manner of bearing witness, and it is helpful if as a start you write these considerations down. Your testimony should not last longer than three minutes, since otherwise it will become a speech and start introducing irrelevant details. It can be arranged under three heads:

(1) My life before the renewal of the Spirit
Describe briefly and concisely the main direction your life takes. What are you striving for? What as far as you are concerned is the best thing in life? What are your main images and goals — success, wealth, reputation? The love of other people? What dreams of the future do you cherish? Read through again what you wrote on the third day of the first week.

(a) Sketch the special circumstances and the actual situations that marked your life before the renewal of the Spirit. Avoid general statements but instead identify important actual details — e.g. 'Formerly I used to spend several hours each evening sitting in front of the television; formerly I had no time for my family but only for my hobby; I hardly ever used to pray; tiny things — name them — used to drive me into a rage; I was enthusiastic about and obsessed by . . .' etc.

(b) Before God consider whether you should mention in detail faults that belong in the confessional. The early Church was not very prudish about the public confession of personal sins. But God does not demand of us that we should strip ourselves psychologically naked in front of people who will not accept such a confession with the respect that is needed. Here it is very much a question of the particular context.

(2) How I was led to the renewal of the Spirit
What was my first contact with people who bear witness to Christ? How did I grow into the movement of renewal — through the testimony of others, through an introductory talk? What has the renewal of the Spirit meant for me? Perhaps you did not feel anything at the laying on of hands, experienced only a vast inner emptiness. Perhaps on the other

hand you were profoundly affected. Was the renewal of the Spirit a turning point in your life?

(a) Describe this event simply and unpretentiously. Avoid extravagant phraseology of the kind that is often used to describe important experiences — terms like fantastic, out of this world, indescribable, or whatever the current superlatives of praise may be.

(b) Be quite open in describing your anxiety and fears and your inhibitions about surrendering yourself to God. Describe your doubts, your critical reflections, your fear of the consequences, etc.

(c) Avoid expressions that outsiders will not understand or that sound too pious and 'saved'.

(3) My life after the renewal of the Spirit

(a) Describe soberly and honestly the changes that have taken place in your life, without exaggeration. Otherwise other people will draw the conclusion that they would never accomplish anything like that, or else they will regard the whole thing as completely improbable: 'Love is not jealous or boastful' (1 Cor. 13:4). Here again mention actual details and facts that other people can verify. Anyone who is honest will have to say of himself or herself that all is not changed utterly. Are there actions or attitudes that cannot be seen as a continuation of your innate or earlier attitudes? The renewal of the Spirit does not make us better than other people but better than we were before.

(b) Avoid giving the impression that the charismatic renewal is the only way to the renewal of the Church. God arouses men and women to a living faith in many different ways. The charismatic renewal is not a movement that gathers adherents, but something brought about by God. It is always threatened by the human tendency to sin and to the abuse of God's gifts.

(c) At your first encounter with other people do not talk about the more spectacular charisms — prophecy, the gift of tongues, healing — if they have been bestowed on you. They are hardly able to imagine what you are talking about. Many people are like the Athenians of Paul's time who liked nothing better than 'telling or hearing something new' (Acts 17:21).

As far as many people are concerned the gift of tongues has something of the sensational about it, and it becomes the one thing they are interested in. Although Paul himself spoke in tongues more than the rest (1 Cor. 14:18) not a word of such activity is mentioned in his missionary speeches as presented by Luke in the Acts of the Apostles. The essential condition that has to be fulfilled before receiving any of the gifts of the Spirit is dying with Christ, the acceptance of one's own death — cf. the seventh day of the first week (2 Tim. 1:7-8):

> For God did not give us a spirit of timidity but a spirit of power and love and self-control. Do not be ashamed then of testifying to our Lord.

Appendix

I: The Renewal of the Church
(text for a leaflet on the charismatic renewal)

1: Witness to faith as a result of personal encounter

The charismatic renewal is a form of evangelization in which on the basis of the common priesthood of all believers Christians lead each other by means of their personal witness to the faith to a direct encounter with Christ himself. Its essence is the conversion that is a necessary pre-requisite for baptism, a missionary liturgy, and the renewal of the Spirit.

Many people who are Christians merely by virtue of infant baptism and their upbringing have found their lives changed by the personal growth prompted by this renewal.

They talk about God and Christ on the basis of a real personal encounter and are set free to bear personal witness to their faith in a world that has grown indifferent or even hostile to Christianity. Many, often to their own surprise, experience in themselves a new love for scripture and for prayer, a new openness to other people's problems and needs and for a social commitment founded in Christian motivation.

This renewal is growing in all countries of the world to an astonishing degree and is a great sign of hope. It is not however a new movement in which we have the aim or the ability to organise something out of our own resources. Nor is it simply a new pastoral technique that can be introduced more or less mechanically. It is rather a gift bestowed by the Lord of the Church who summons each individual man and woman to give a personal response and thus leads them to a vigorous exercise of the common priesthood of all believers.

> Lord, renew your Church
> and begin with me.

2: The gap between faith and experience can be closed

How and why does one become a Christian? Is it enough to be baptized as a baby, and does one become a Christian simply by means of a nominally Christian upbringing? Is it enough to be a decent man or woman and to fulfil one's religious 'duties'? Have we not turned Christianity basically into a collection of unwelcome demands?

In keeping with the New Testament we have to say: You become a Christian quite decisively through your personal turning to Christ and through the experience of his actual presence in your life. But this turning to Christ and this experience of him in your life are not things that come just from you alone. They are instead a gift of God that is aroused and supported by other people's witness to the faith. Nobody believes in isolation. So we too must express our faith in personal witness in each other's presence. Many mambers of prayer groups confirm that the disastrous gap between faith and experience, between intellect and emotion, that so many are concerned about today, can be overcome.

3: God's Spirit is present in a way that can be experienced by the senses

How does God's tangible presence in our life come about? Genuine experience always has something to do with our senses. God, the almighty Father, is however someone we can neither see nor hear. As far as we are concerned he has no voice and no form (John 5:37). He dwells in unapproachable light, he 'whom no man has ever seen or can see' (1 Tim. 6:16). But in Jesus Christ God's love of man and his kindness towards him took on bodily form and became capable of being perceived by our senses, so that the witnesses of what Jesus said and did proclaim what they themselves have seen and heard (1 John 1:1-3). After the Ascension we can no longer see and hear Jesus's earthly form. But he has left his Spirit behind among us, and this Spirit powerfully makes his presence felt, in a way that can be perceived by our senses (1 Cor. 12:7), if people gather in the name of Jesus and testify to their faith before each other. When we see and hear how other people surrender themselves to God in praise, thanksgiving and faith, then we see and hear something of the Spirit of Jesus himself (Acts 2:33). This experience cuts us to the heart (Acts 2:37), lays hold not just of our understanding, not just of our will, but of all our being and resources.

God is thus not only the almighty Creator who is over us. He is also powerfully present among us as the Spirit of Jesus Christ (1 Cor. 14:25). By this means the power is bestowed on us to decide totally for Christ and to bear witness for him.

Lord, be present among us again
and let us behold your glory.

4: Missionary liturgy as a social experience of God

The charismatic renewal's constant source of life is a missionary liturgy — the service of prayer conducted in small compact groups. It is something to which each one contributes (cf. 1 Cor. 14:26) in free, spontaneous prayers that emerge from the shared silence. These prayers are basically a response to the word of God which places demands on the whole man and intensifies his activity: it does not call for a sinking into one's self with the extinction of the ego as its goal. The person who is praying directs himself with his whole being through Christ to the Father. Because the prayers and invocations are said out loud and in the presence of others, they have at the same time the character of proclamation and, if God so ordains, serve the faith of others.

Prayer as a service to the faith of others is at the same time a social experience of God. We experience the presence of the Holy Spirit not apart from or beyond other people but when we accept their prayer into ourselves (even if in certain circumstances this may be a critical acceptance) and allow ourselves to be affected by it. The deepest dimension of this social form of prayer is worshipping God for his own sake. This is at the same time something that is taking place in God himself. The Spirit of God prays within us and with us through Christ to the Father (Rom. 8:15-16, 26; Gal. 4:6). Inasmuch as this Spirit of God is one and the same in all of us, it makes possible an experience of fellowship and community that far transcends other forms of human togetherness.

The Holy Spirit is also called our counsellor and advocate. We experience him to the extent that in his power we help others, stand by others, serve the faith of others.

5: The charisms — qualification for the common priesthood

Being qualified for serving the faith of others and thereby for the common priesthood is something for which the New Testament uses the term charism (gift of grace). On every man and woman certain abilities are bestowed, and these the Spirit of Christ can change, purify and make use of for the building up of Church and society. All charisms flow out of the love that through the Holy Spirit has been poured into our hearts (Rom. 5:5). They appear both in the form of verbal charisms (contributing to prayer services, personal witness) and in the form of active charisms. The gifts of grace in their fullness were bestowed on the Church at the first Pentecost. Among them belong the gift of prophecy, the gift of tongues and the gift of healing (Mark 16:17-18; 1 Cor. 12:4-11; Acts 2:4, 10:46, 19:6). These more outstanding and spectacular charisms (cf. Vatican II Constitution on the Church, *Lumen gentium,* 12) are being bestowed more abundantly on the Church today and in fact belong to the normal everyday life of a living Christian community.

> Lord, let us be at the priestly service of each other
> as good stewards of your varied grace,
> each with the gift he or she has received.
>   (cf. 1 Pet. 4:10)

6: The central event: the renewal of the Spirit

The Christian's initiation into the Christian life in its fullness has since time immemorial taken place in a number of steps brought about by the Holy Spirit in us (but not without our help) (cf. Acts 2:38), and these steps must continually be renewed in the lifelong process of becoming a Christian. We provide mutual help towards this 'renewal of the Spirit' in suitable introductory talks and meetings. It comprises the following aspects:

(a) *Conversion*: 'Put off your old nature which belongs to your former manner of life . . ., and be renewed in the spirit of your minds' (Eph. 4:22-23; cf. Col. 3:9-10, Rom. 12:2). Conversion is the renewal of our human spirit, of our emotion, will, intellect, of our whole person, in the power of the Holy Spirit. Its starting-point is surrender to God's plan and will, and an initial acceptance of one's own death — the latter the pre-condition for all charismatic activity. According to Hebrews 6:4-6 such conversion is something that takes place at a very profound level in our lives and that cannot be repeated with the same effect but nevertheless must continually be renewed.

(b) Renewal of baptismal promises: Baptism with water for the forgiveness of sins is 'the washing of regeneration and renewal in the Holy Spirit' (Titus 3:5). The renewal of baptism takes place in the sacrament of penance and in prayer for healing from the injuries and wounds other people are responsible for (original sin).

(c) Renewed participation in Jesus's baptism of the Spirit: In the New Testament view of things the experience of Pentecost begins with Jesus's baptism (cf. Acts 10:37-38, Luke 4:18). In it Jesus himself was baptized with the Holy Spirit. While he was praying, this divine power came upon him in a manner that could be seen and heard and thus could be experienced both by himself and by those present (Luke 3:21-22, and parallel passages in the other gospels). From this point on he emerged as the original charismatic, as God's unique witness, as prophet, teacher, victor over disease, demons and death.

The Catholic view is that the sacrament of confirmation is the historical continuation of Jesus's experience of the Spirit and of the first Pentecost (Paul VI, 1971) and thus the sacramental offer of the baptism of the Spirit, in other words being made competent to exercise the gifts of the Spirit at the service of others. The Evangelical rite of confirmation also includes the invocation of the Holy Spirit. The renewal of the Spirit is therefore also the renewal of confirmation.

(d) Guidance by the Holy Spirit. The person who has become a new man or woman is no longer afraid, whether of God or of the future, and lets himself or herself be led by the Spirit of God (Rom. 8:14). He or she continually remains open to God's intervention in his or her own life and in that of the Church.

(e) Deepened understanding of the eucharist as the one spiritual food and the one spiritual drink, as the sign of unity.

Making oneself over to Christ and asking for the renewal of the Spirit take on profundity and seriousness if they are expressed in personal and for the most part extempore prayer before witnesses. Those present lay their hands on the person praying and utter prayers of intercession, praise and thanksgiving. This procedure is not a new sacrament but an exercise of the common priesthood of all believers, on the basis of which Christians help and strengthen one another in the faith.

In this moment many experience a new joy in existing for God, worshipping him and serving others. Others looking back some weeks or months afterwards state that their life has changed: 'But the fruit of the Spirit is love, joy, peace, patience, kindness, goodness, faithfulness, gentleness, self-control' (Gal. 5:22-23), and all these are things we can and should really experience in ourselves (Gal. 3:2-5). The person who surrenders himself or herself to others will find himself or herself.

> Lord Jesus Christ, today I surrender to you afresh my life and my death. I renounce suspicion of you and pray you to be the Lord over my thoughts, my will and my emotions. Change me into the person you want me to be so that I may bring your joy to others. I ask you for all the gifts of your Holy Spirit.

⌐7: *A taboo must be broken*
Anyone who attends a charismatic prayer service for the first time as an outside observer — and everyone starts as such — may perhaps find it to begin with a distressing experience. This is quite normal, because we have behind us a long history of inhibition and taboo surrounding our personal relationship to God: 'Religion is a private affair,' is our attitude. 'As far as religion is concerned certain things are private and personal. I can't tell other people about my personal relationship to God.' This kind of inner resistance that is born of fear is something everyone must reckon with at the start.

(*a*) Surrounding belief with a false sense of privacy. The gospels may tell us: 'When you pray, go into your room and shut the door' (Matt. 6:6), but this is said to the Pharisees who used prayer as a means of impressing people. There is also the saying: 'Every one who acknowledges me before men, the Son of man also will acknowledge before the angels of God' (Luke 12:9) and the apostles' conviction that 'we cannot but speak of what we have seen and heard' (Acts 4:20).

(b) The taboo on the emotion of faith. Especially since the Enlightenment we have been told: 'Religion is a matter of the intellect. Emotions connected with belief cannot prove anything and are absolutely uncertain. You should never under any circumstances display publicly anything like joy in God.' This is a taboo that must be broken.

The Second Council of Orange in 529 taught explicitly that the beginning of faith is the disposition to believe which is awakened in us by the Spirit of Christ and by which we believe in Christ (DS 375). What are we fascinated by, affected by, attracted by? Have our emotions really been made Christian, or are we not rather 'led astray to dumb idols' (1 Cor. 12:2), to the many powers that determine our life in our modern civilization — technology, sport, personalities, material well-being? Making our emotions Christian is at the same time a contribution to political and social progress that only Christians can make.

(c) The idea of religious competitiveness. Someone who tries for the first time to pray freely and spontaneously with others discovers within himself or herself a fear not only of his or her own inner emptiness but also of what the others will think: 'Am I doing well enough? What will the others think?' Even in prayer we are begging for recognition and approval. Many people also shrink back from the consequences of making their life over to Christ — 'I had to change my life radically overnight' — and so their freedom to decide becomes inhibited.

'Take heart, it is I; have no fear: (Matt. 14:27).

8: Ecumenical perspectives

To an astonishing degree the charismatic renewal has sprung up almost simultaneously in all the still divided Churches and traditions. It shows an undreamed of power to renew them from within according to their own particular individuality, to free them and to change them from onesidedness and exaggeration due to historical circumstances. Even if a joint Eucharist is not yet possible, all the same a mutual unity is experienced in prayer-groups that in a surprising way is the start of a common tradition. This presupposes that each individual Christian remains firmly rooted in his or her own tradition.

9: Pastoral and ecclesiastical considerations

The charismatic renewal is a way towards a living community and affects the Church from its innermost core in all the forms its life takes. It has to start by growing in small groups — of young people, families, candidates for confirmation — and in this context can penetrate existing groups such as societies, councils, committees, etc. and can illuminate them and bring them to a new pitch of intensity. Everywhere where two or three are gathered together the renewal qualifies people for personal and social evangelization. Only in a later phase will it be able to embrace Church structures and institutions in their totality (positions of responsibility in the Church as a ministry to the other ministries). Hence the renewal, relaxation and deepening of the parish liturgy presupposes an evangelization of the parish as a new form of the parish mission in which every individual will have made his or her life over to Christ. A possible fruit of this would be the renewal of the Spirit bestowed on individuals in the Pentecost liturgy of the parish, lay sermons as personal witness every Sunday, extempore bidding prayers, exchange of the kiss of peace.

> Come into our life, Holy Spirit,
> give us your gifts, change us, renew your Church.

II. A testimony of faith

There are many new professions of faith besides the Apostles' Creed and the Nicene Creed which are known to us from their use in the liturgy and in instruction, which come from the first centuries of the life of the early Church and which are thus common to all Christians.

Fresh formulations of our belief are a good thing, because our profession of faith has continually to be translated into terms of the contemporary situation. Of course they can also run the risk of being misunderstood as some kind of substitute or replacement for the old creeds. This is undesirable because clearly they only express part of the totality of Christian truth. Hence for example the Evangelical Bishop Hermann Dietzfelbinger once suggested that instead of new professions of faith we should talk about testimonies of faith. We would like to take over this concept of a testimony of faith with the following example of a comprehensive and precisely formulated profession of faith that arose in a charismatic community (on the basis of a preliminary draft the origin of which is not known).

This helps to fulfil two functions. First, it offers for meditation a text that uses precisely thought out expressions to present the central experiences of faith in such a way that it can serve us who read it continually to make our faith our own and actual, in keeping with its content. Second, initiation into the basic Christian experience cannot, as has often been said, be a substitute for a doctrine of the faith. For that recourse must be had to the available catechisms and handbooks of doctrine. But the text that follows can perhaps provide in an easily available form the most important features and statements which Christian faith is concerned with, seen in a certain perspective, for the benefit of someone who may not have yet learned very much in the way of doctrine and is looking for words to express the faith he or she confesses. In this sense it can also be recited in groups, perhaps antiphonally, or used in a service as a creed, as 'a sacrifice of praise to God, that is, the fruit of lips that acknowledge his name' (Heb. 13:15).

I know that of my own strength I cannot believe in God.
Faith is God's gift.
Through his Holy Spirit
and through his Word
God has awakened faith within me.

I do not need to ask for proofs,
since faith is trust in God,
confidence that lives in my heart.

So I am relaxed and happy.
For trust in God prevents me
from losing myself in fear and anxiety,
from rigid concern to make a living,
and from barricading myself against everything that
    threatens me.

Because I stand under God and trust in him
I stand over the things of this world
and keep them at a distance.
The need for things and the urge to compete
shall not take me prisoner;
the standards of this world
shall not lord it over me.
For God has set me free.

This is the God I believe in:
the one, true, personal God
who created heaven and earth,
to whom the Bible bears witness,
of whom Jesus says
we should call him our Father.

I have experienced that God is love.
I recognize this love by the fact
that for the sake of us men
he became man in Jesus of Nazareth.
So the good news rang out on our earth,
and everyone can hear it.

For Jesus proclaimed God's new creation.
More than just in what he said,
in everything he did, in his whole being,
he is God's gift of himself to us made visible.
The outcasts and those who were repudiated he accepted,
those sick in mind and body he healed,
those who were weak he set upright and strengthened;

sinners he called to himself in compassion
and granted them forgiveness.
In everything he showed and lived God's love,
and he maintained this love
even when they took him prisoner,
declared him guilty, mocked and struck him —
him, who knew no sin.
Up to death on the cross
he remained true to his Father's will.
He was forsaken by God
so that we may never again be godforsaken.
He sacrificed his life
so that we might gain life.
Thus he freed us
from the fetters of sin,
from the power of the devil
and from the might of death.

God raised him up from death
as the first-born of a new creation,
and thereby he promised eternal life
to us, too, who belong to him:
life marked by eternity and abundance.
I extol the resurrection of Jesus, my saviour,
and rejoice that for all eternity
he is raised up at the right hand of the Father.
In keeping with his promise
the ever-living God, our creator and Lord,
sent his Spirit
on the waiting disciples
to kindle within them
the fire of faith and love.

To us too, his children,
he has granted life
from the abundance of his divine life.
When he created us
he breathed his breath into us;
when he called us to faith
he gave us his Spirit,
the source of all life and of all holiness;

and through his Spirit he equips us
with the gifts that we need
on our pilgrimage to him
and in the service of his kingdom.

I praise him for the fact
that I can experience his Spirit
alive and at work in his community
and within myself, weak human being that I am.
Continually I reach my hand out afresh
in prayer to him, the Spirit of God,
experience his gifts
and long for his fruits;
and I praise God
who bestows such gifts on his children.

So I live in the wonderful freedom
into which God has liberated me.
and despite all adversity I firmly believe
that Jesus, the Lord of the Church,
in this age full of disorder and collapse
is true to his community
and wishes to give it a new form.

What is broken will die away;
what is sound and promotes life will grow
so that the community of his disciples
will shine forth brightly once again
as the city on the hill and the salt of the earth,
not entrenched in positions of power,
modest, poor,
often despised,
but ready to love the Lord
and to serve men:
a free place of refuge,
of comfort and of joy,
where the words spoken from the cross
raise men up again and make them new
and enable them to find their brothers and sisters.

I thank Jesus from my whole heart
that he continually through his word and his sacrificial
    meal
gives me and all my sisters and brothers
new strength to follow and imitate him.

In following him I would like to make a reality
the love that Jesus lived and taught.

I would like to return the love
that comes to me from Jesus:
love that makes the other person happy
and gives him joy;
love that is modest, gentle and humble,
kind, merciful,
eschewing violence, unarmed;
love that has mercy on the outcasts,
that helps those in misery,
that overcomes inhumanity in men's hearts
and in the conditions of life of this world;
love that withholds from no one
the forgiveness and the promise of the gospel.

I am sure that Jesus raises me up again
if I fail in love and confess my guilt.

With longing I seek
the fellowship of the holy meal
which he himself instituted
and in which he comes right among us,
in the simple signs
of bread and wine,
with which he himself feeds us
with his body given up for us
and with his blood poured out for us
and strengthens us on the way to our goal
and quickens our earthly body
with the power of the resurrection
to the joys of heaven.

In reverence and thanksgiving
I read the Bible

for — precisely in its human form —
it is God's one, eternal and trustworthy word,
'a lamp to my feet and a light to my path,'
the joy and comfort of my heart.

Thus I am certain that nothing in heaven or on earth,
no power in the universe,
can separate me from the love of God
that is in Christ Jesus.

So I await with confidence
the consummation of our life with him,
his coming again at the end of time,
when his day dawns,
when he finally judges the world
and brings us, his disciples, home
to the eternal kingdom of his Father,
the new Jerusalem that comes down from heaven
like a bride adorned for her bridegroom,
to the wedding feast of heaven
that is without end
where in unceasing fellowship
we shall live with him
in unclouded joy
and unimaginable glory.

For it is 'what no eye has seen,
nor ear heard,
nor the heart of man conceived,
what God has prepared for those who love him.'